# Uncle Charlie's HUNTING SHACK

## By Bruce Cochran

WILLOW CREEK PRESS

MINOCQUA, WISCONSIN

ISBN 1-57223-019-3  Softcover
ISBN 1-57223-018-5  Hardcover

Published by  WILLOW CREEK PRESS
              an imprint of Outlook Publishing
              P.O. Box 881
              Minocqua, WI 54548

For information on other Willow Creek titles,
write or call 1-800-850-WILD.

Printed in the U.S.A.

# Spring

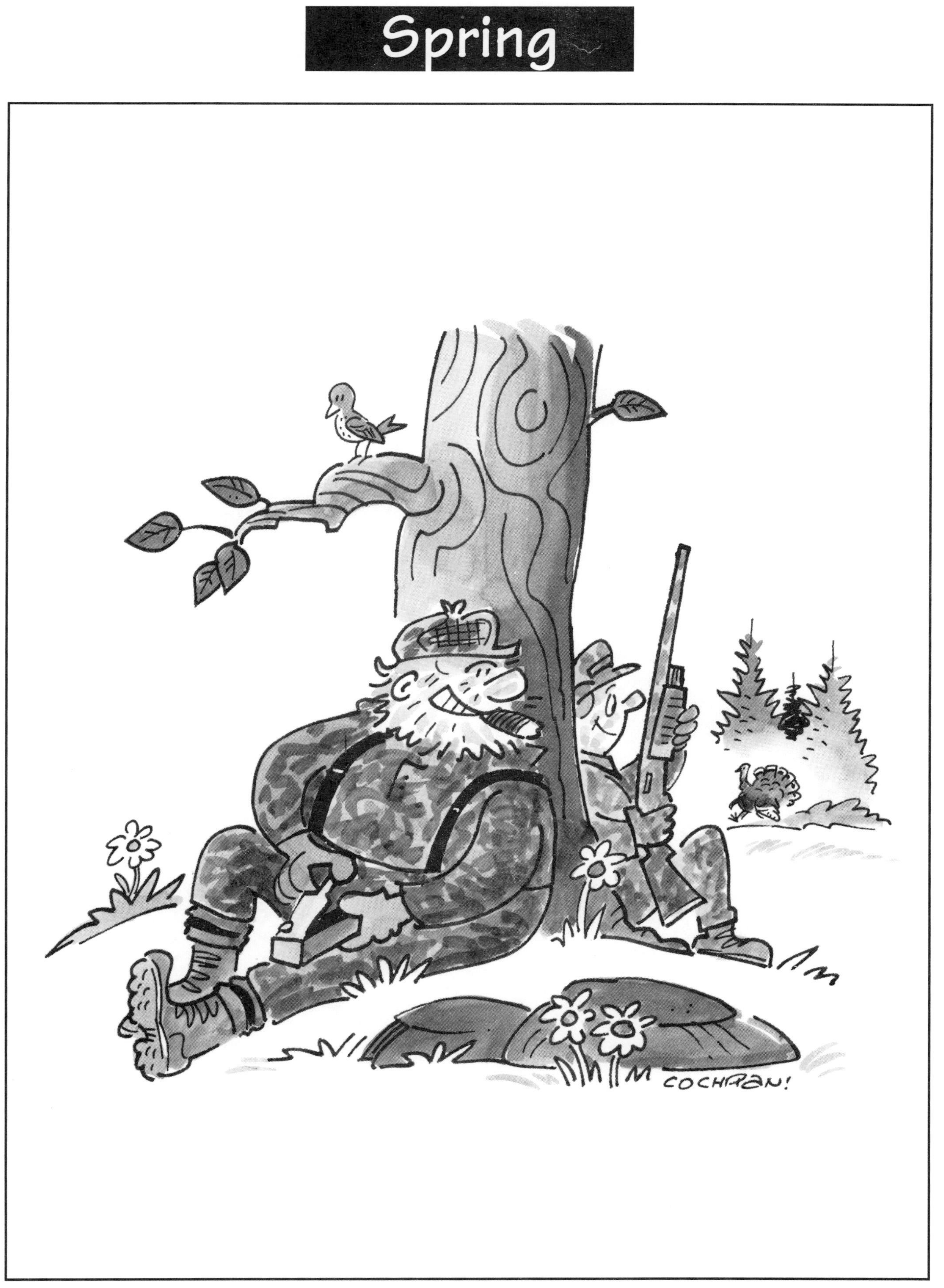
COCHRAN!

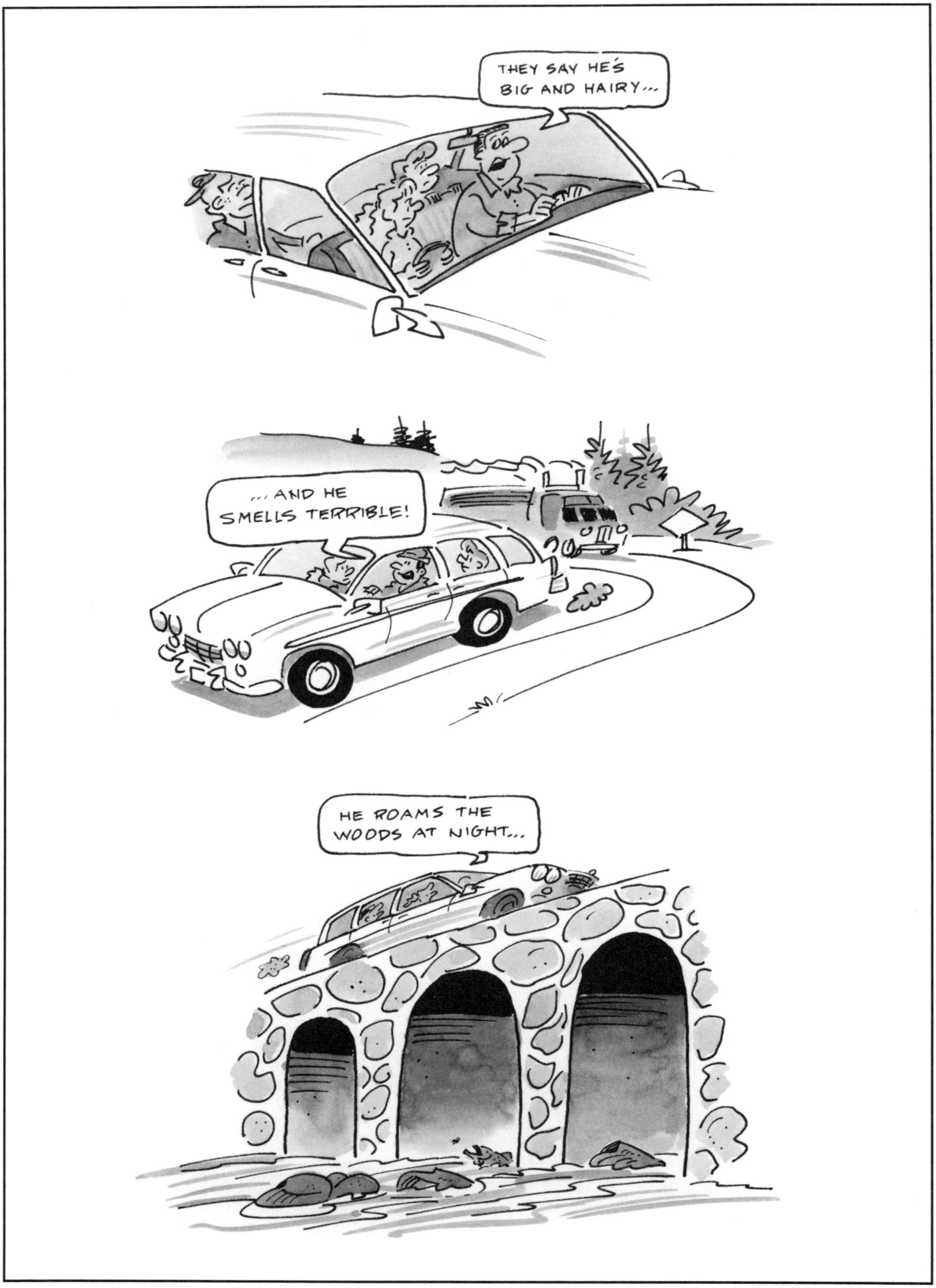
THEY SAY HE'S BIG AND HAIRY...
...AND HE SMELLS TERRIBLE!
HE ROAMS THE WOODS AT NIGHT...

... KNOCKING OVER GARBAGE CANS, SCARING LIVESTOCK, AND SOMETIMES KILLING A GOAT OR A CHICKEN.
THE ABOMINABLE SNOWMAN?!
BIGFOOT?!
NO. UNCLE CHARLIE.
COCHRAN!

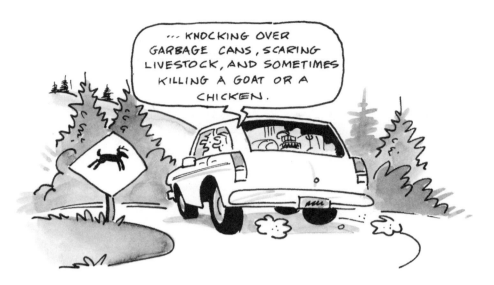

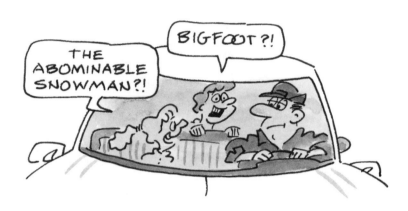

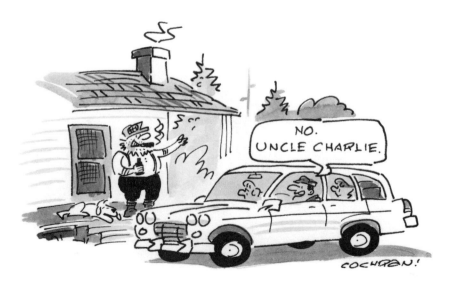

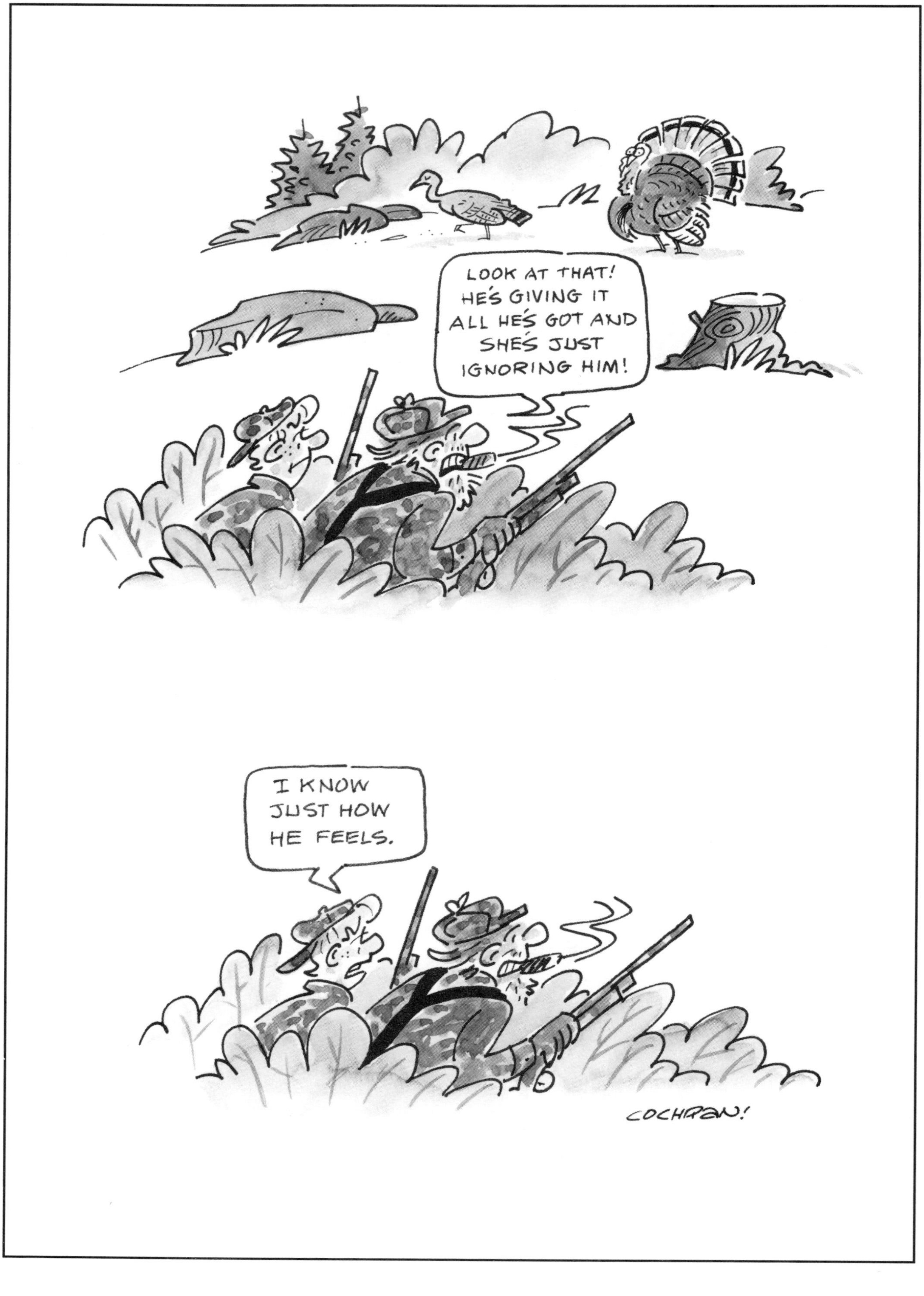
LOOK AT THAT! HE'S GIVING IT ALL HE'S GOT AND SHE'S JUST IGNORING HIM!
I KNOW JUST HOW HE FEELS.
COCHRAN!

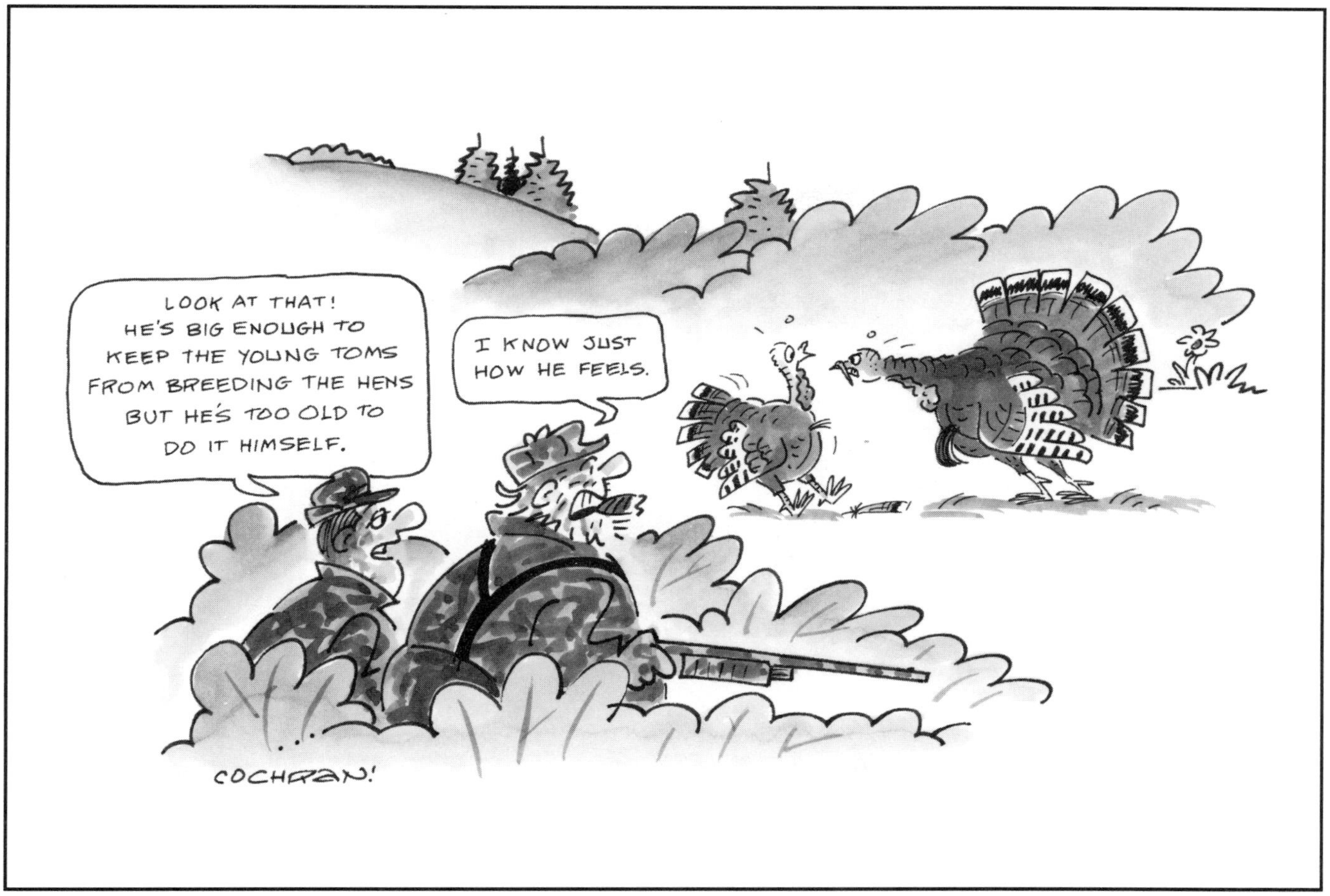
LOOK AT THAT! HE'S BIG ENOUGH TO KEEP THE YOUNG TOMS FROM BREEDING THE HENS BUT HE'S TOO OLD TO DO IT HIMSELF.
I KNOW JUST HOW HE FEELS.
COCHRAN!

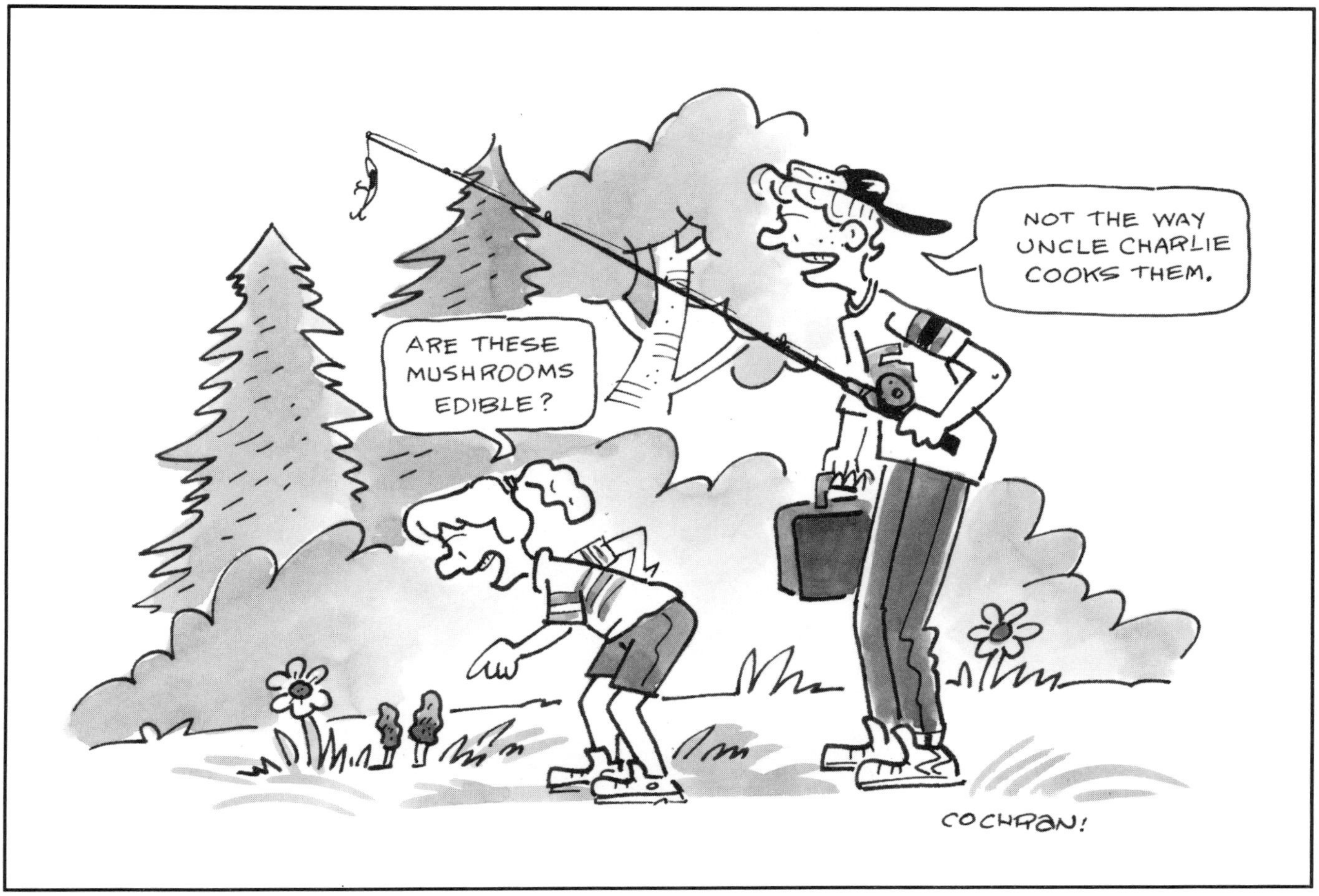
ARE THESE MUSHROOMS EDIBLE?
NOT THE WAY UNCLE CHARLIE COOKS THEM.
COCHRAN!

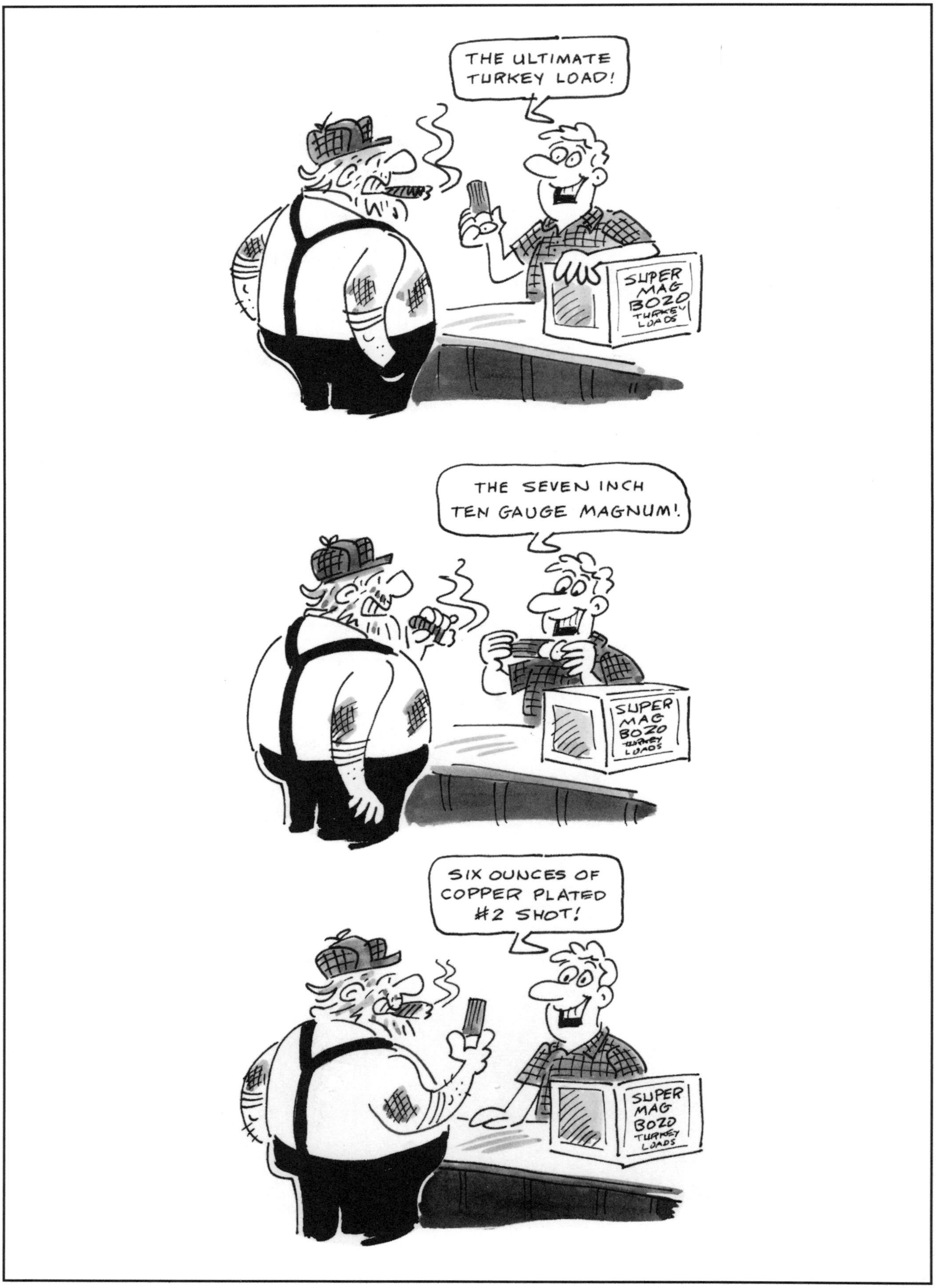
THE ULTIMATE TURKEY LOAD!
SUPER MAG BOZO TURKEY LOADS
THE SEVEN INCH TEN GAUGE MAGNUM!
SUPER MAG BOZO TURKEY LOADS
SIX OUNCES OF COPPER PLATED #2 SHOT!
SUPER MAG BOZO TURKEY LOADS

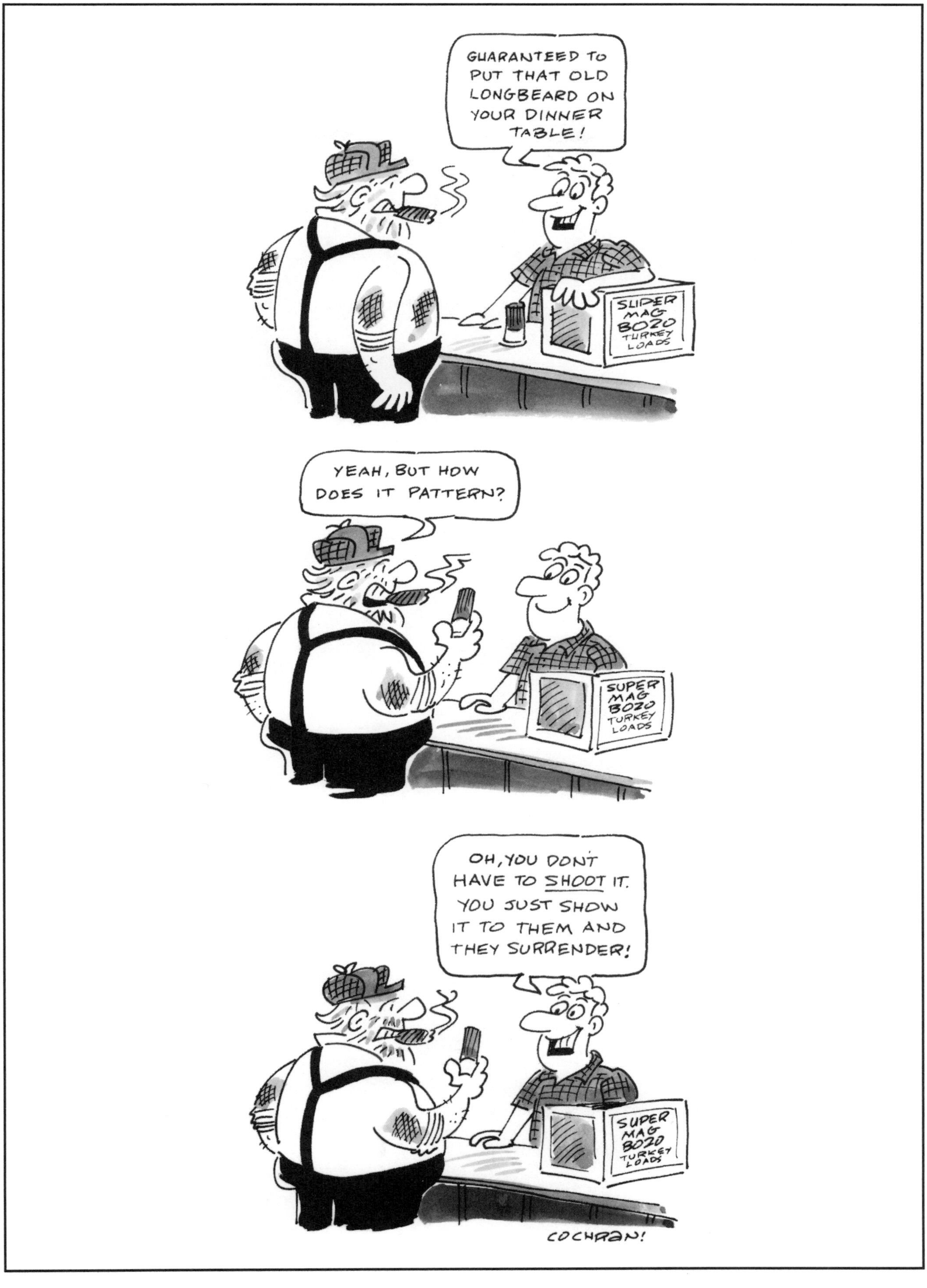
GUARANTEED TO PUT THAT OLD LONGBEARD ON YOUR DINNER TABLE!
SUPER MAG BOZO TURKEY LOADS
YEAH, BUT HOW DOES IT PATTERN?
SUPER MAG BOZO TURKEY LOADS
OH, YOU DON'T HAVE TO SHOOT IT. YOU JUST SHOW IT TO THEM AND THEY SURRENDER!
SUPER MAG BOZO TURKEY LOADS
COCHRAN!

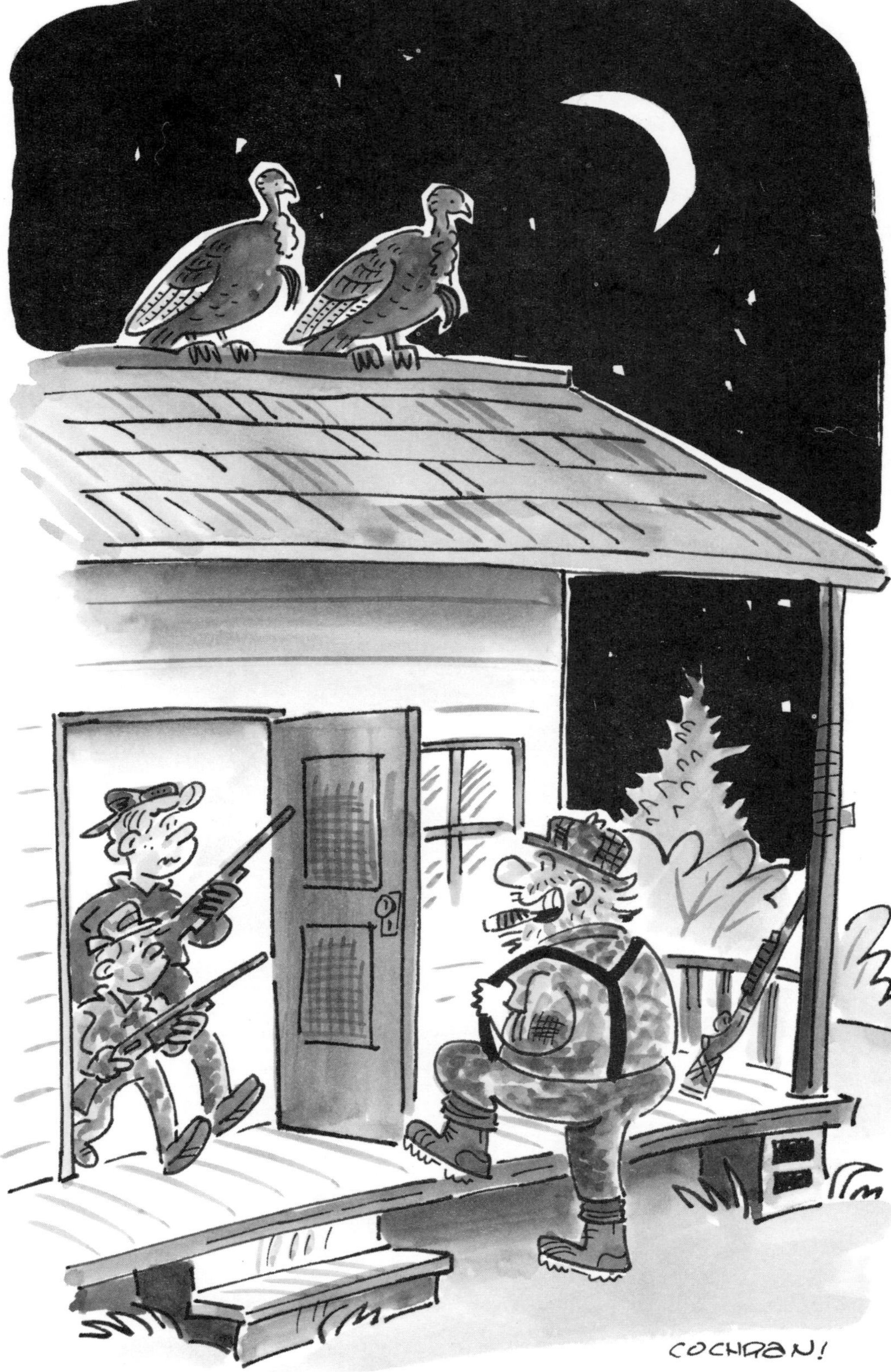
COCHRAN!

*"You kids get a move on. It's a long walk to where the turkeys are roostin' and we gotta be there by daylight."*

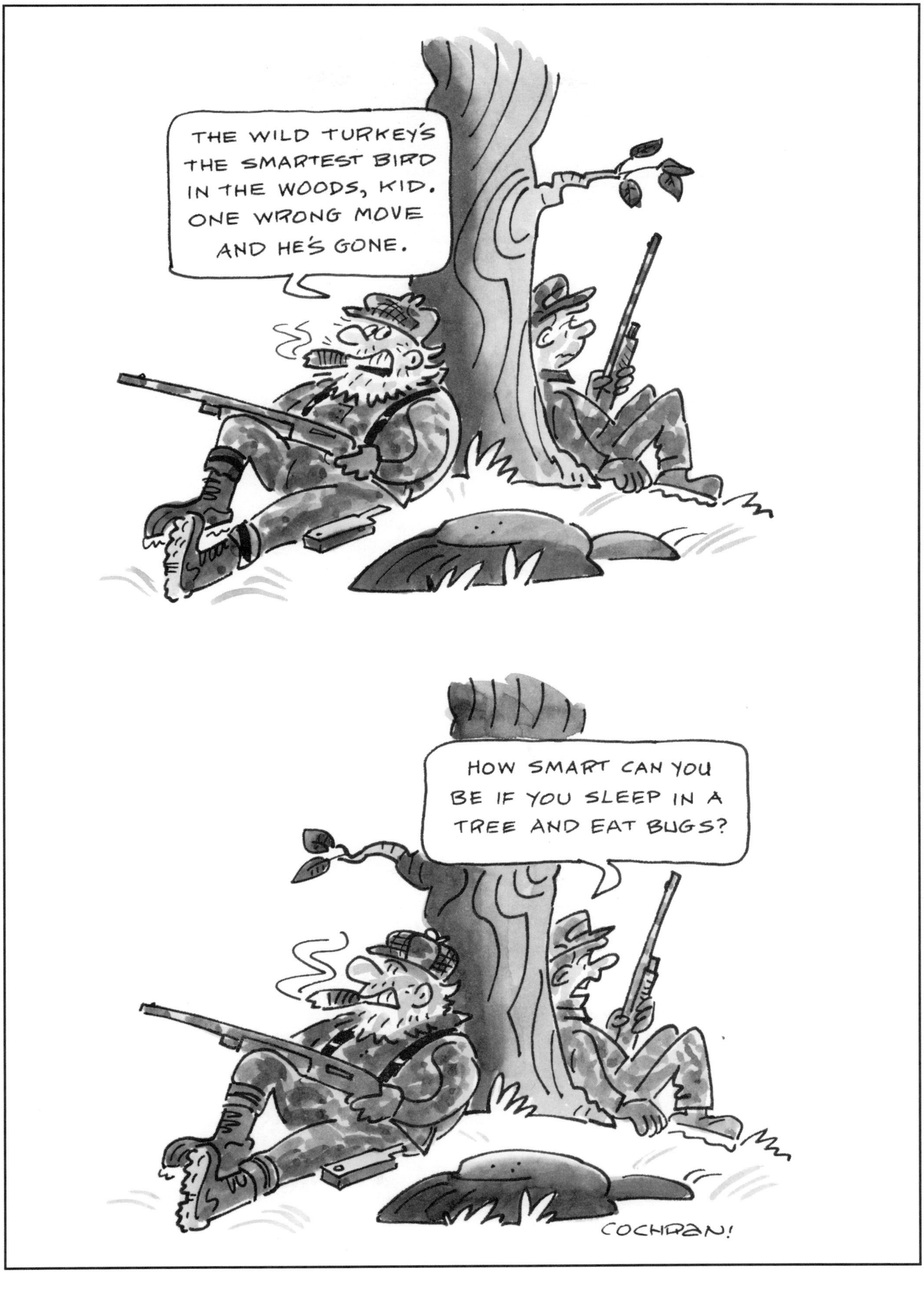
THE WILD TURKEY'S THE SMARTEST BIRD IN THE WOODS, KID. ONE WRONG MOVE AND HE'S GONE.
HOW SMART CAN YOU BE IF YOU SLEEP IN A TREE AND EAT BUGS?
COCHRAN!

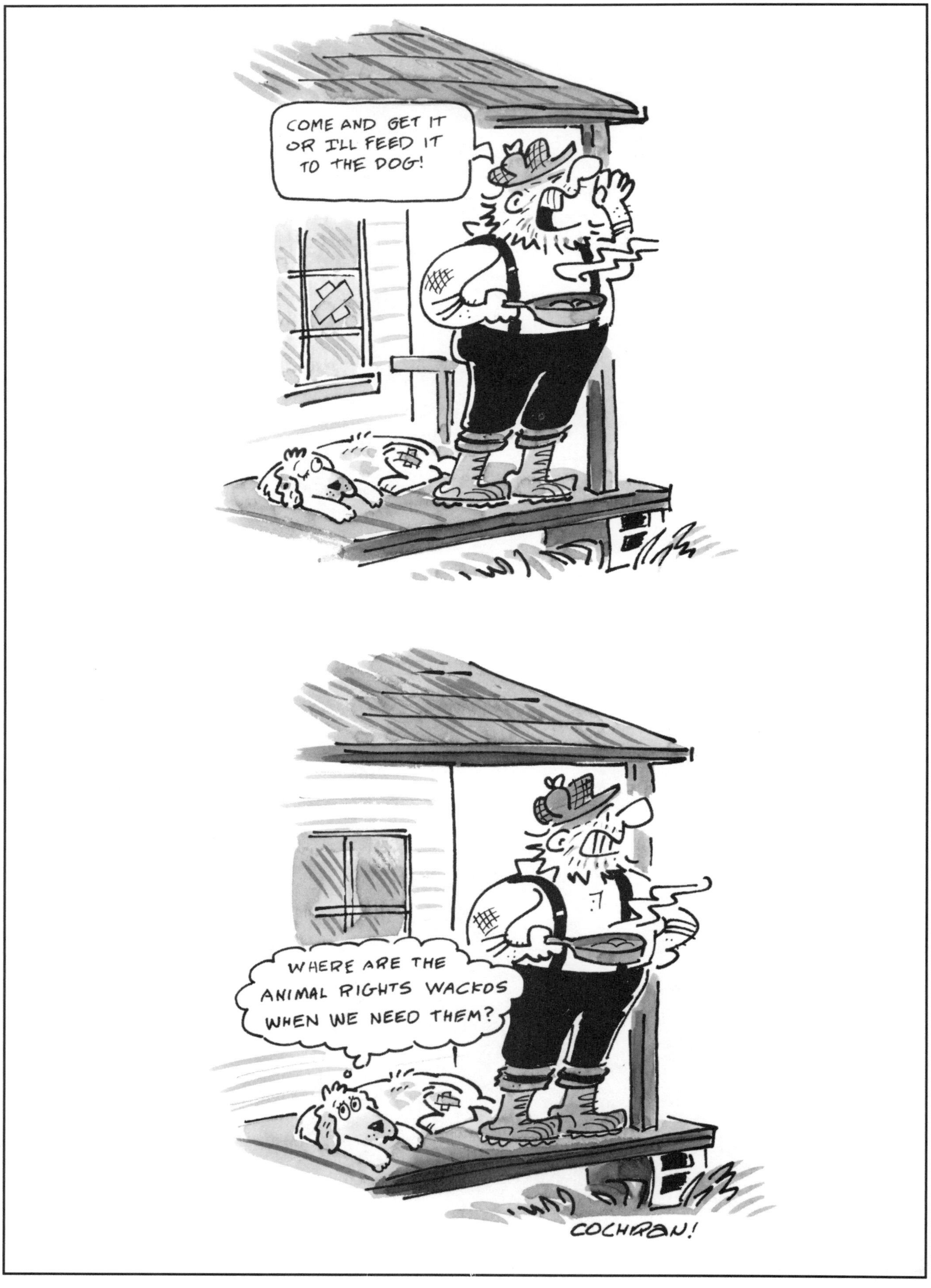
COME AND GET IT OR I'LL FEED IT TO THE DOG!
WHERE ARE THE ANIMAL RIGHTS WACKOS WHEN WE NEED THEM?
COCHRAN!

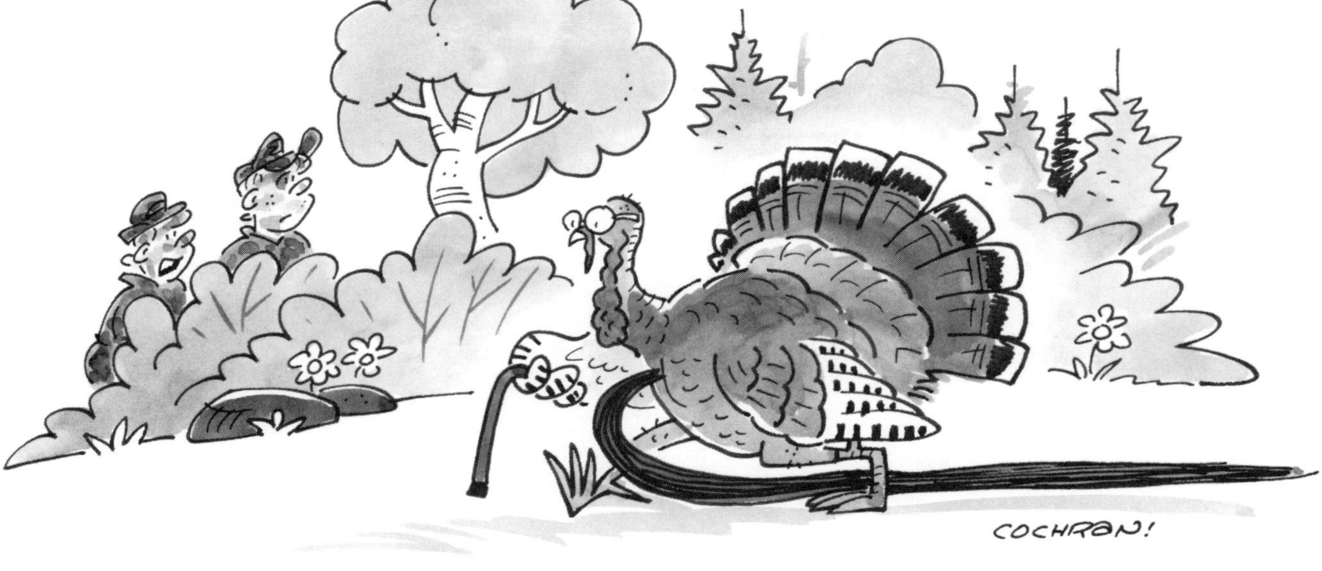
COCHRAN!

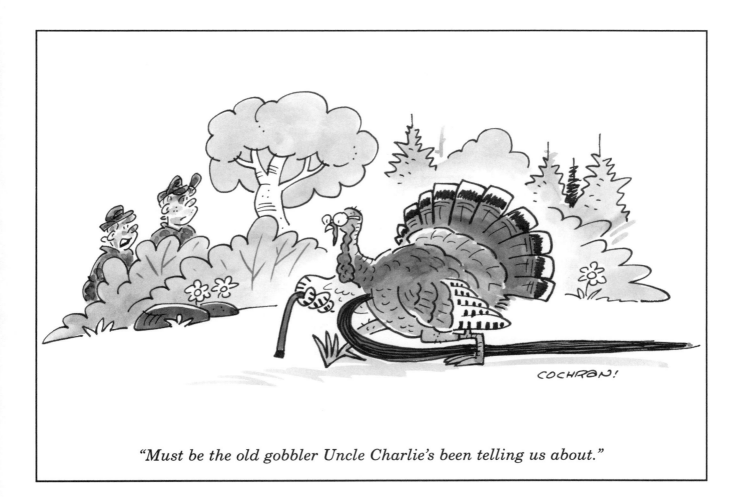

*"Must be the old gobbler Uncle Charlie's been telling us about."*

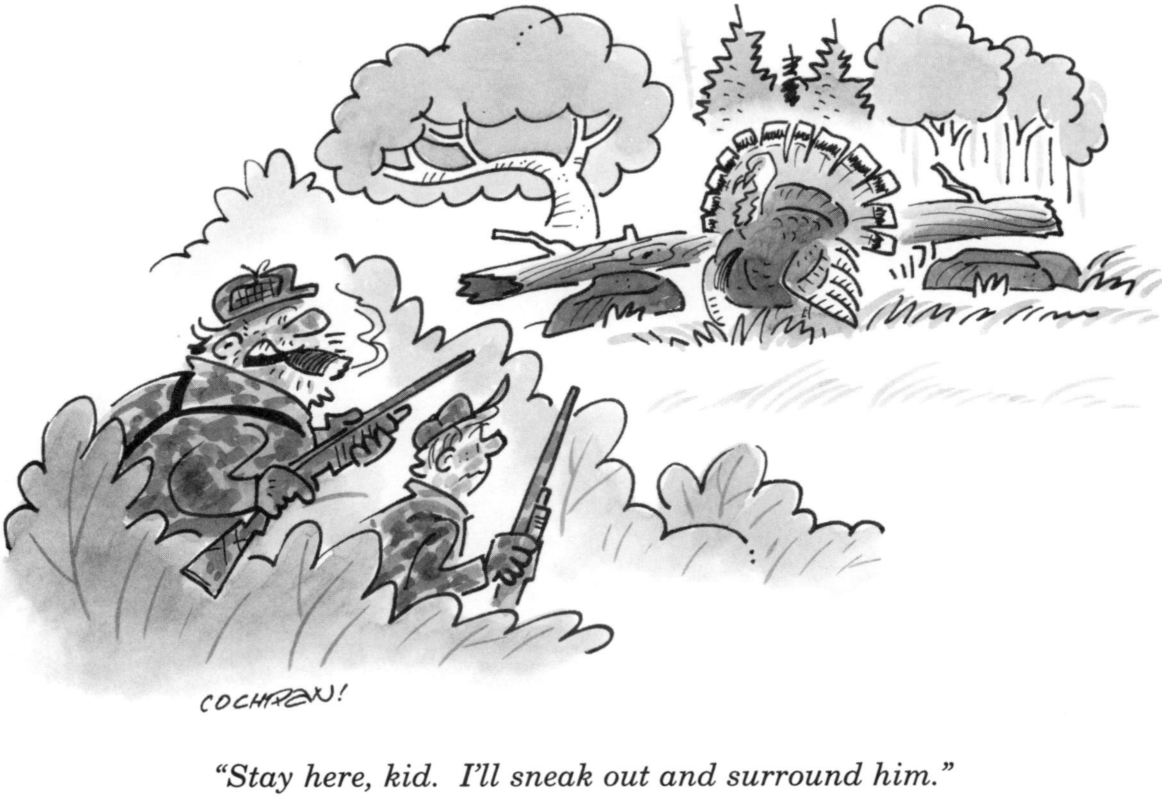
COCHRAN!

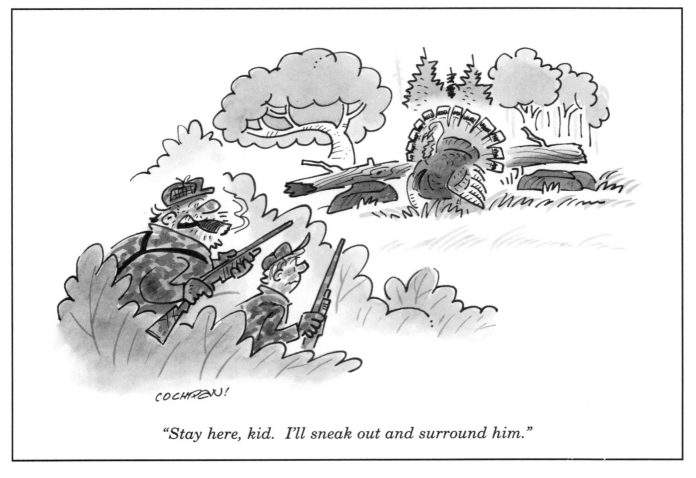

*"Stay here, kid.  I'll sneak out and surround him."*

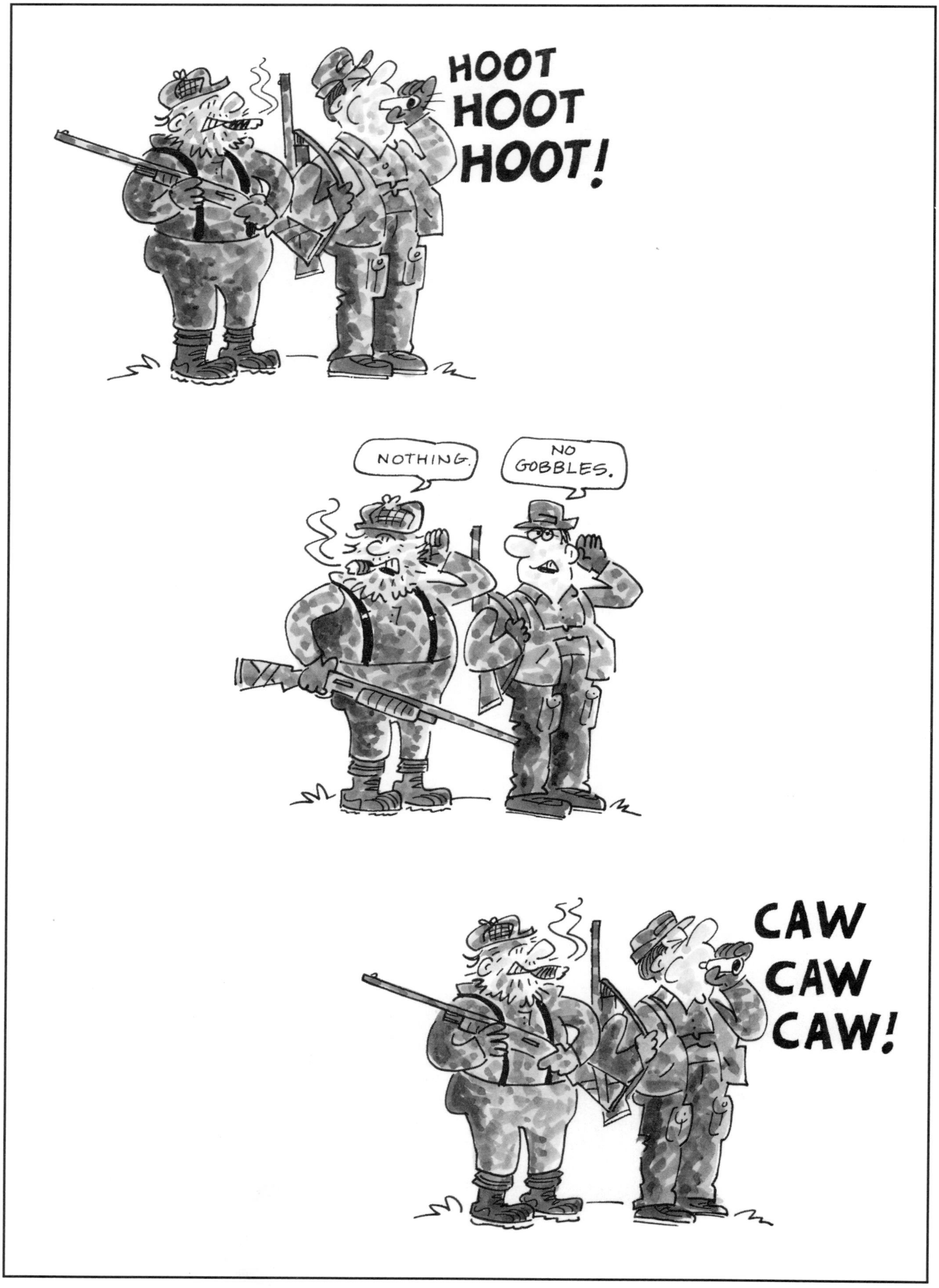
HOOT
HOOT
HOOT!
NOTHING.
NO GOBBLES.
CAW
CAW
CAW!

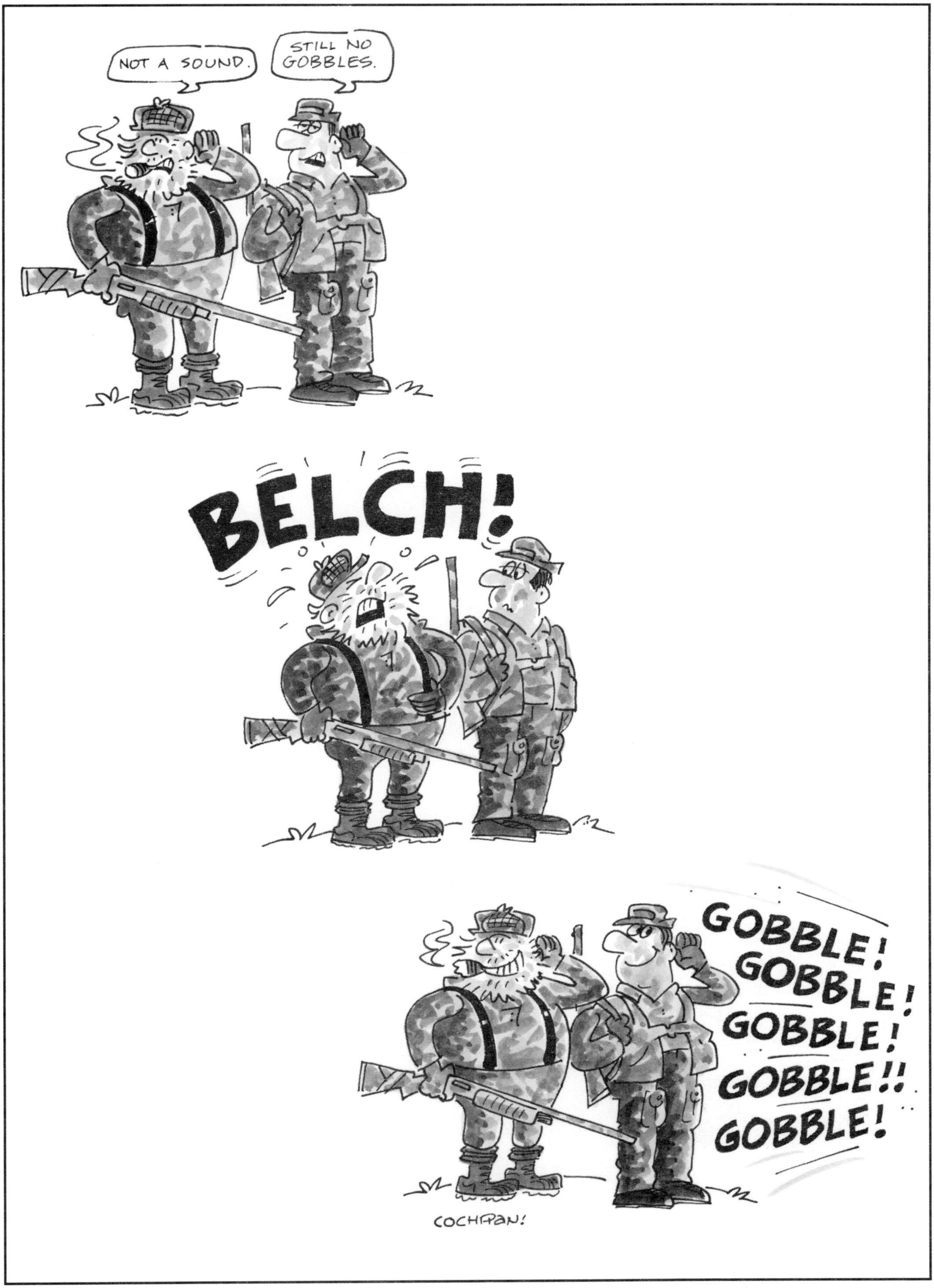
NOT A SOUND.
STILL NO GOBBLES.
BELCH!
GOBBLE! GOBBLE! GOBBLE! GOBBLE!! GOBBLE!
COCHRAN!

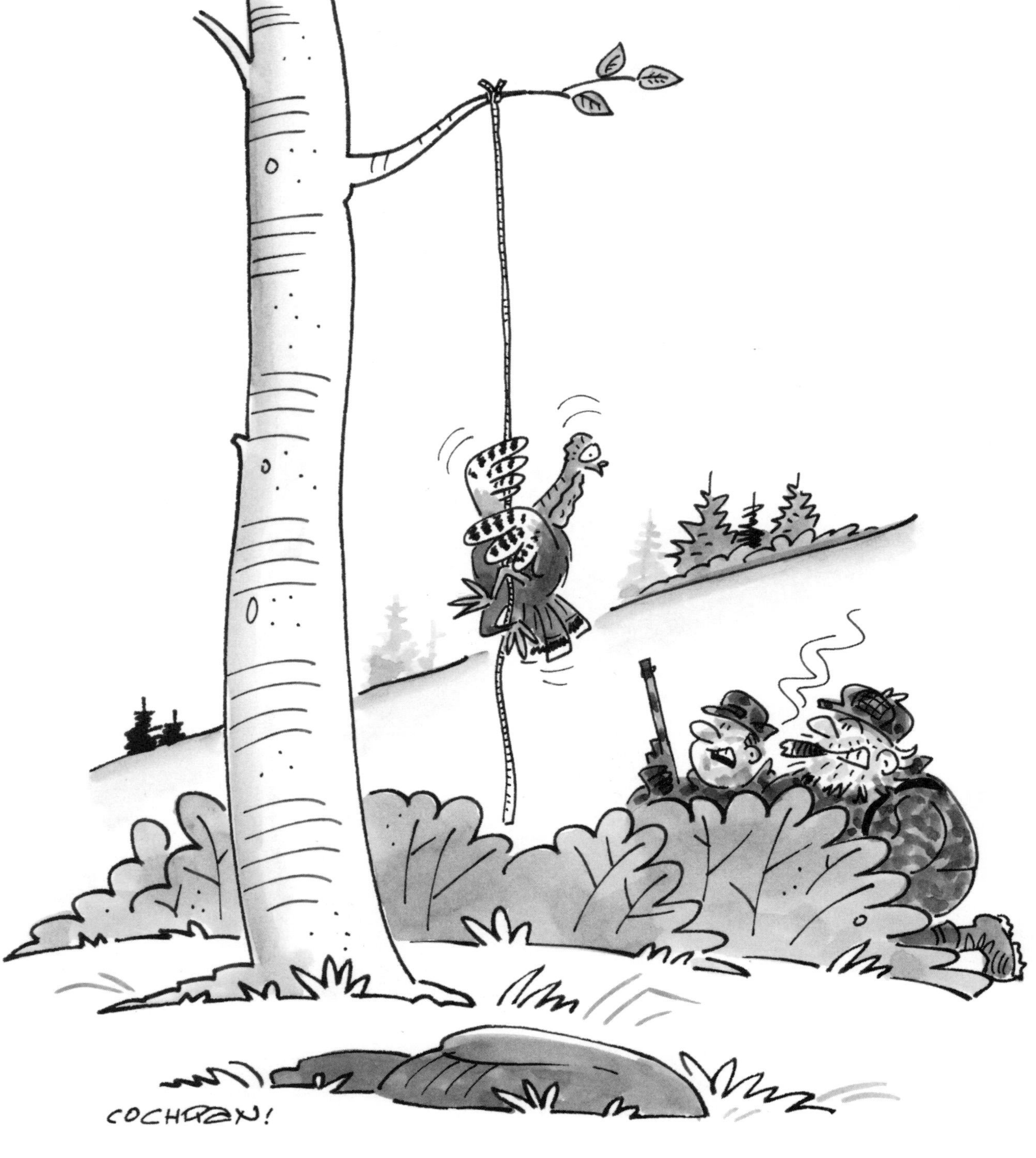
COCHRAN!

*"I always thought they* **FLEW** *down from the roost."*

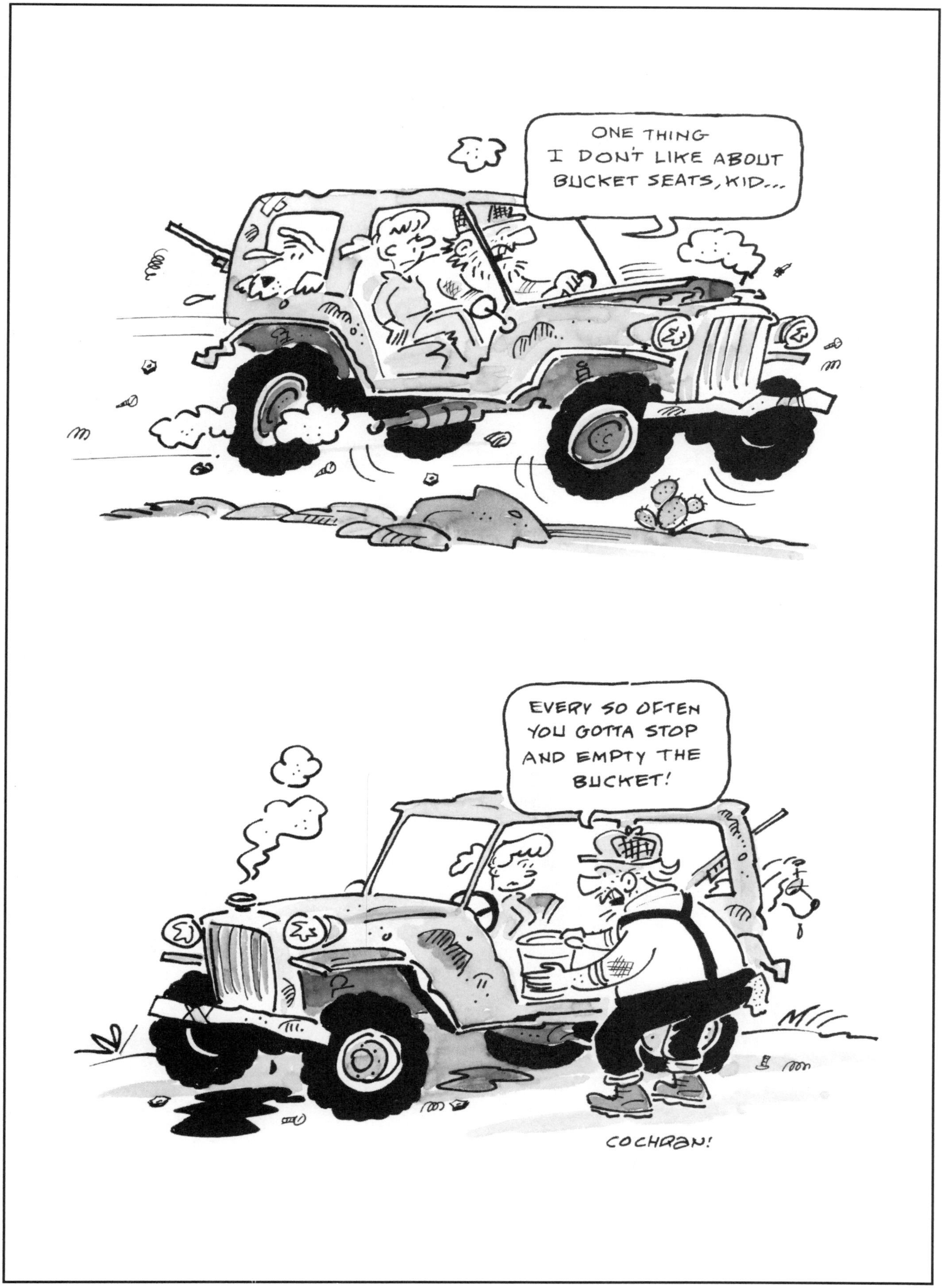
ONE THING I DON'T LIKE ABOUT BUCKET SEATS, KID...
EVERY SO OFTEN YOU GOTTA STOP AND EMPTY THE BUCKET!
COCHRAN!

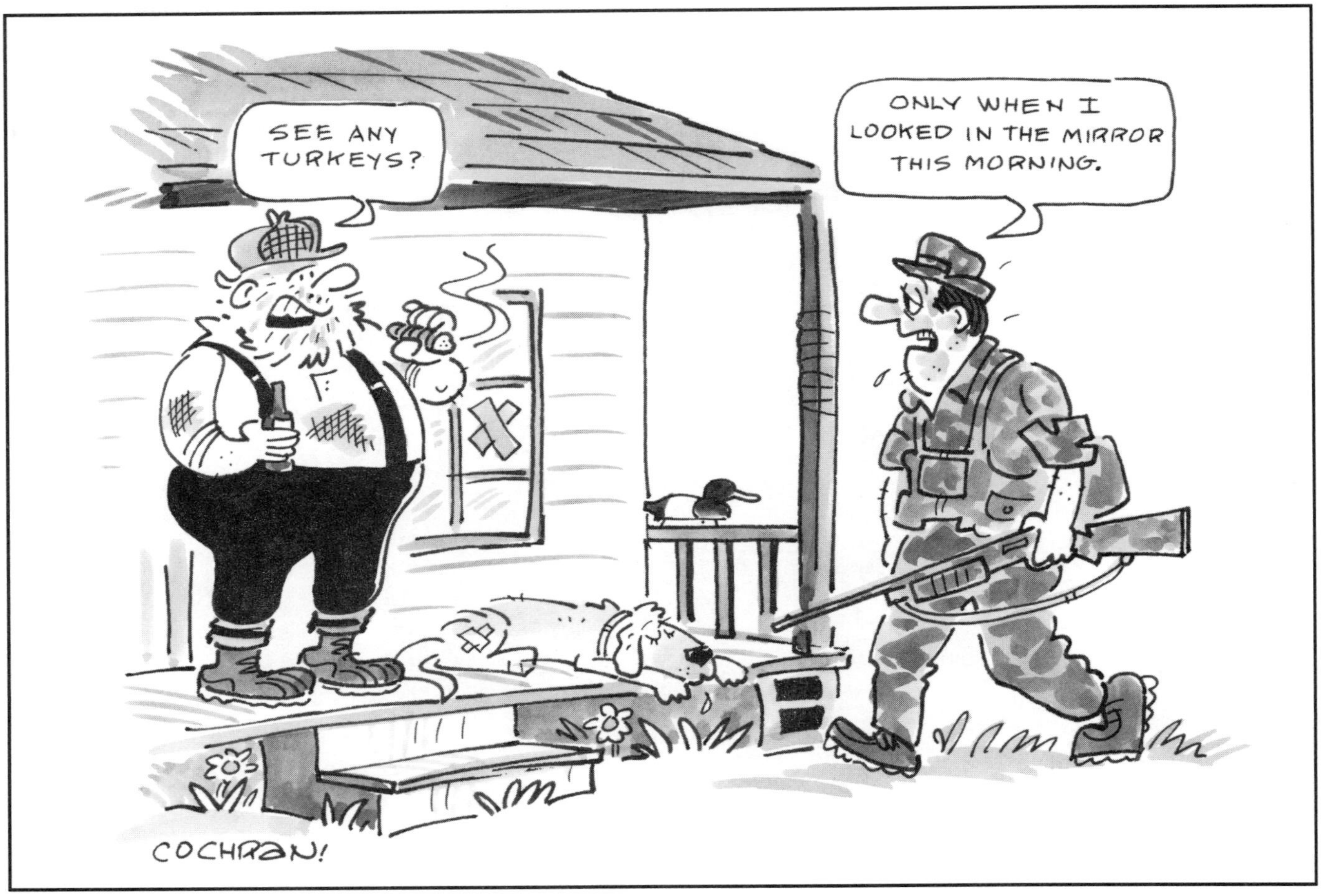
SEE ANY TURKEYS?
ONLY WHEN I LOOKED IN THE MIRROR THIS MORNING.
COCHRAN!

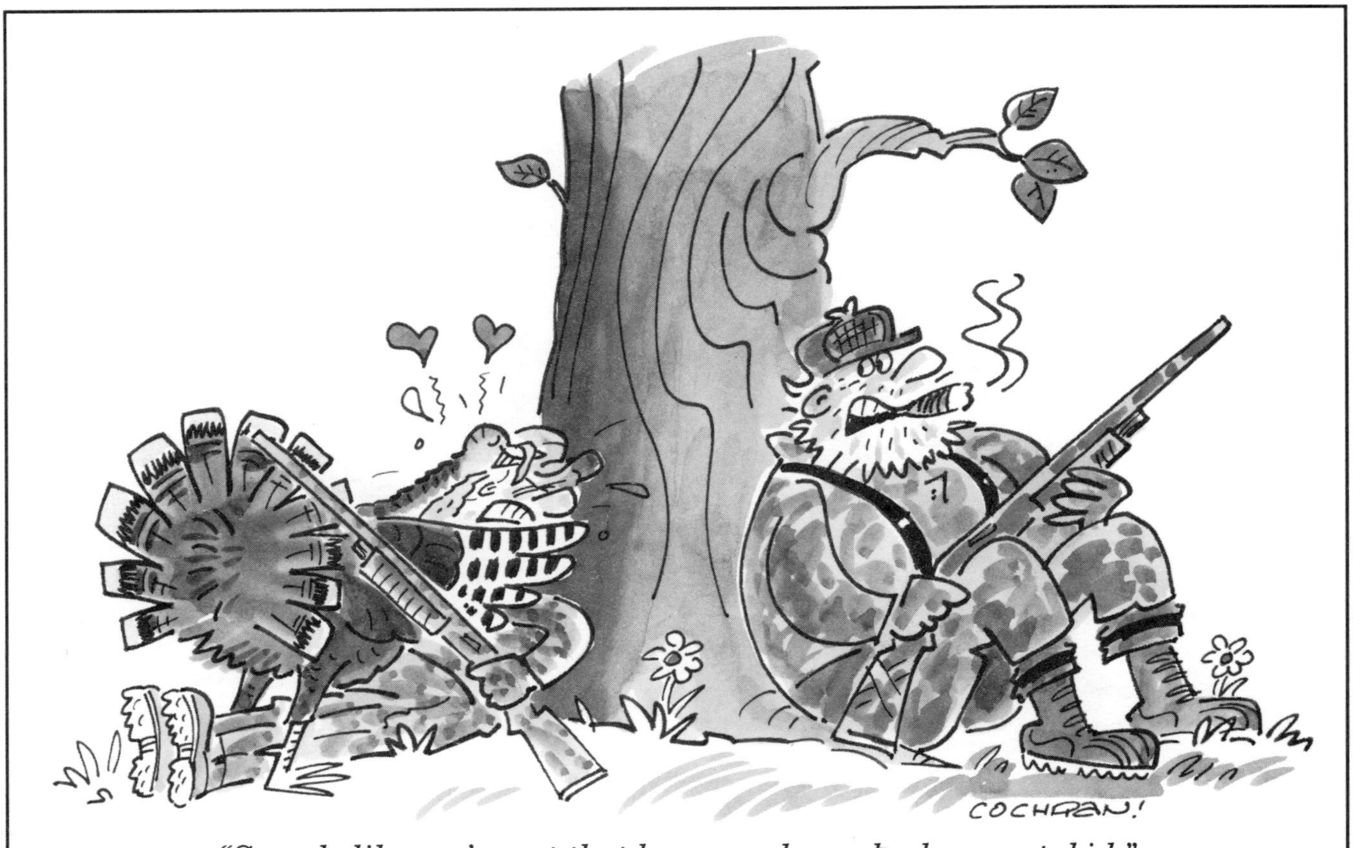
COCHRAN!

*"Sounds like you've got that lonesome hen yelp down pat, kid."*

YELP!
YELP!
YELP!
SPLAT!
YELP THIS!
COCHRAN!

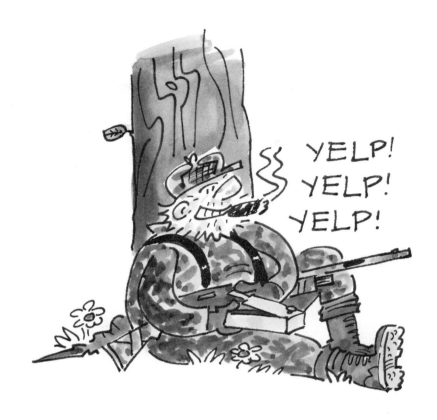

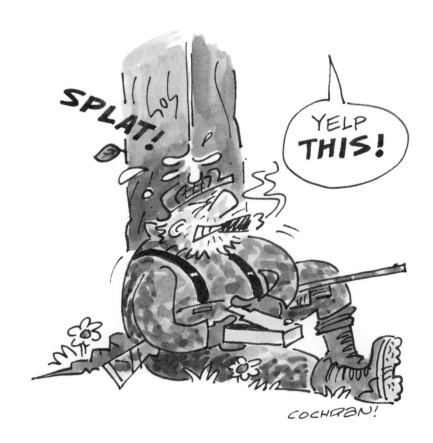

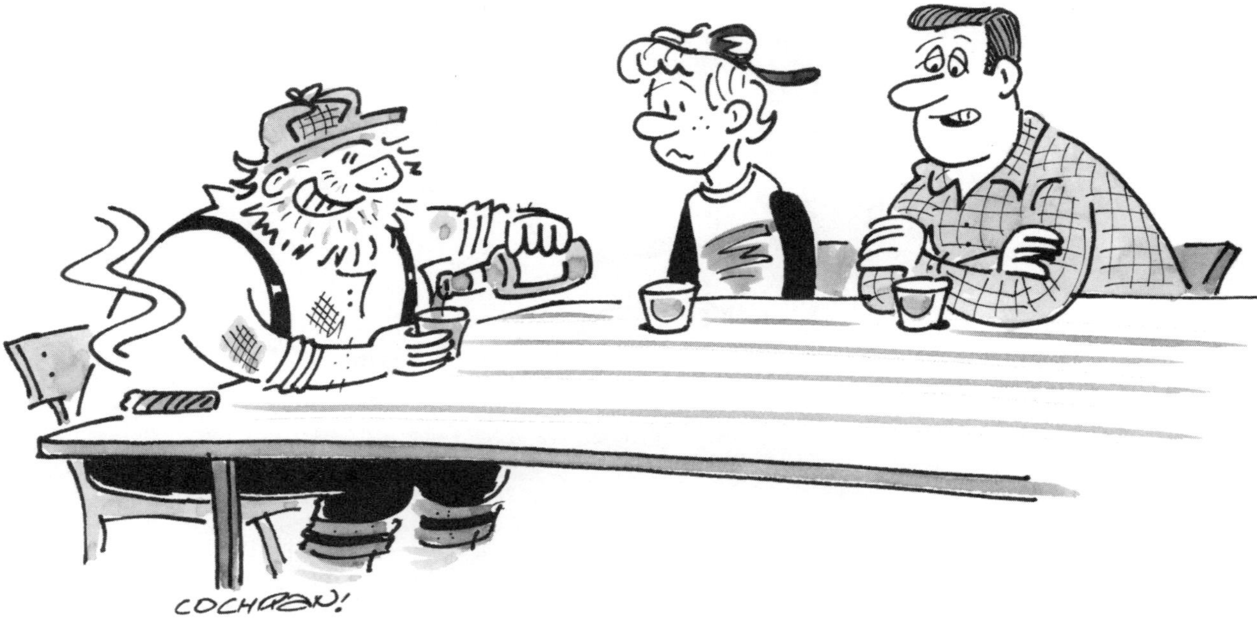
COCHRAN!

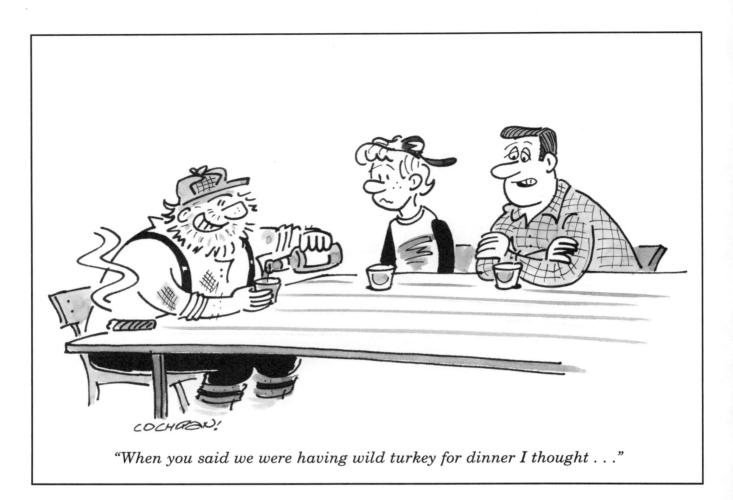

*"When you said we were having wild turkey for dinner I thought . . ."*

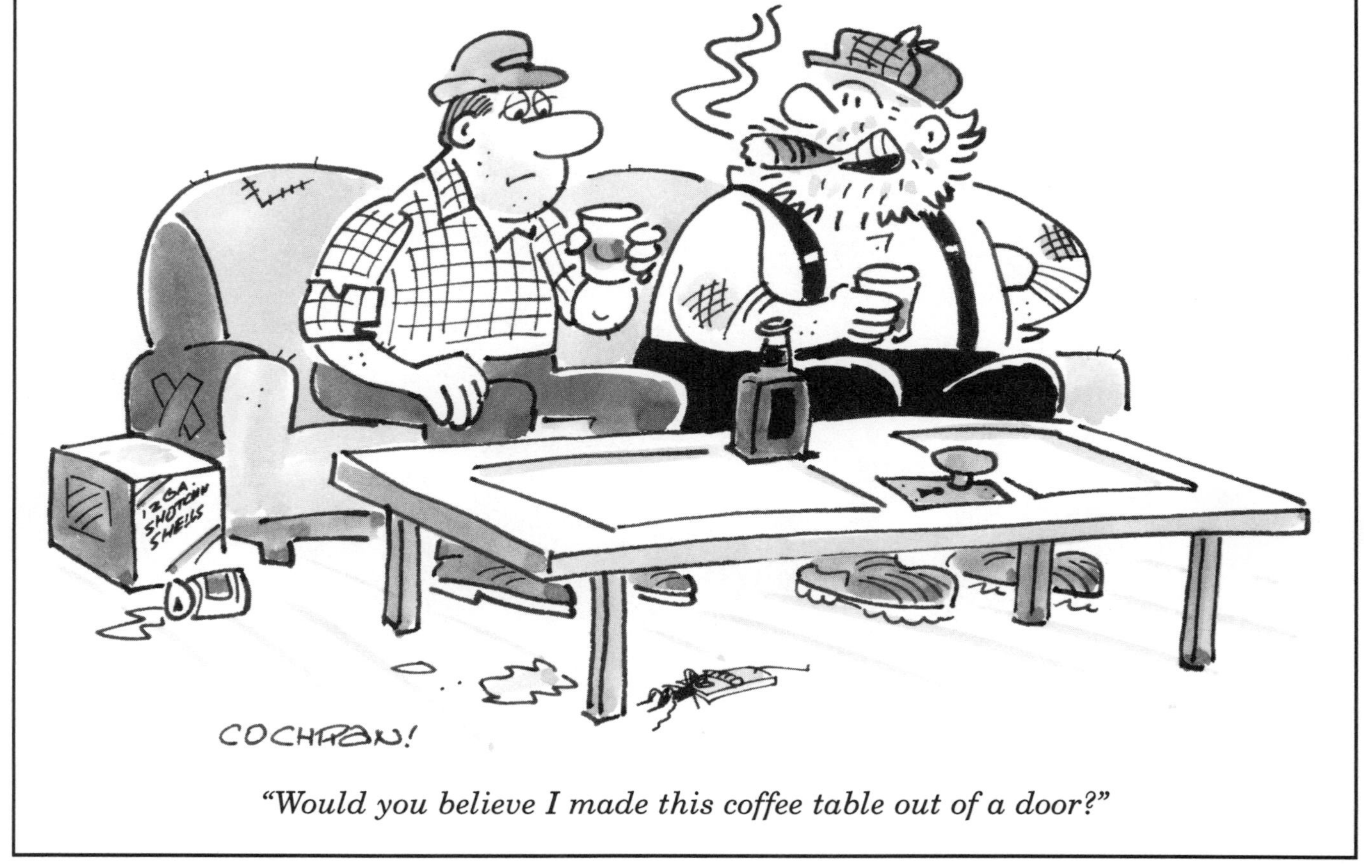
12 GA SHOTGUN SHELLS
COCHRAN!

*"Would you believe I made this coffee table out of a door?"*

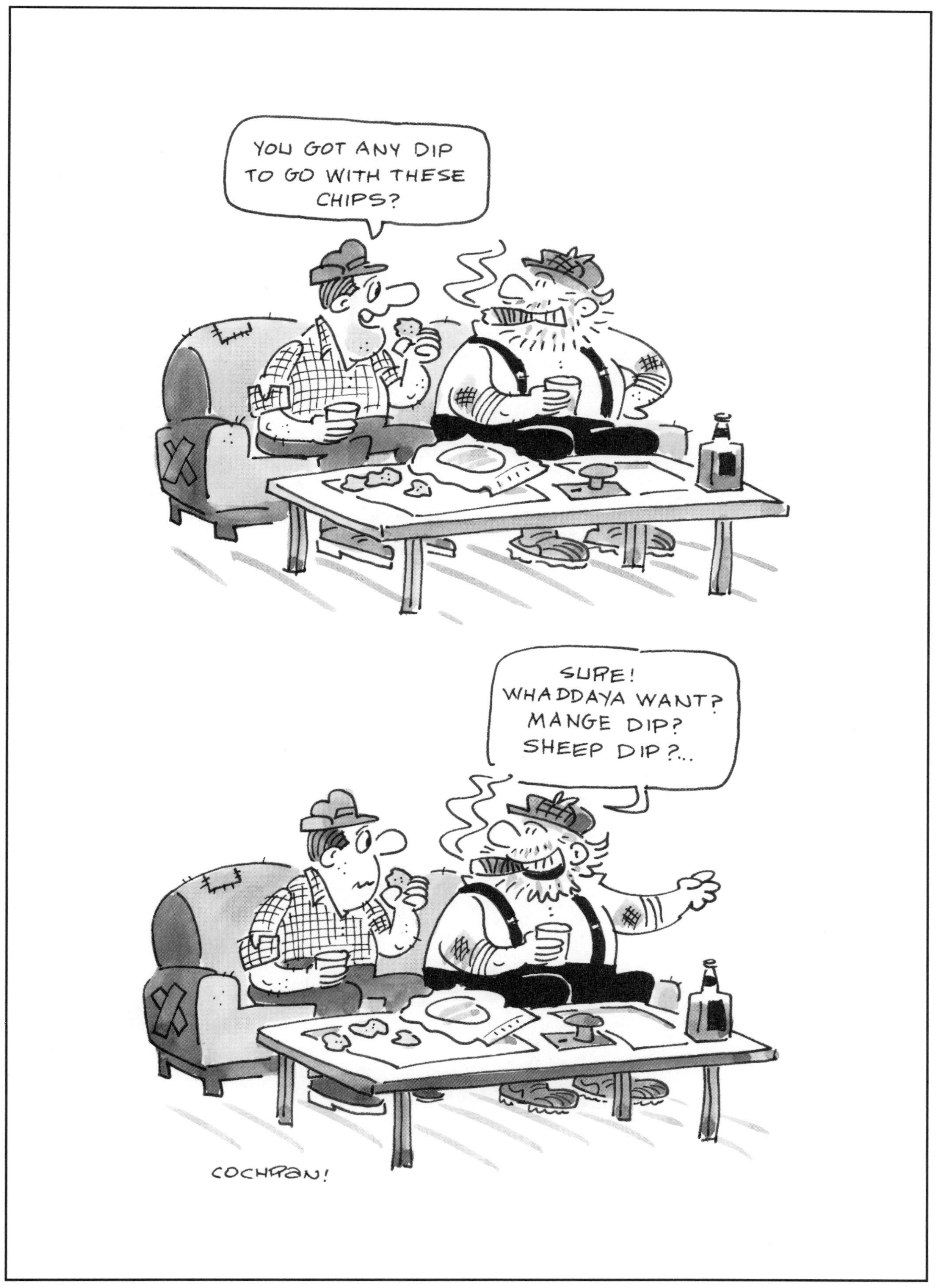

YOU GOT ANY DIP TO GO WITH THESE CHIPS?
SURE! WHADDAYA WANT? MANGE DIP? SHEEP DIP?...
COCHRAN!

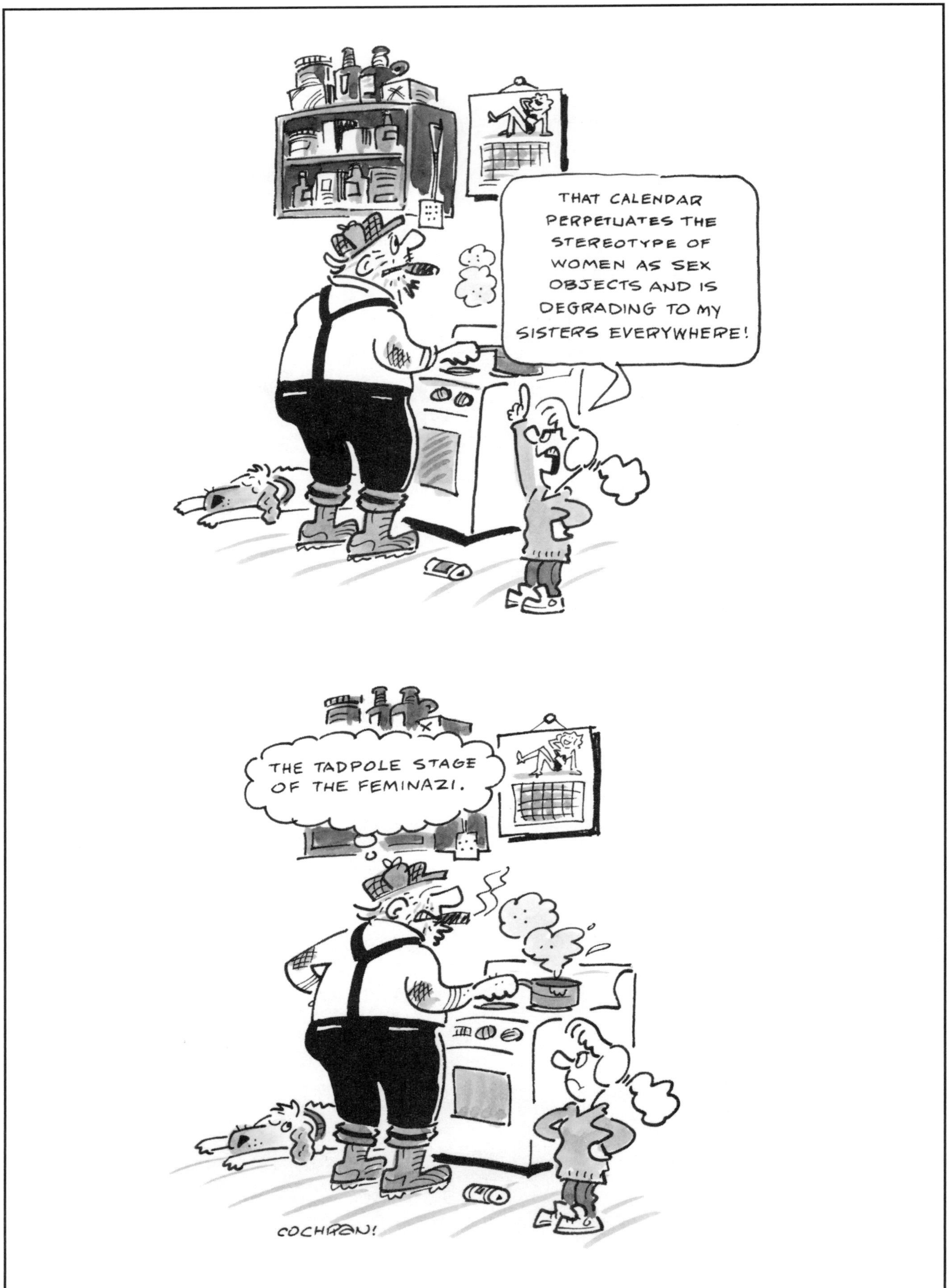
THAT CALENDAR PERPETUATES THE STEREOTYPE OF WOMEN AS SEX OBJECTS AND IS DEGRADING TO MY SISTERS EVERYWHERE!
THE TADPOLE STAGE OF THE FEMINAZI.
COCHRAN!

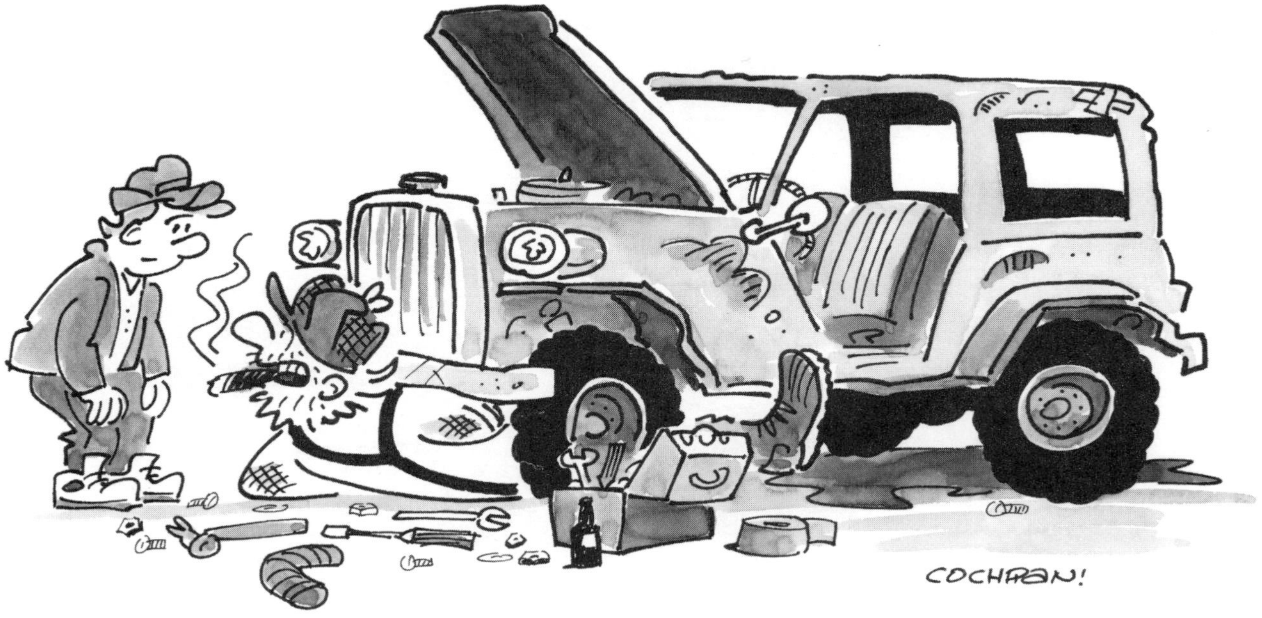
COCHRAN!

*"One of the bushings is gone, kid. Go find my tackle box and get me a plastic worm."*

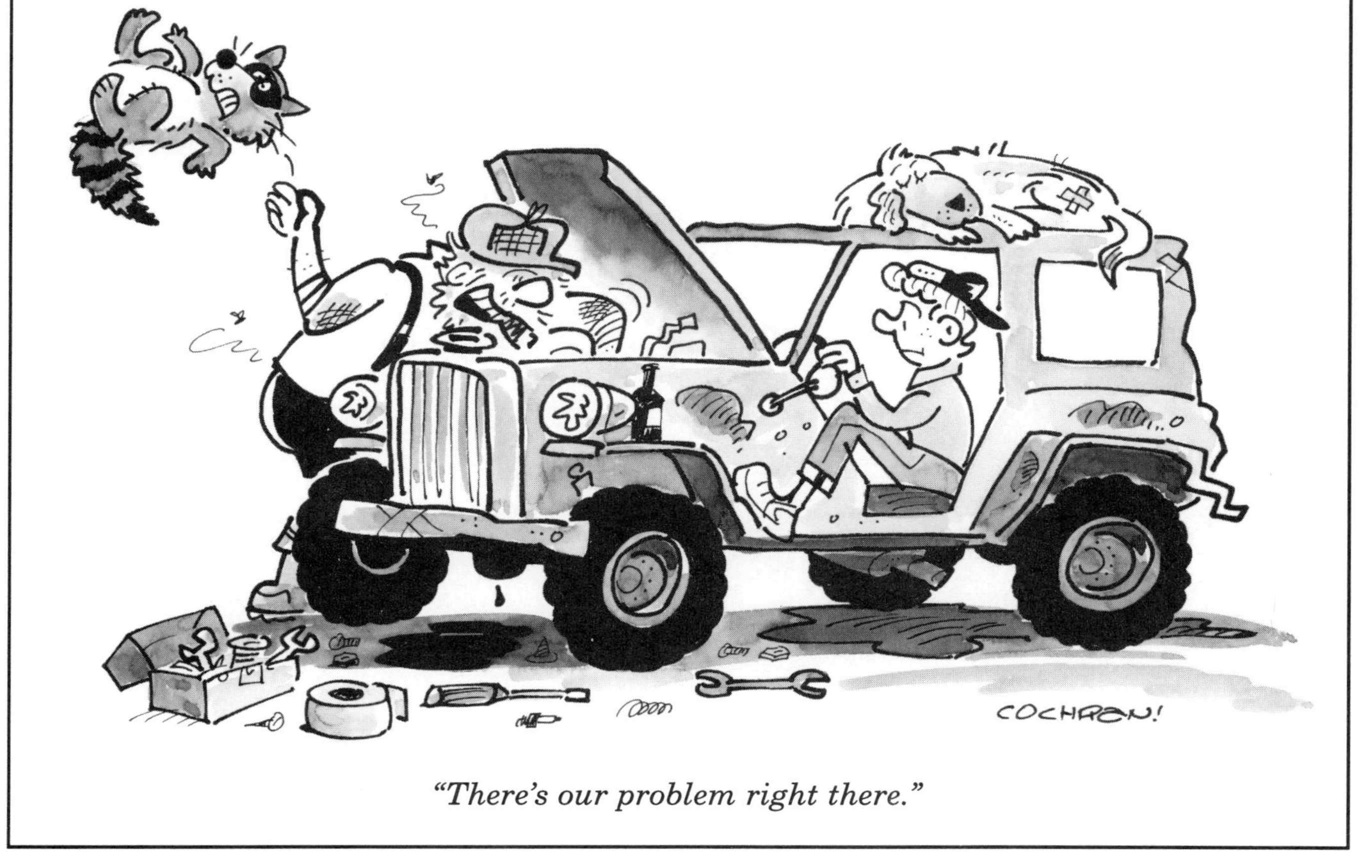
COCHRAN!

*"There's our problem right there."*

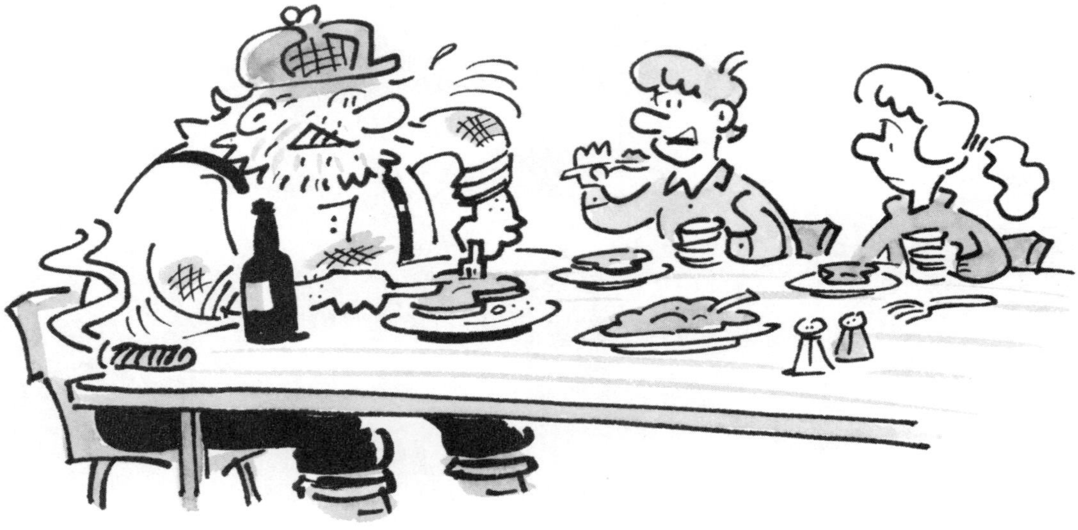

*"This meat's cold, Uncle Charlie."*

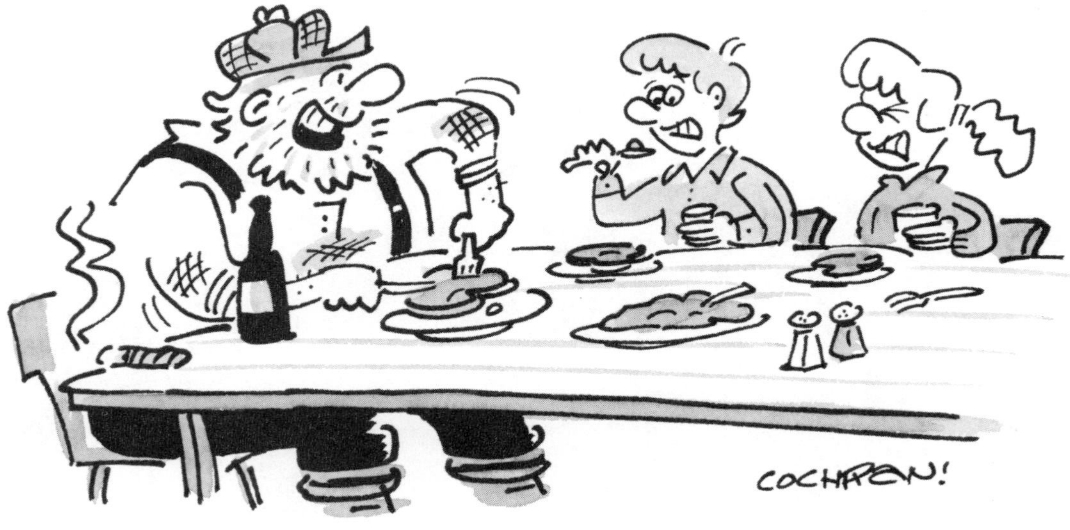
COCHRAN!

*"Shouldn't be. It was warm when I scraped it off the bumper."*

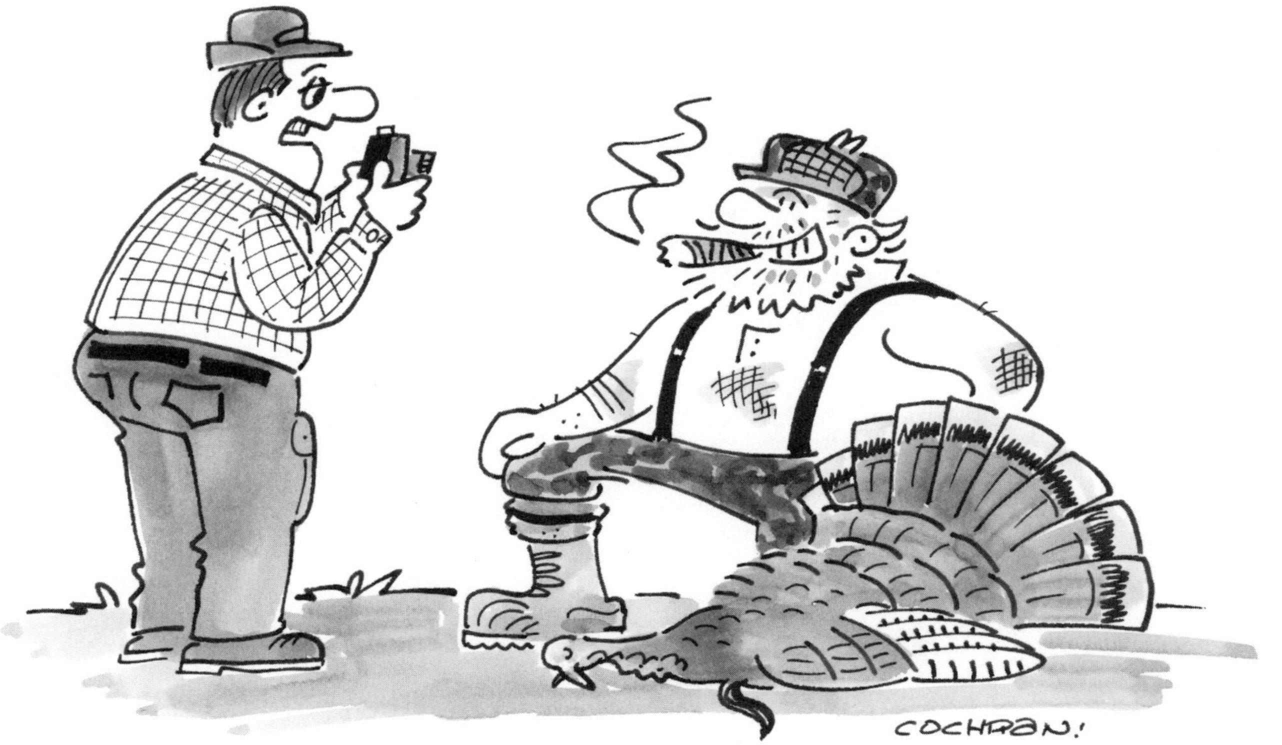
COCHRAN!

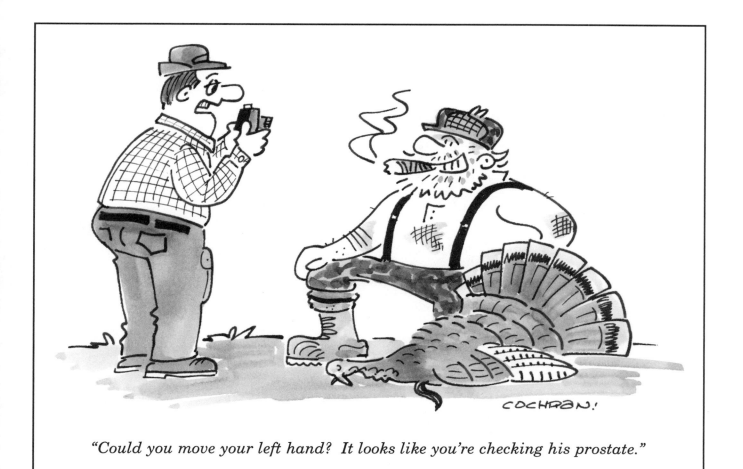

*"Could you move your left hand? It looks like you're checking his prostate."*

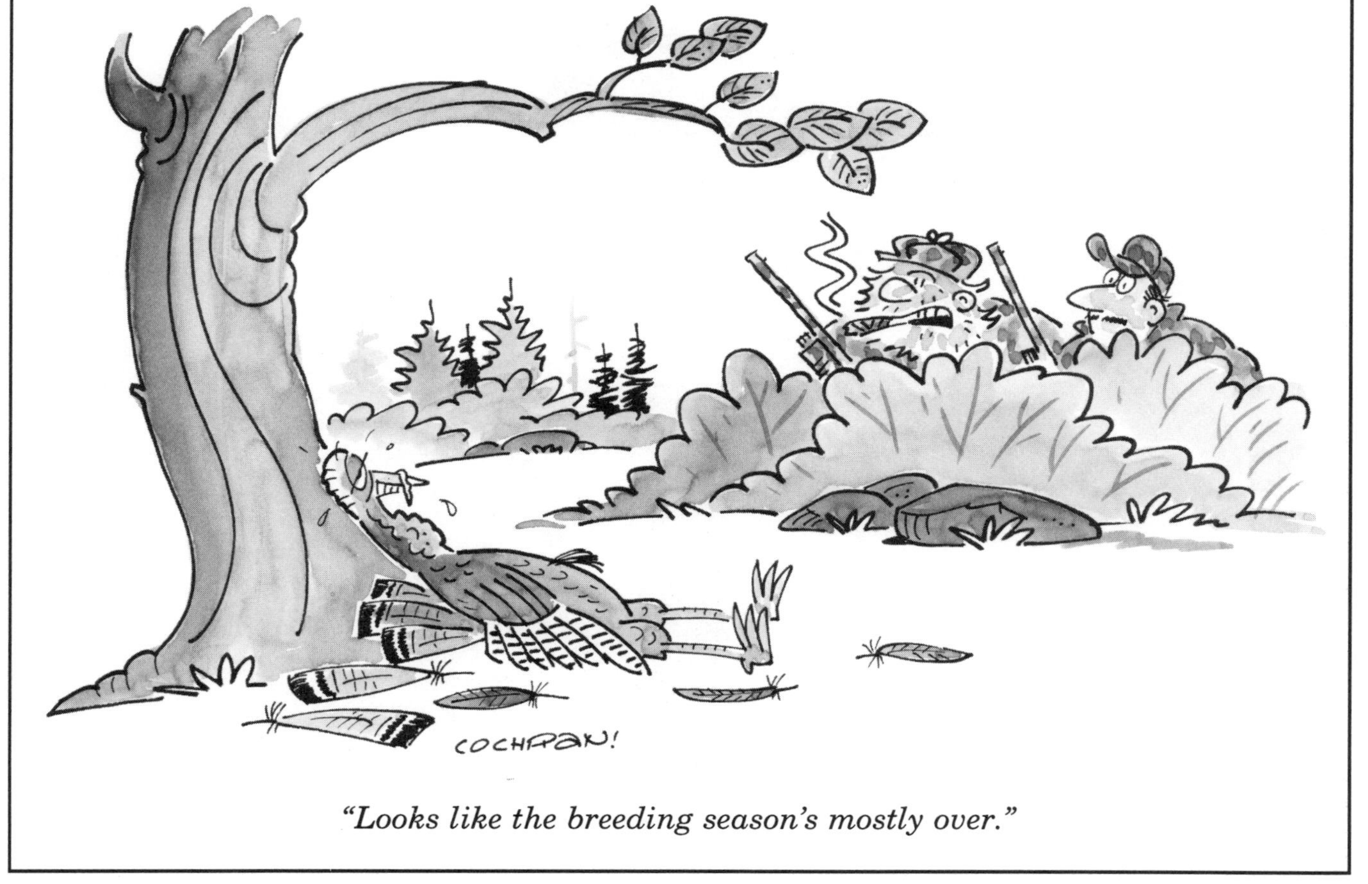
COCHRAN!

*"Looks like the breeding season's mostly over."*

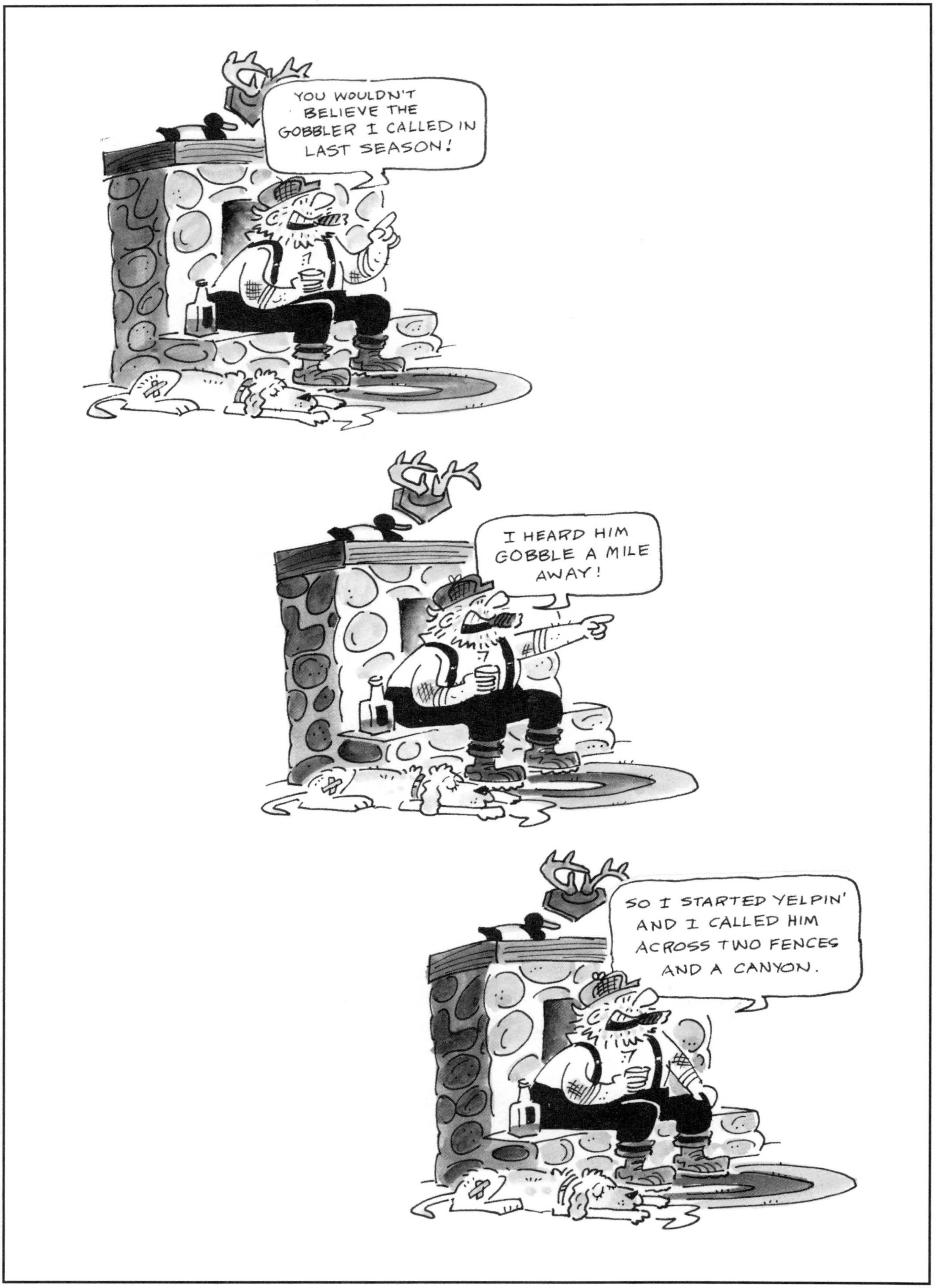
YOU WOULDN'T BELIEVE THE GOBBLER I CALLED IN LAST SEASON!
I HEARD HIM GOBBLE A MILE AWAY!
SO I STARTED YELPIN' AND I CALLED HIM ACROSS TWO FENCES AND A CANYON.

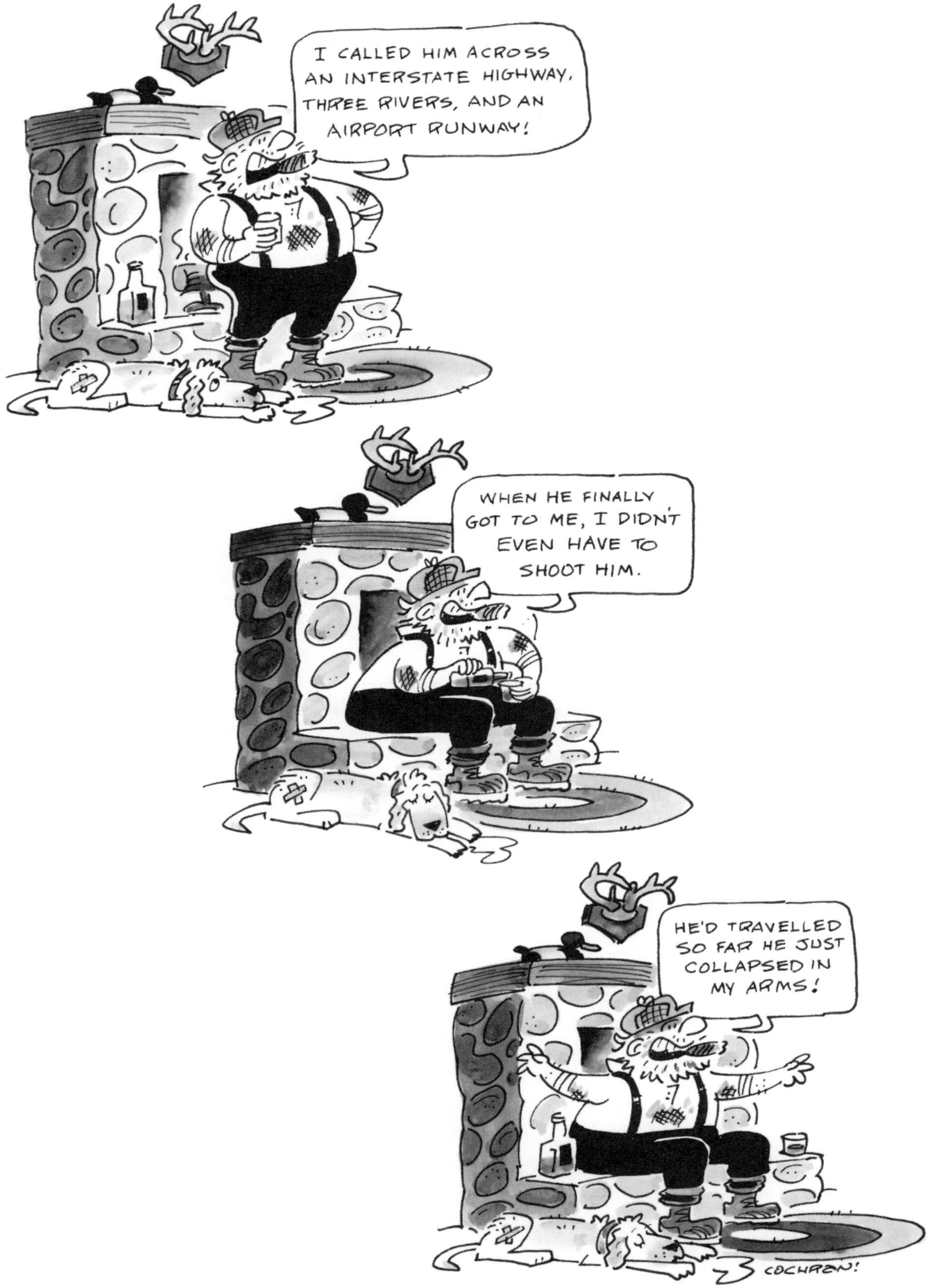
I CALLED HIM ACROSS AN INTERSTATE HIGHWAY, THREE RIVERS, AND AN AIRPORT RUNWAY!
WHEN HE FINALLY GOT TO ME, I DIDN'T EVEN HAVE TO SHOOT HIM.
HE'D TRAVELLED SO FAR HE JUST COLLAPSED IN MY ARMS!
COCHRAN!

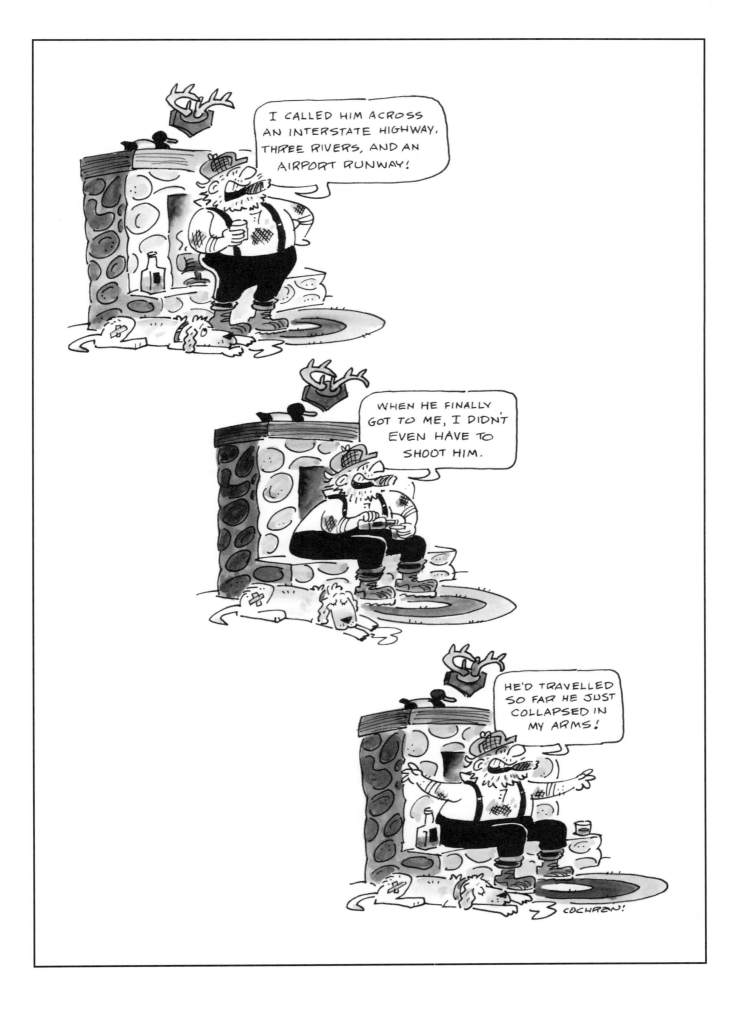

# Summer

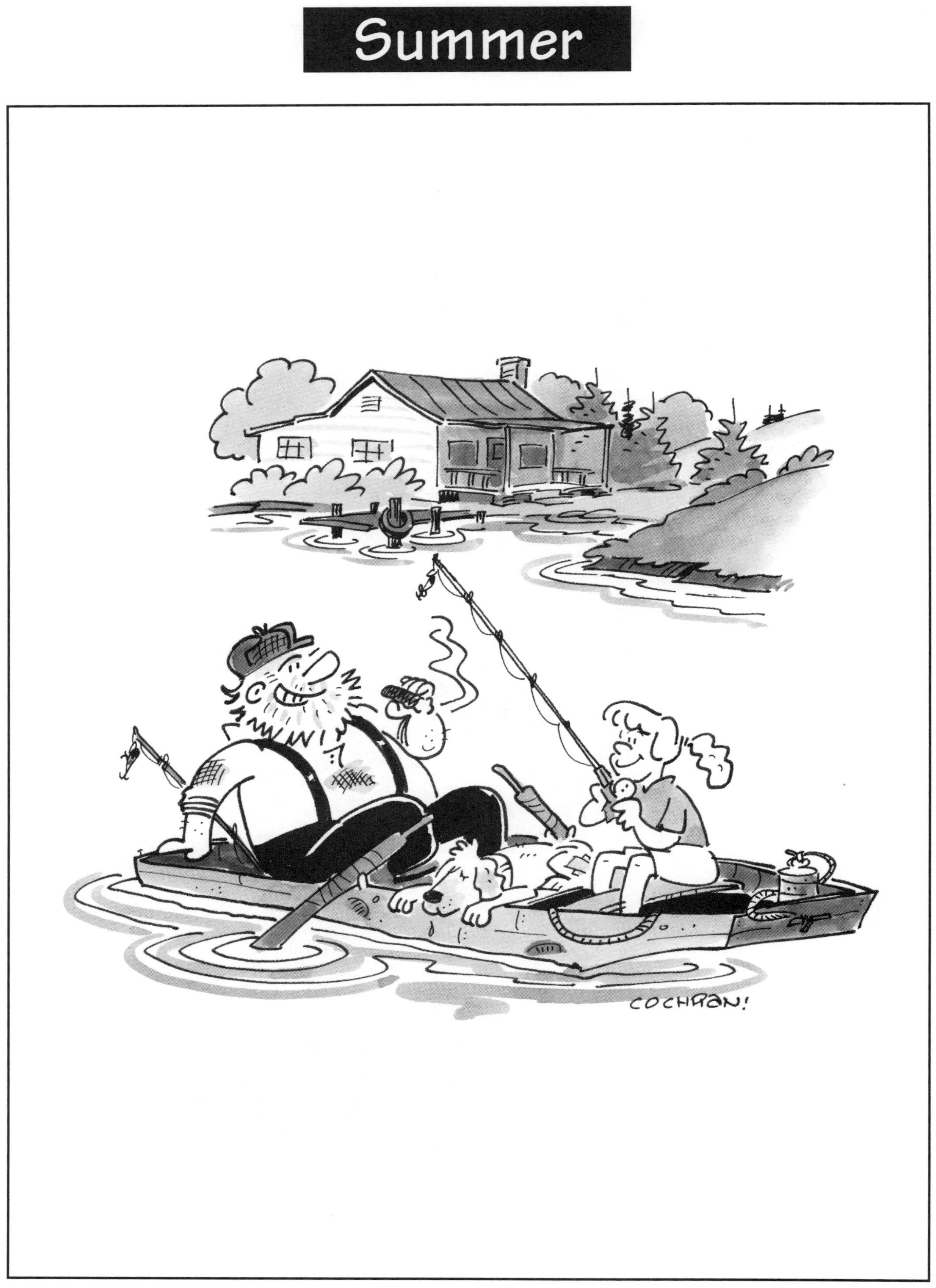
COCHRAN!

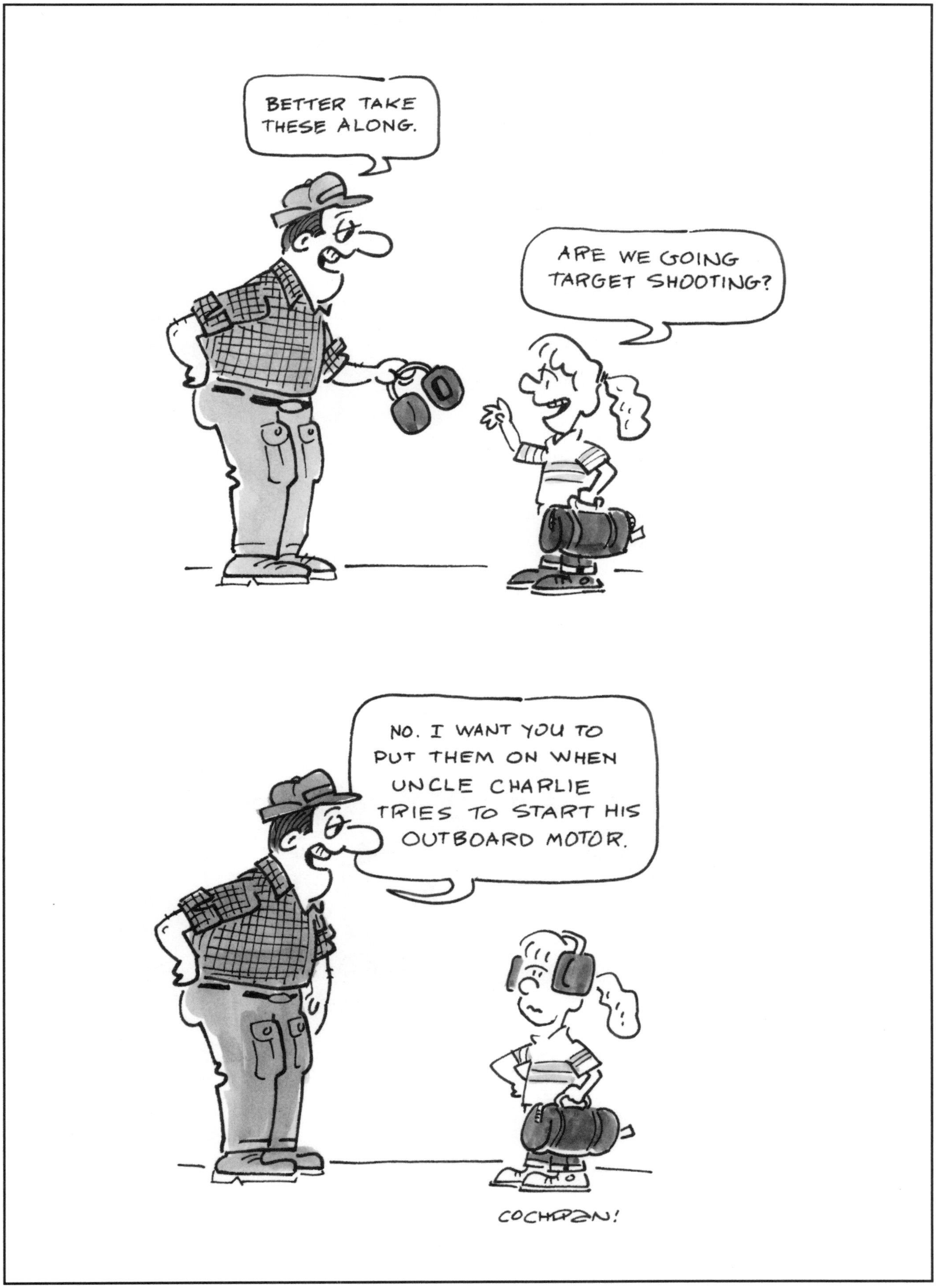

BETTER TAKE THESE ALONG.
ARE WE GOING TARGET SHOOTING?
NO. I WANT YOU TO PUT THEM ON WHEN UNCLE CHARLIE TRIES TO START HIS OUTBOARD MOTOR.
COCHRAN!

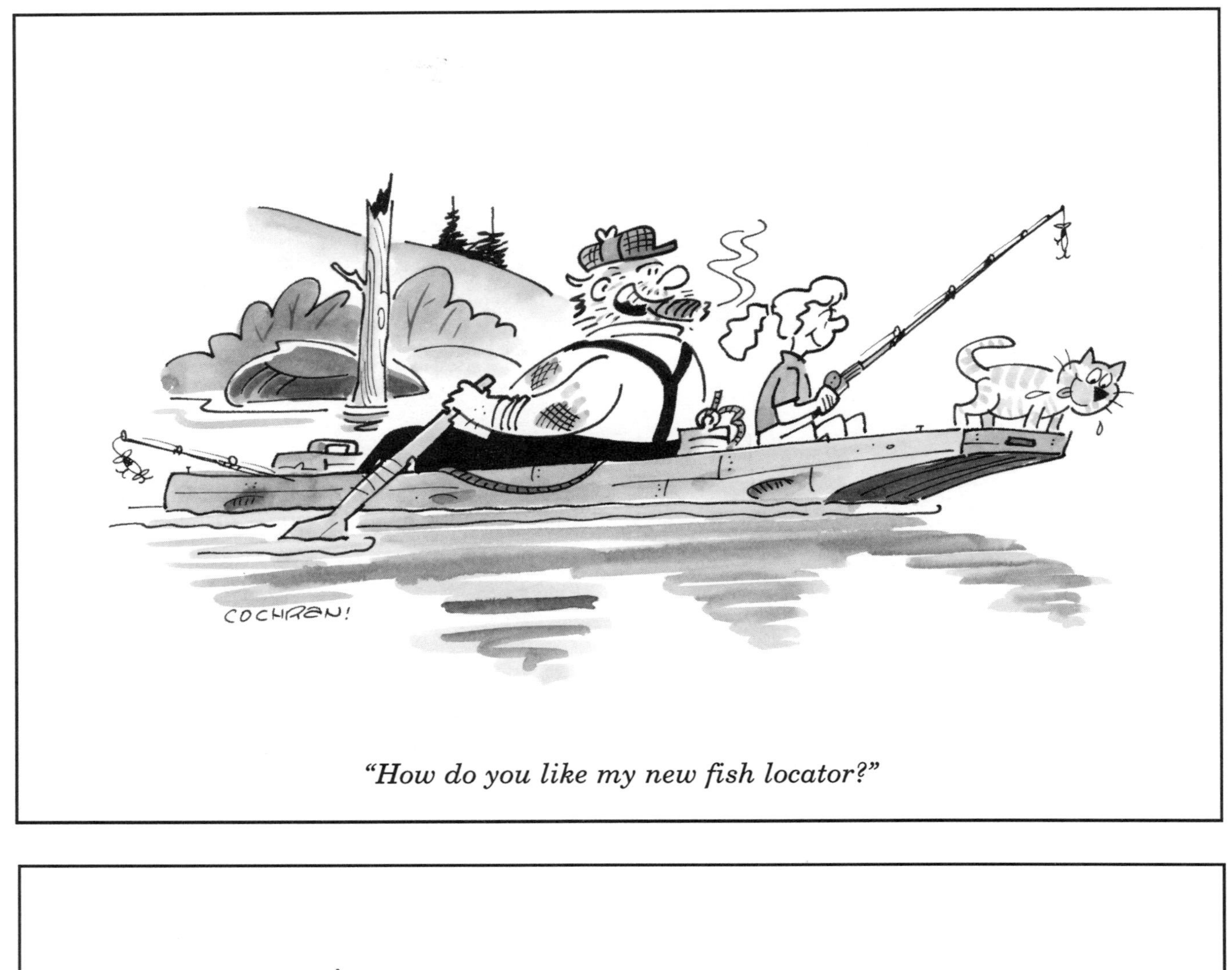
COCHRAN!

*"How do you like my new fish locator?"*

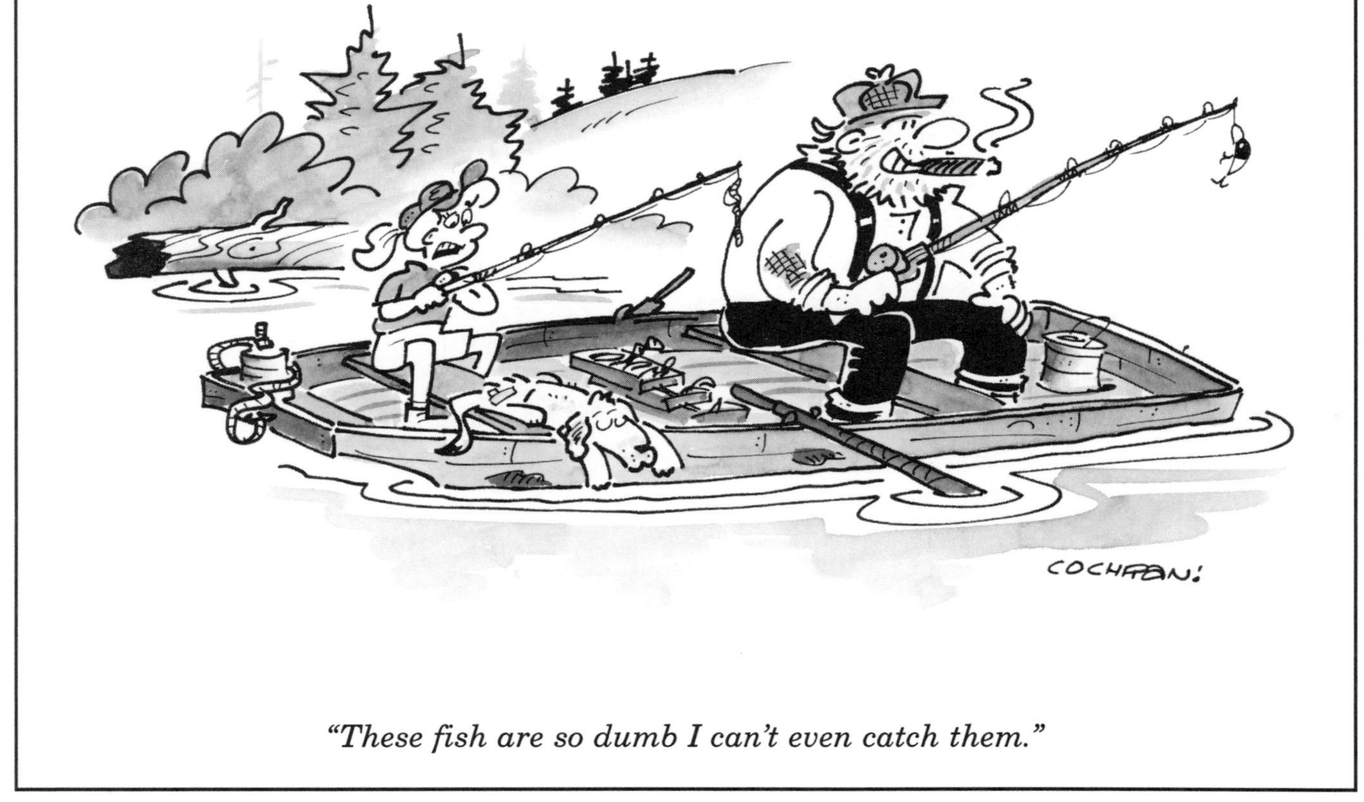
COCHRAN!

*"These fish are so dumb I can't even catch them."*

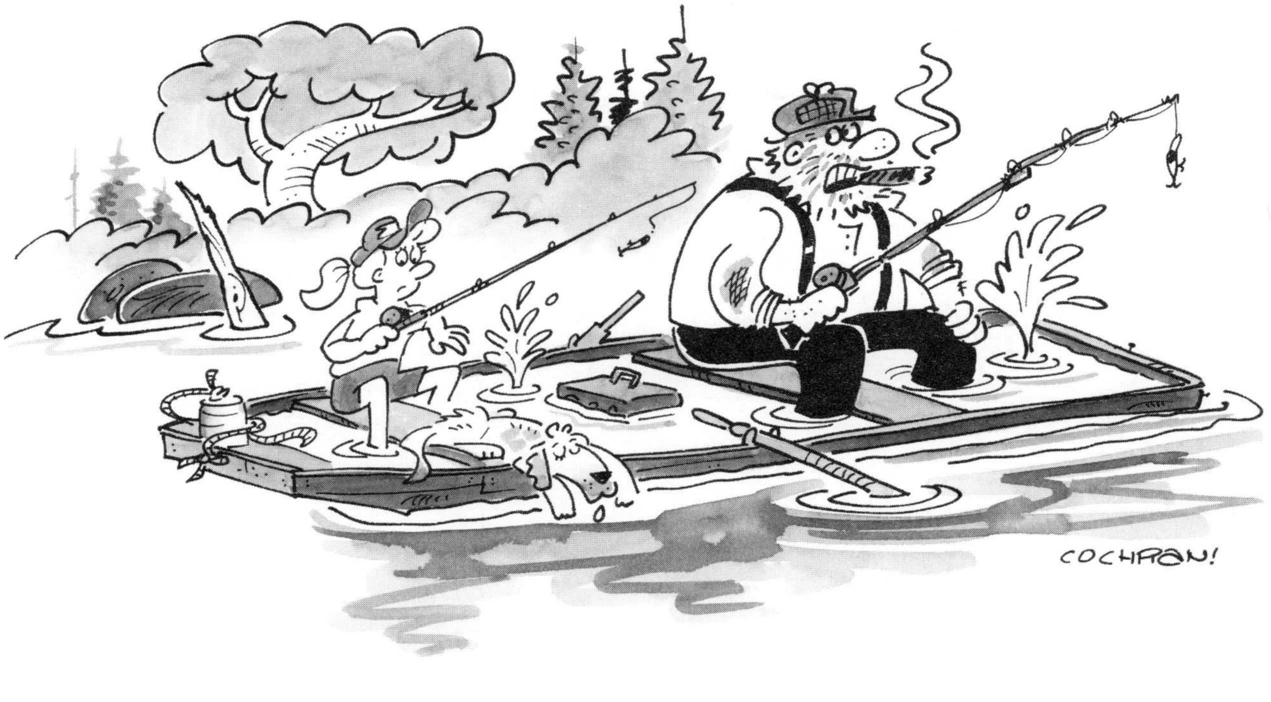
COCHRAN!

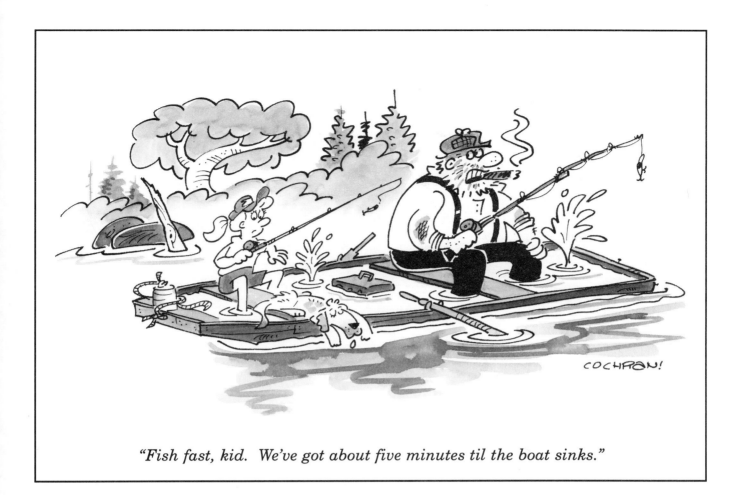

*"Fish fast, kid. We've got about five minutes til the boat sinks."*

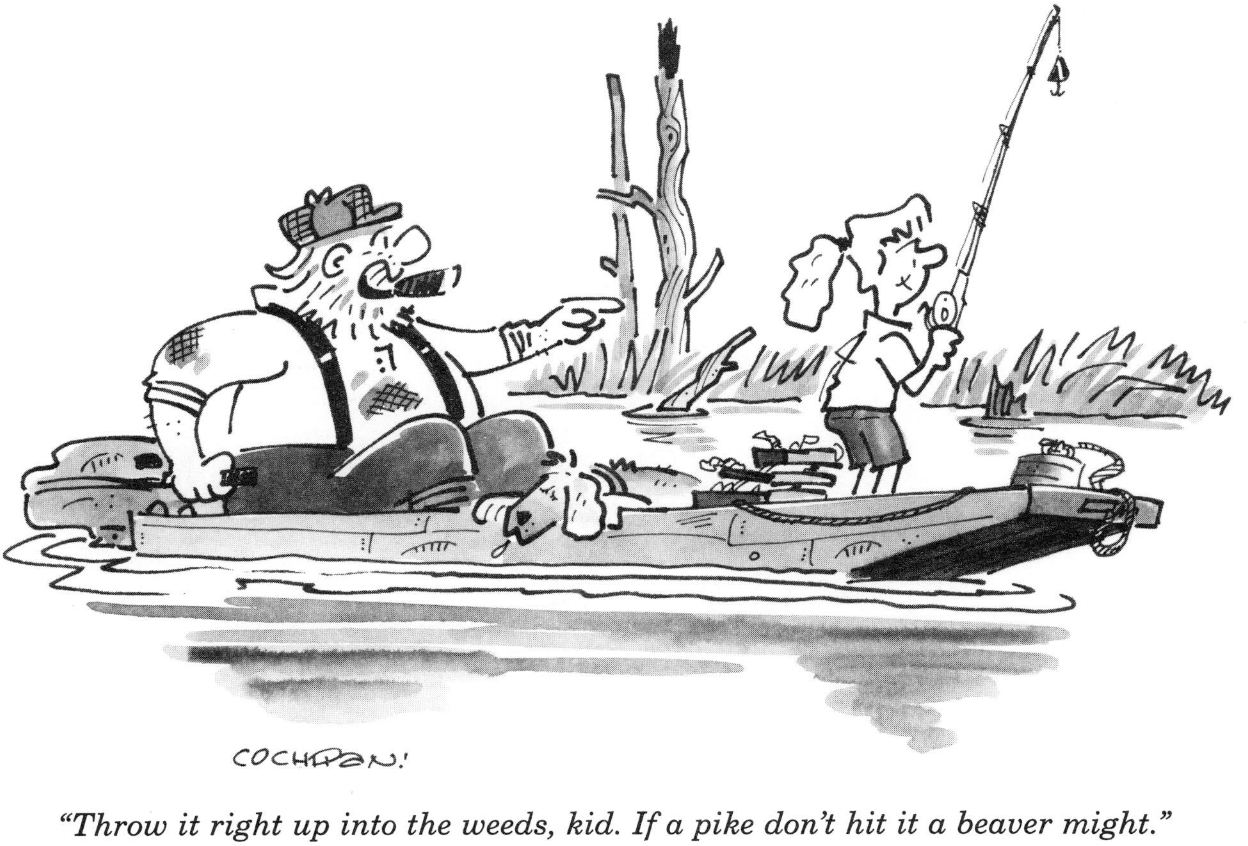
COCHRAN!

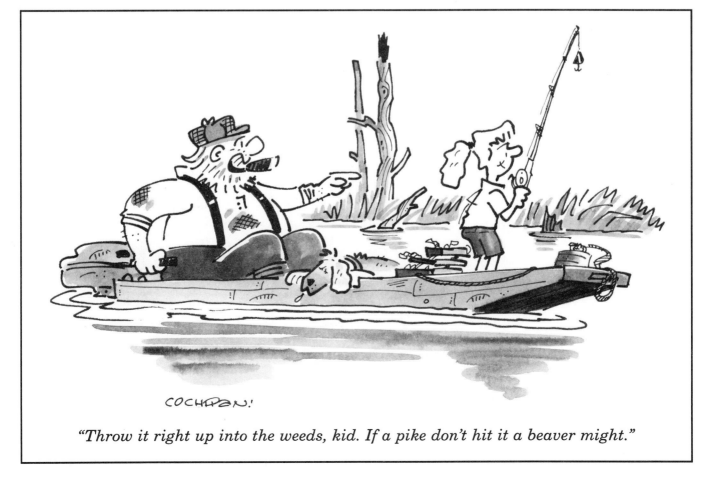

*"Throw it right up into the weeds, kid. If a pike don't hit it a beaver might."*

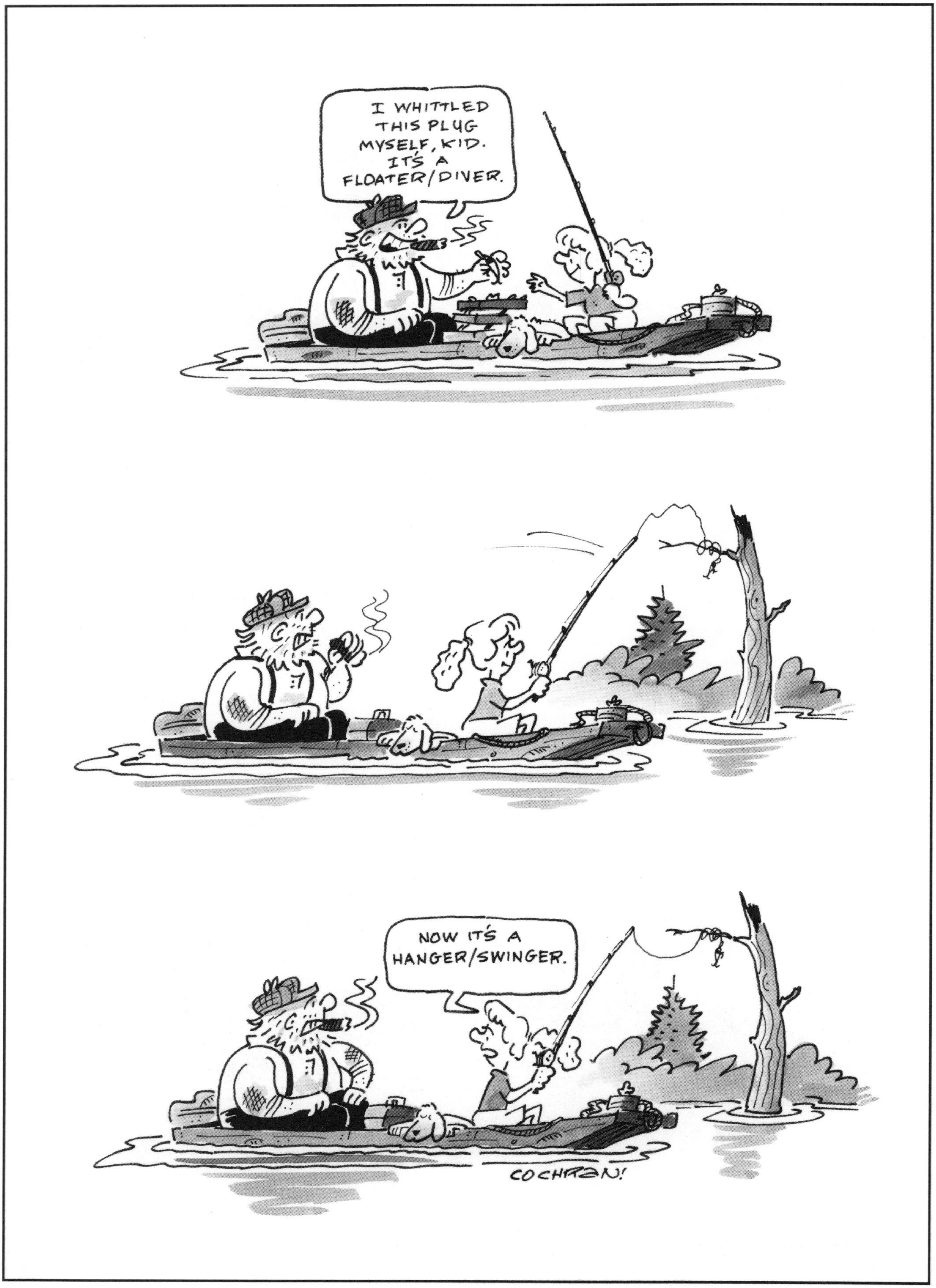
I WHITTLED THIS PLUG MYSELF, KID. IT'S A FLOATER/DIVER.
NOW IT'S A HANGER/SWINGER.
COCHRAN!

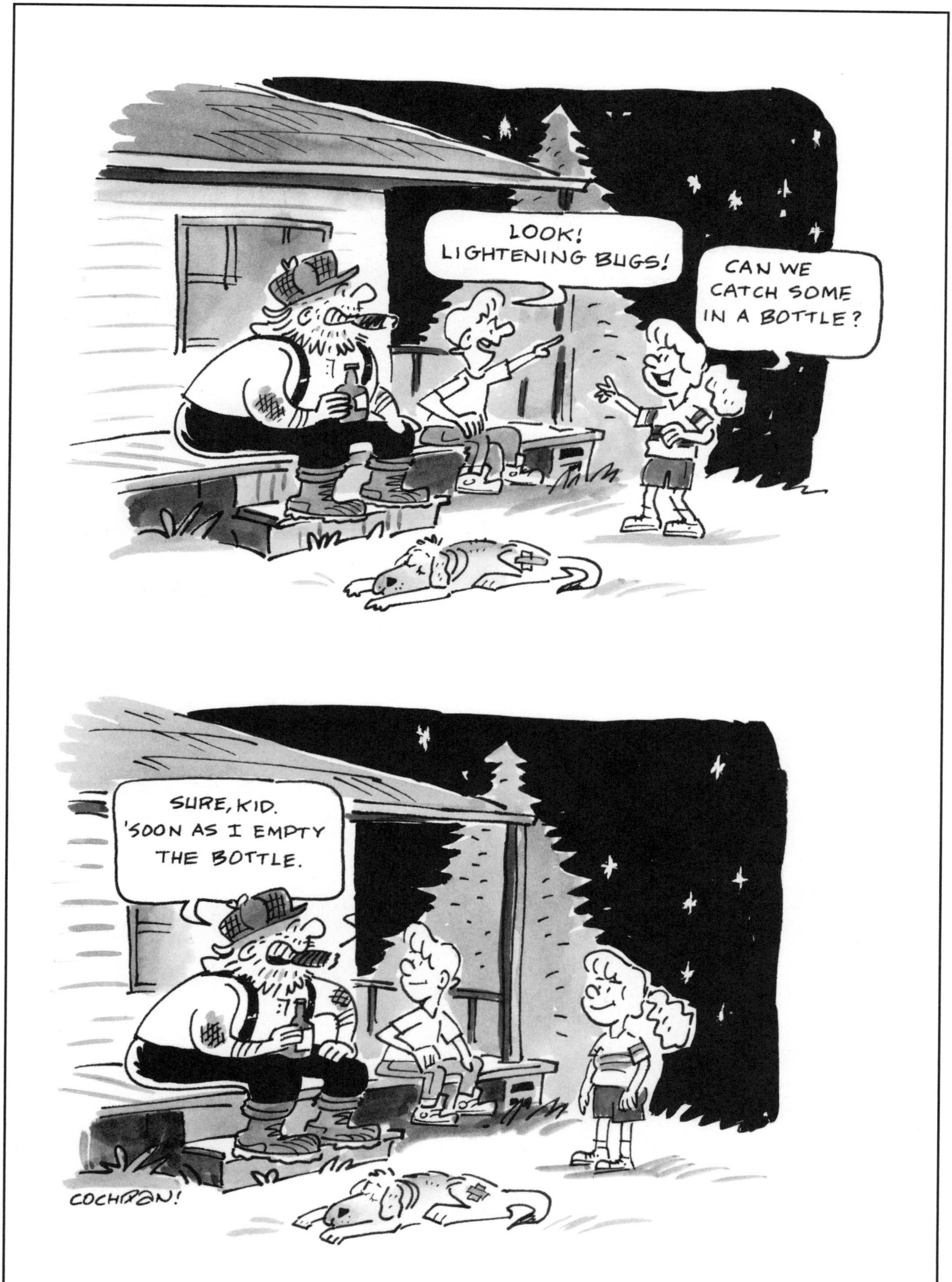
LOOK! LIGHTENING BUGS!
CAN WE CATCH SOME IN A BOTTLE?
SURE, KID. 'SOON AS I EMPTY THE BOTTLE.
COCHRAN!

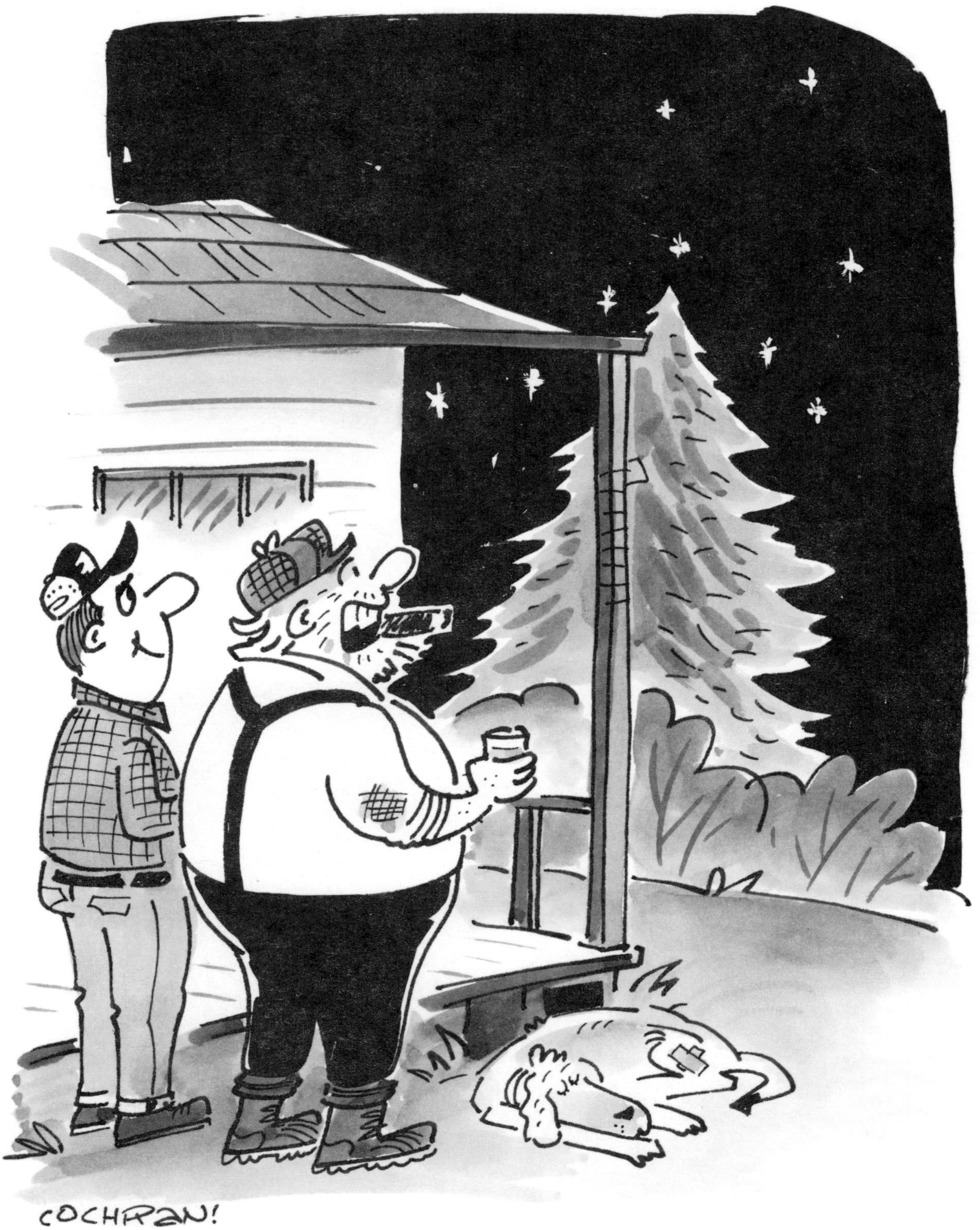
COCHRAN!

*"Orion's belt, huh. I always thought it looked like a roll of duct tape."*

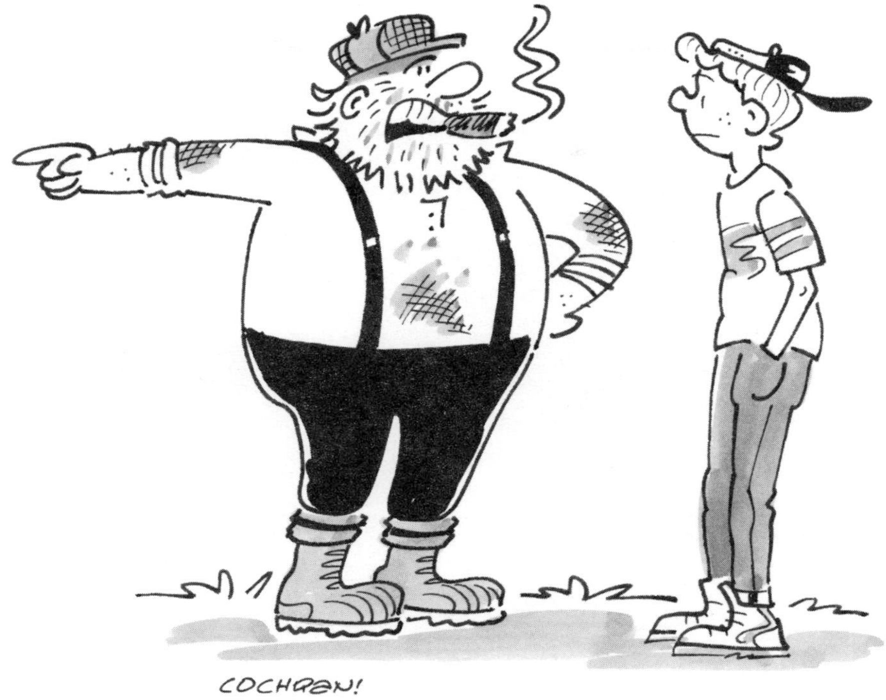
COCHRAN!

*"Whaddaya mean there's nothing to do at night around here? You can go down to the Dairy Queen and watch the bug zapper!"*

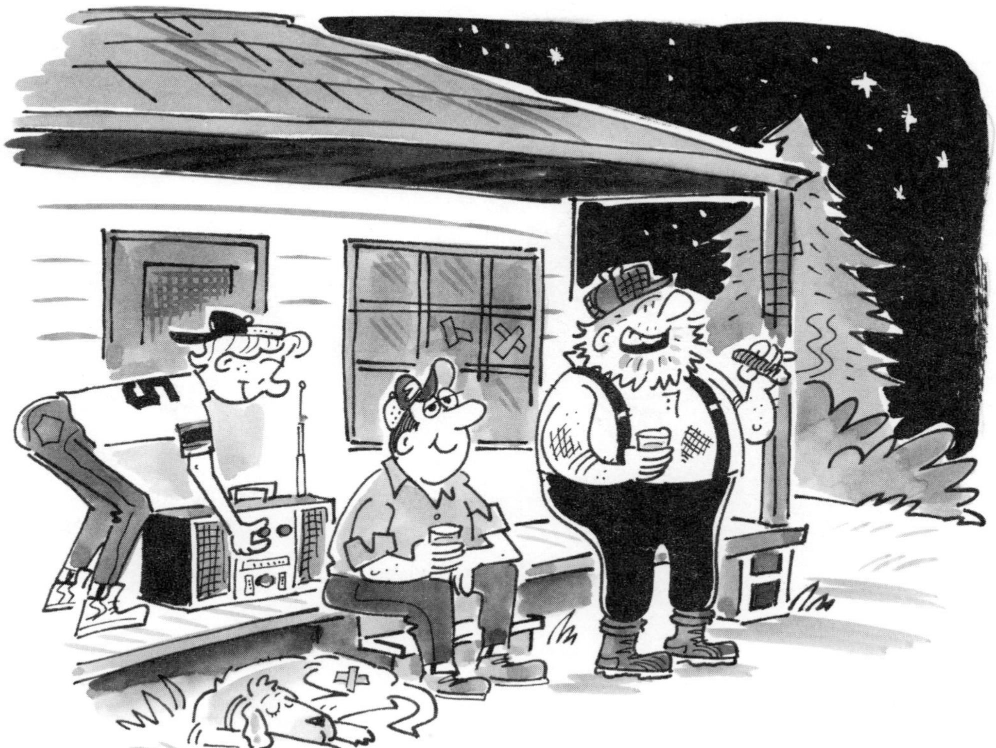
COCHRAN!

*"Sure is peaceful, isn't it."*

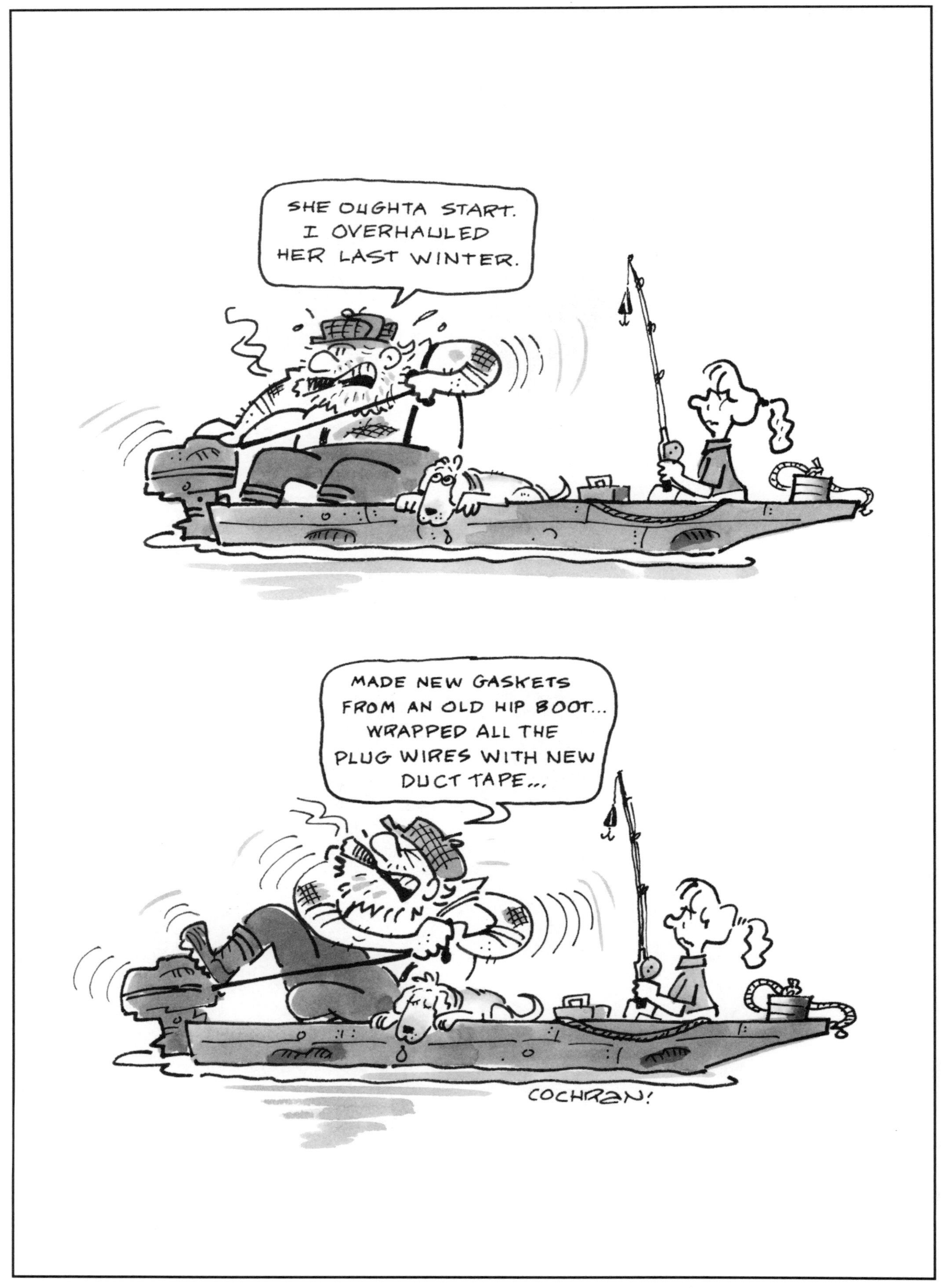
SHE OUGHTA START. I OVERHAULED HER LAST WINTER.
MADE NEW GASKETS FROM AN OLD HIP BOOT... WRAPPED ALL THE PLUG WIRES WITH NEW DUCT TAPE...
COCHRAN!

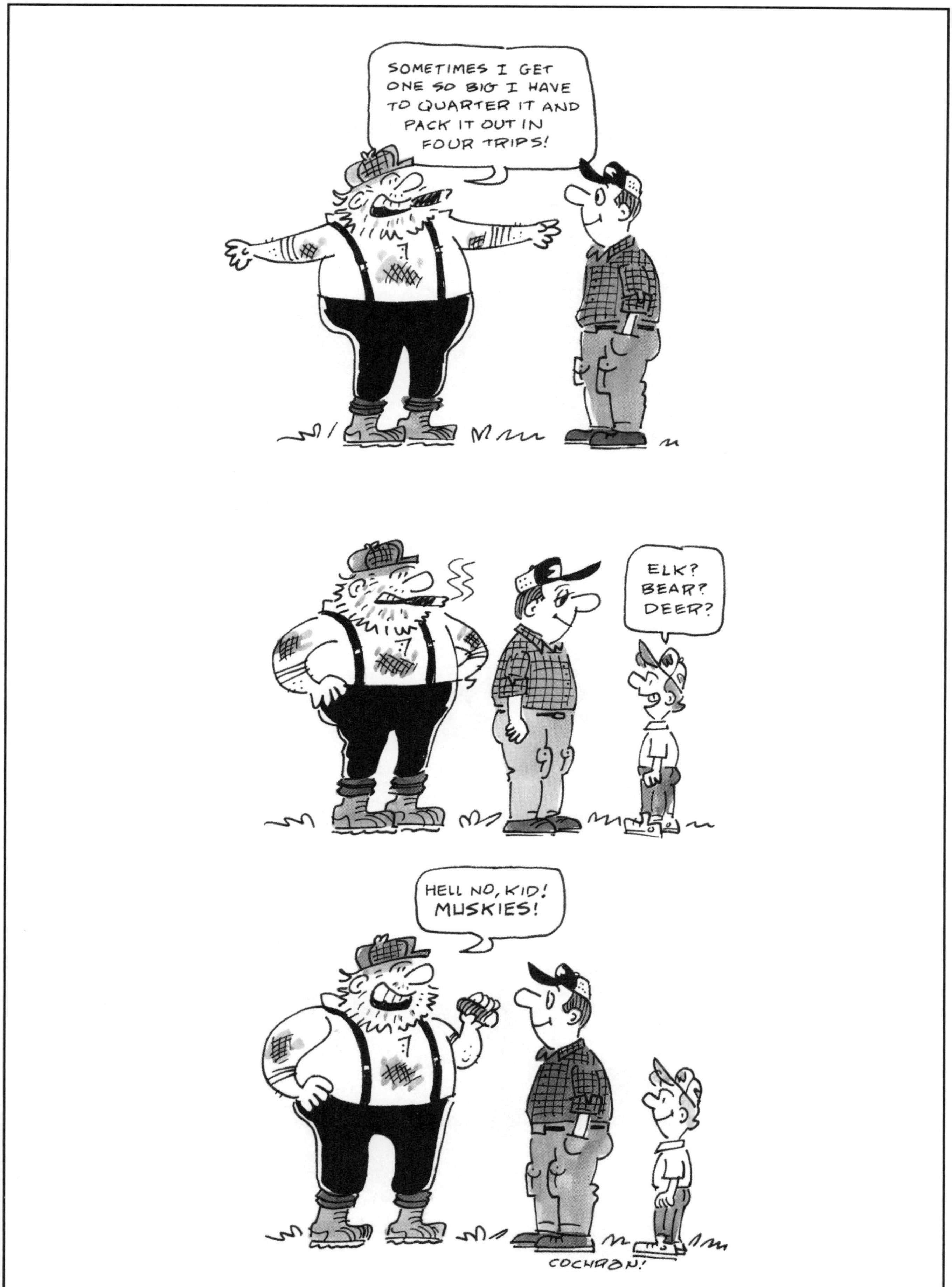
SOMETIMES I GET ONE SO BIG I HAVE TO QUARTER IT AND PACK IT OUT IN FOUR TRIPS!
ELK? BEAR? DEER?
HELL NO, KID! MUSKIES!
COCHRAN!

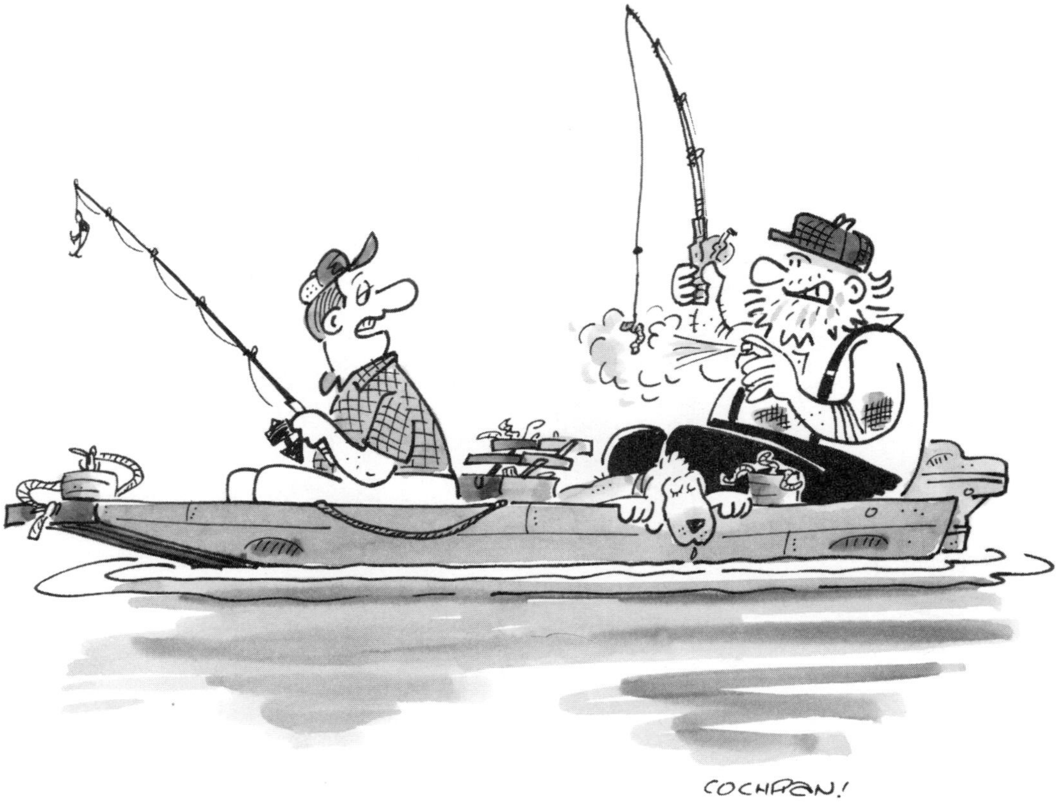
COCHRAN!

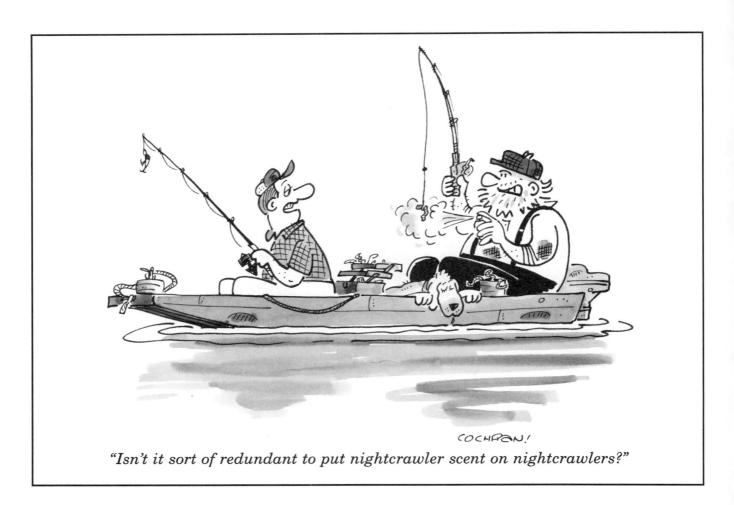

*"Isn't it sort of redundant to put nightcrawler scent on nightcrawlers?"*

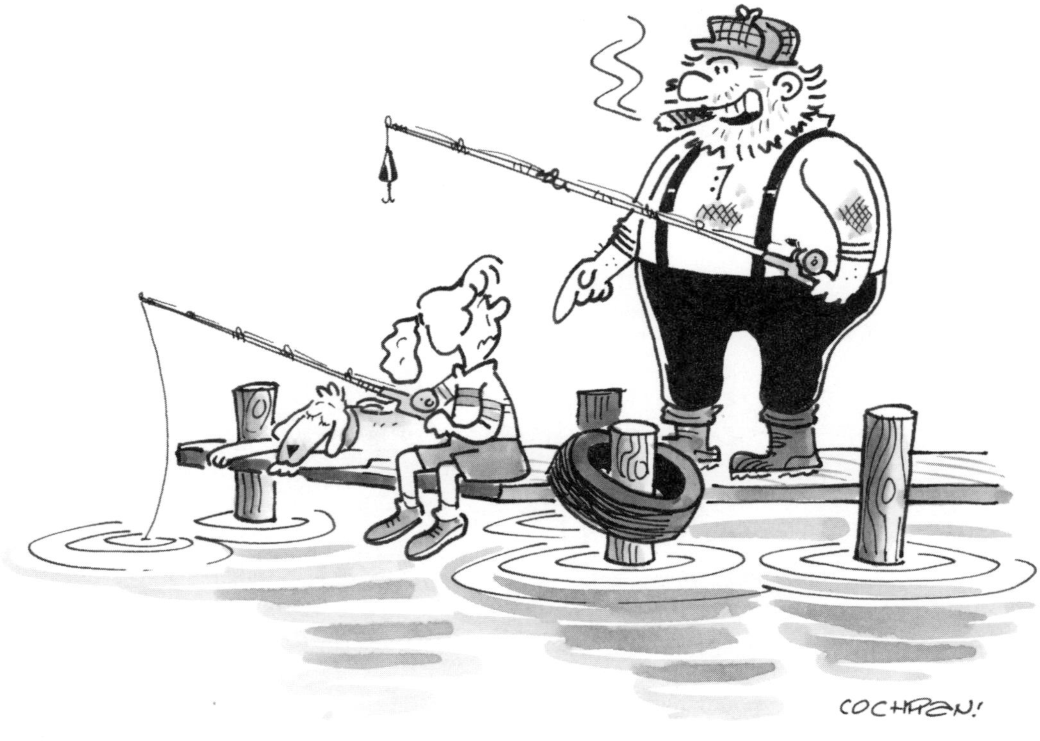
7
COCHRAN!

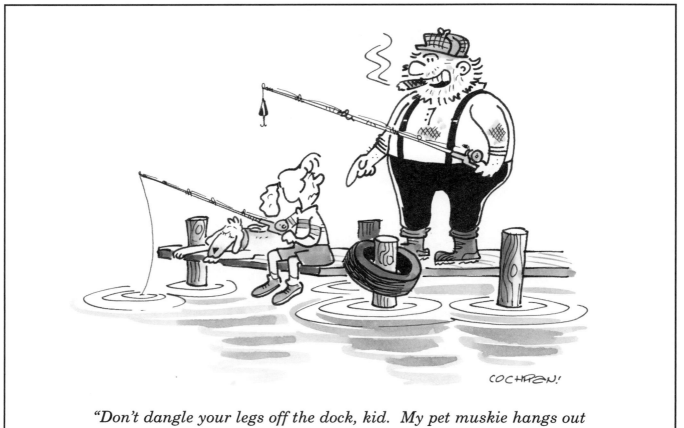

*"Don't dangle your legs off the dock, kid. My pet muskie hangs out under there and he might be in a bad mood."*

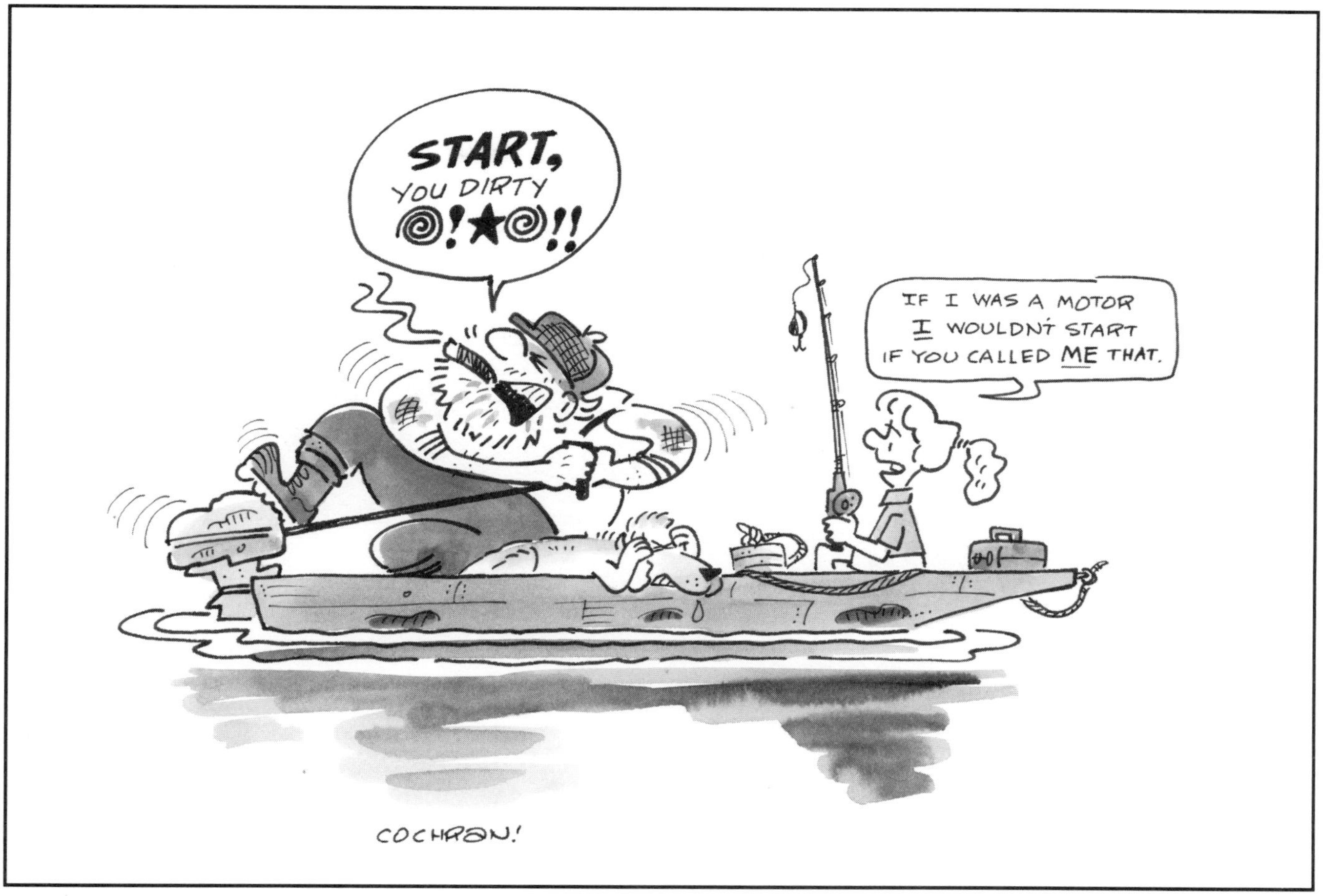
START, YOU DIRTY @!★@!!
IF I WAS A MOTOR I WOULDN'T START IF YOU CALLED ME THAT.
COCHRAN!

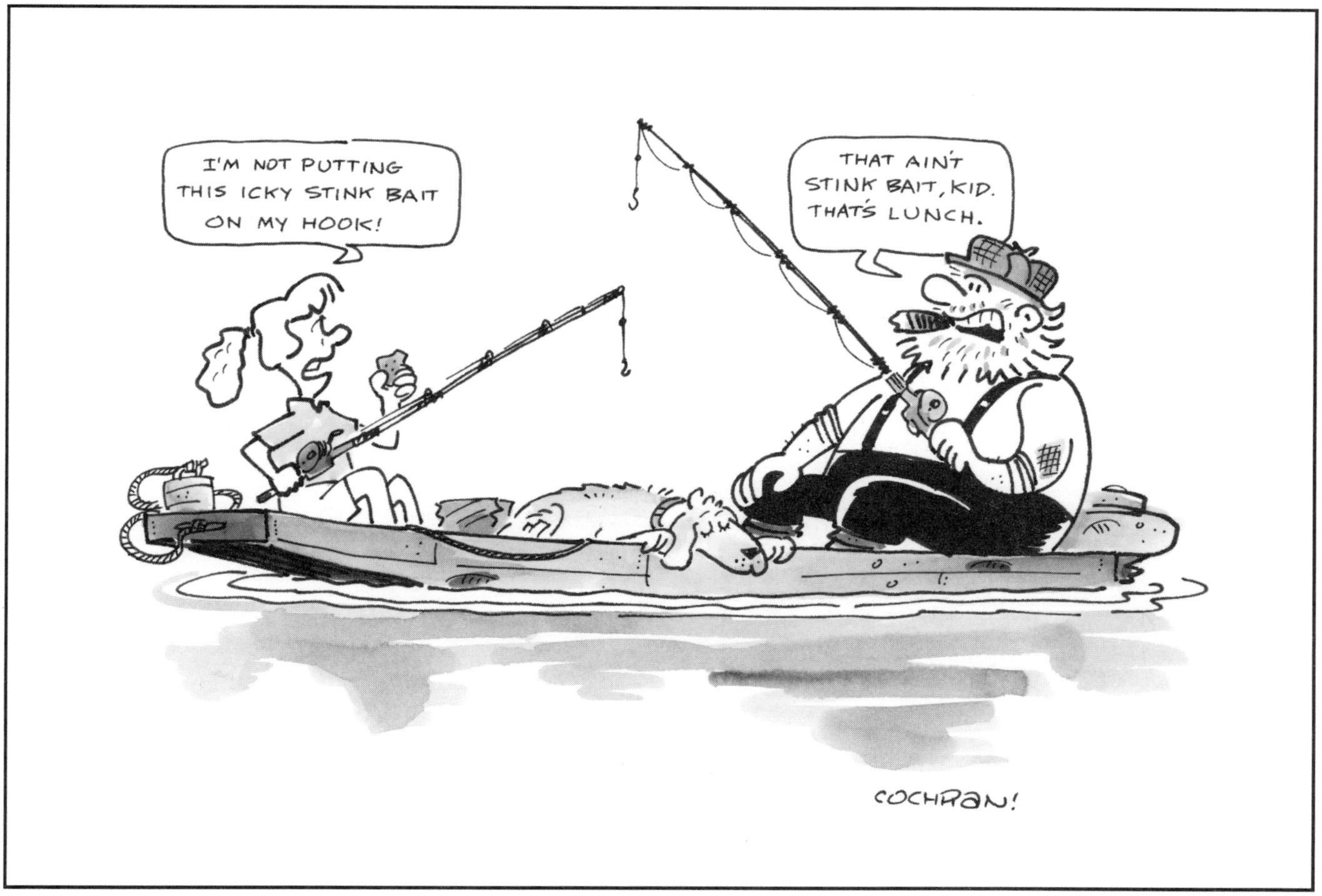
I'M NOT PUTTING THIS ICKY STINK BAIT ON MY HOOK!
THAT AIN'T STINK BAIT, KID. THAT'S LUNCH.
COCHRAN!

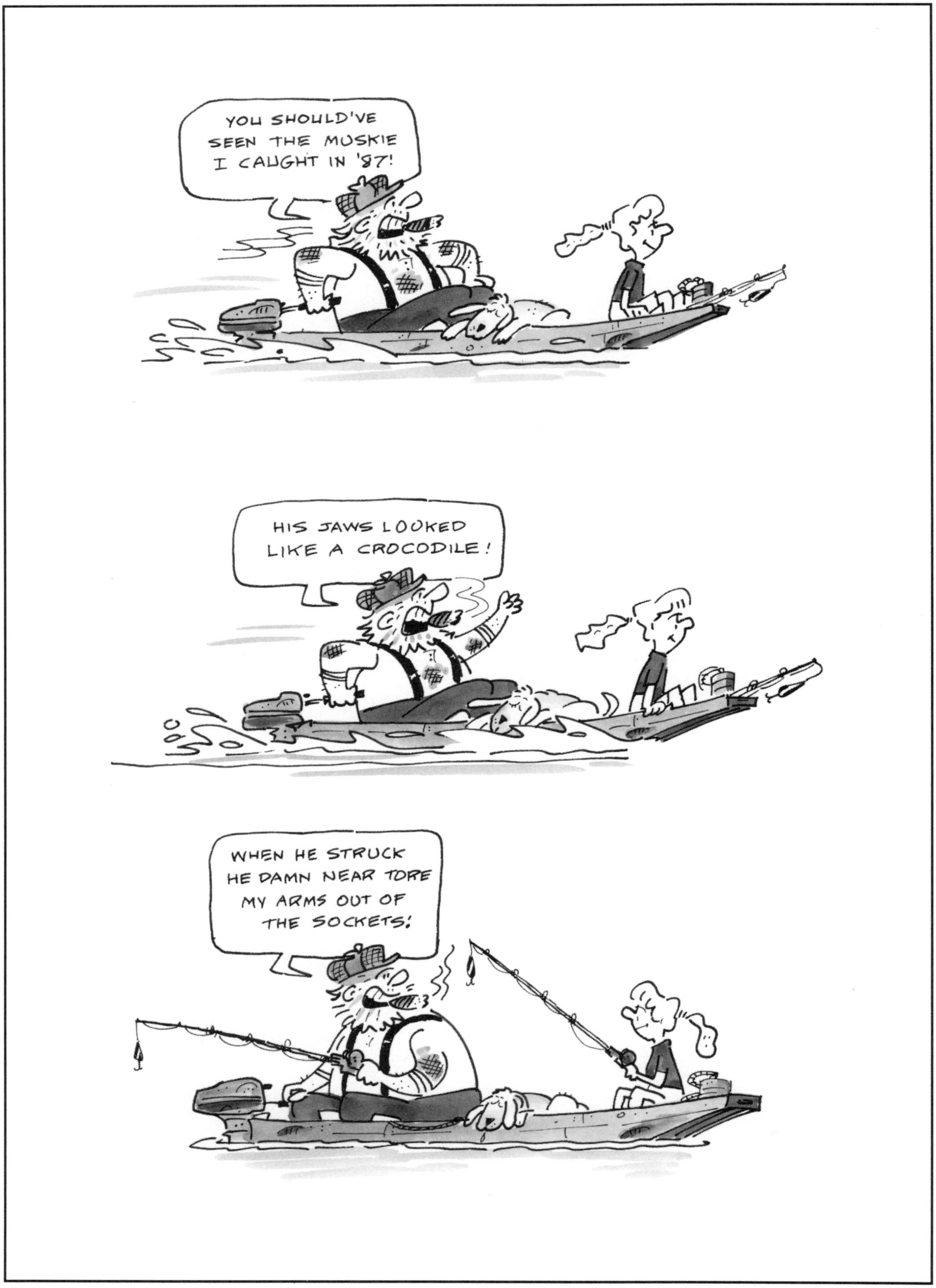
YOU SHOULD'VE SEEN THE MUSKIE I CAUGHT IN '87!
HIS JAWS LOOKED LIKE A CROCODILE!
WHEN HE STRUCK HE DAMN NEAR TORE MY ARMS OUT OF THE SOCKETS!

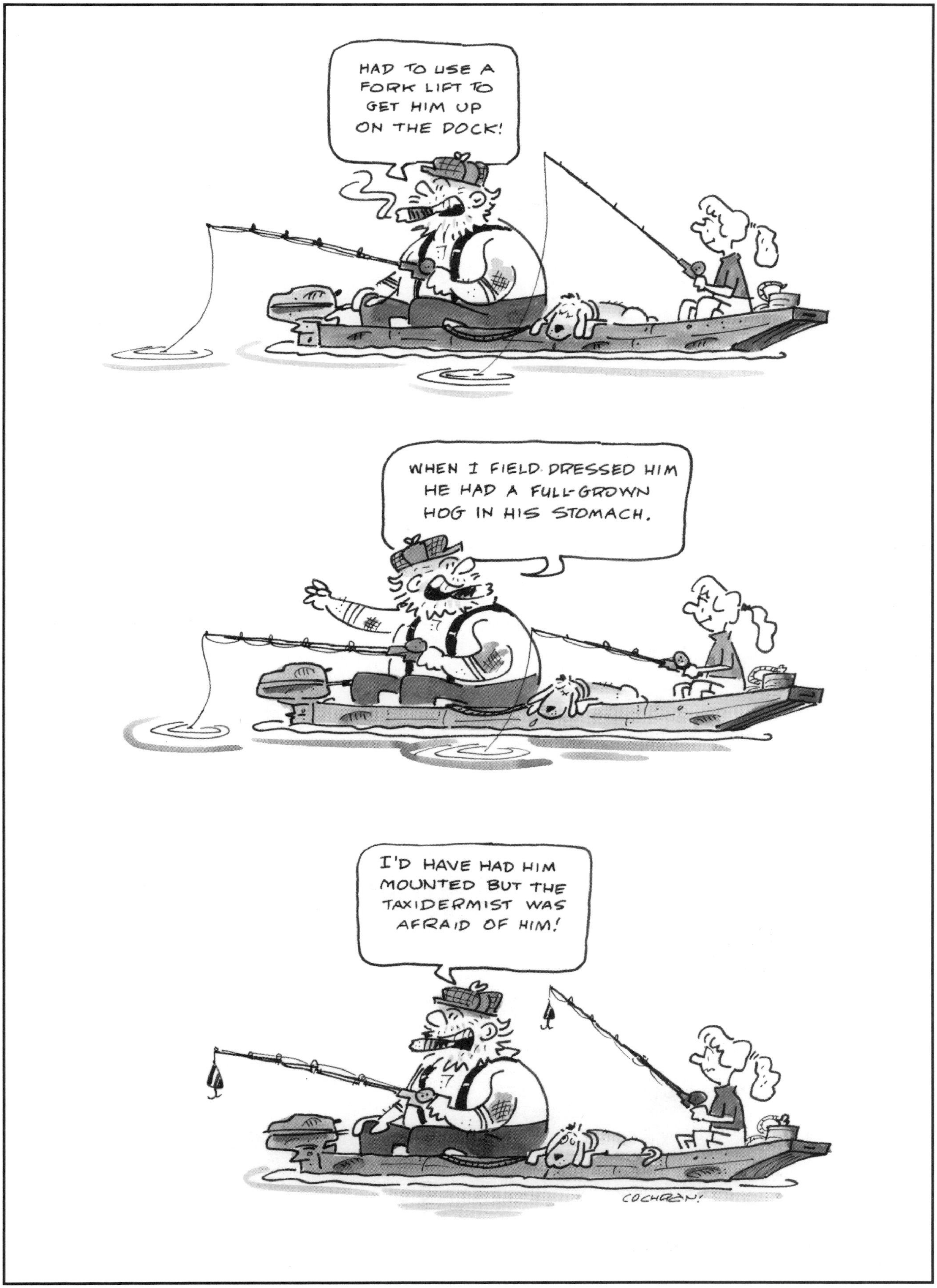
HAD TO USE A FORK LIFT TO GET HIM UP ON THE DOCK!
WHEN I FIELD DRESSED HIM HE HAD A FULL-GROWN HOG IN HIS STOMACH.
I'D HAVE HAD HIM MOUNTED BUT THE TAXIDERMIST WAS AFRAID OF HIM!
COCHRAN!

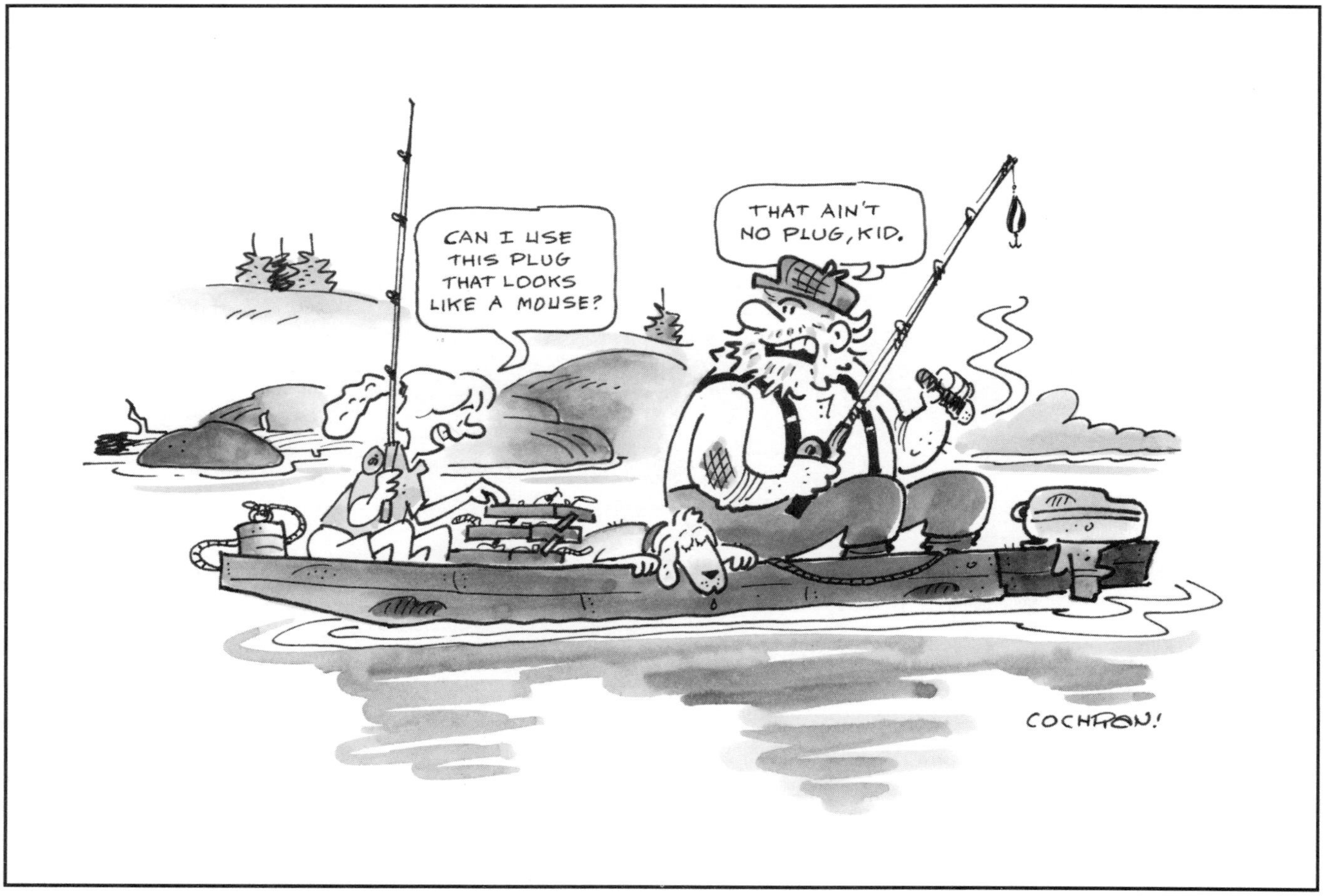
CAN I USE THIS PLUG THAT LOOKS LIKE A MOUSE?
THAT AIN'T NO PLUG, KID.
COCHRAN!

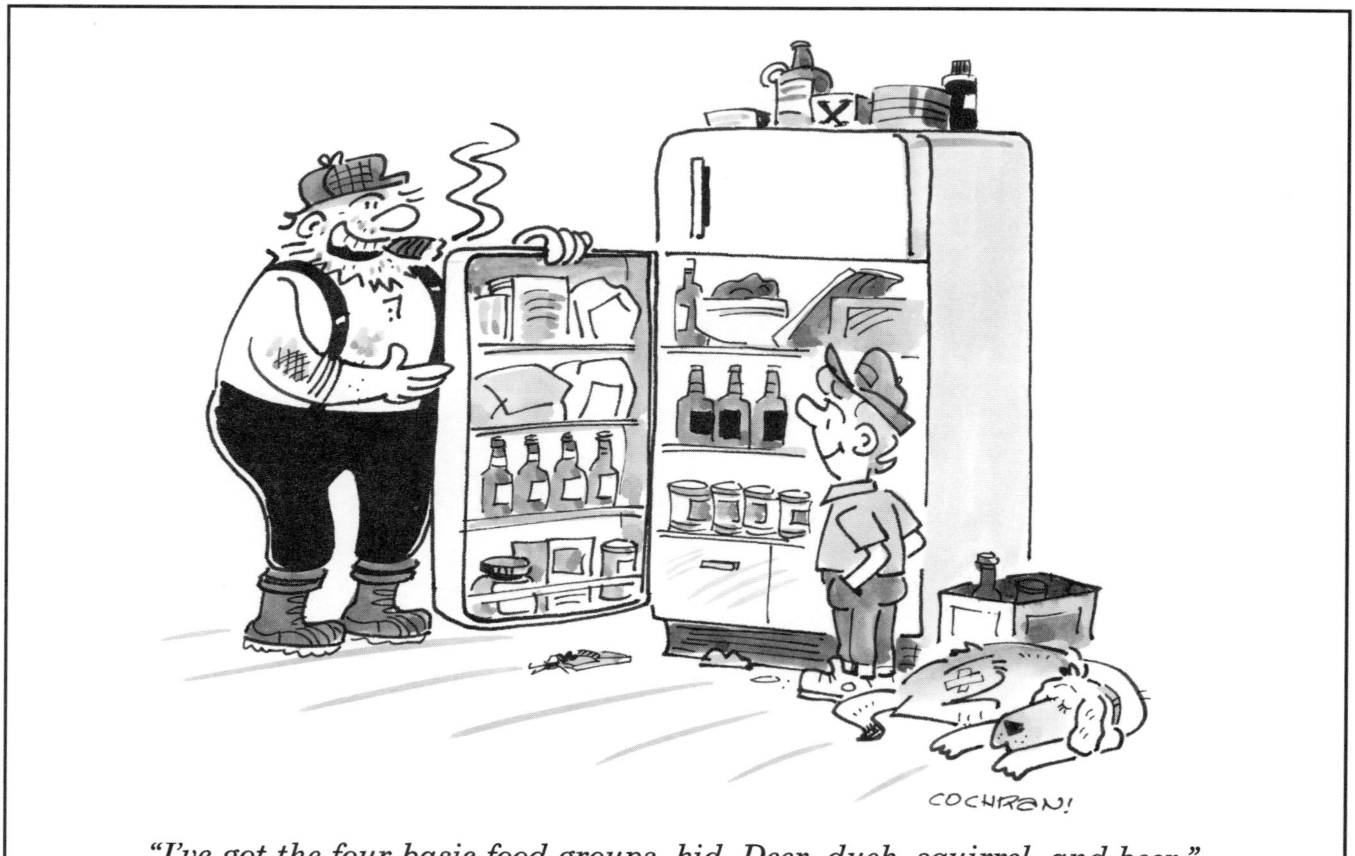
X
COCHRAN!

*"I've got the four basic food groups, kid. Deer, duck, squirrel, and beer."*

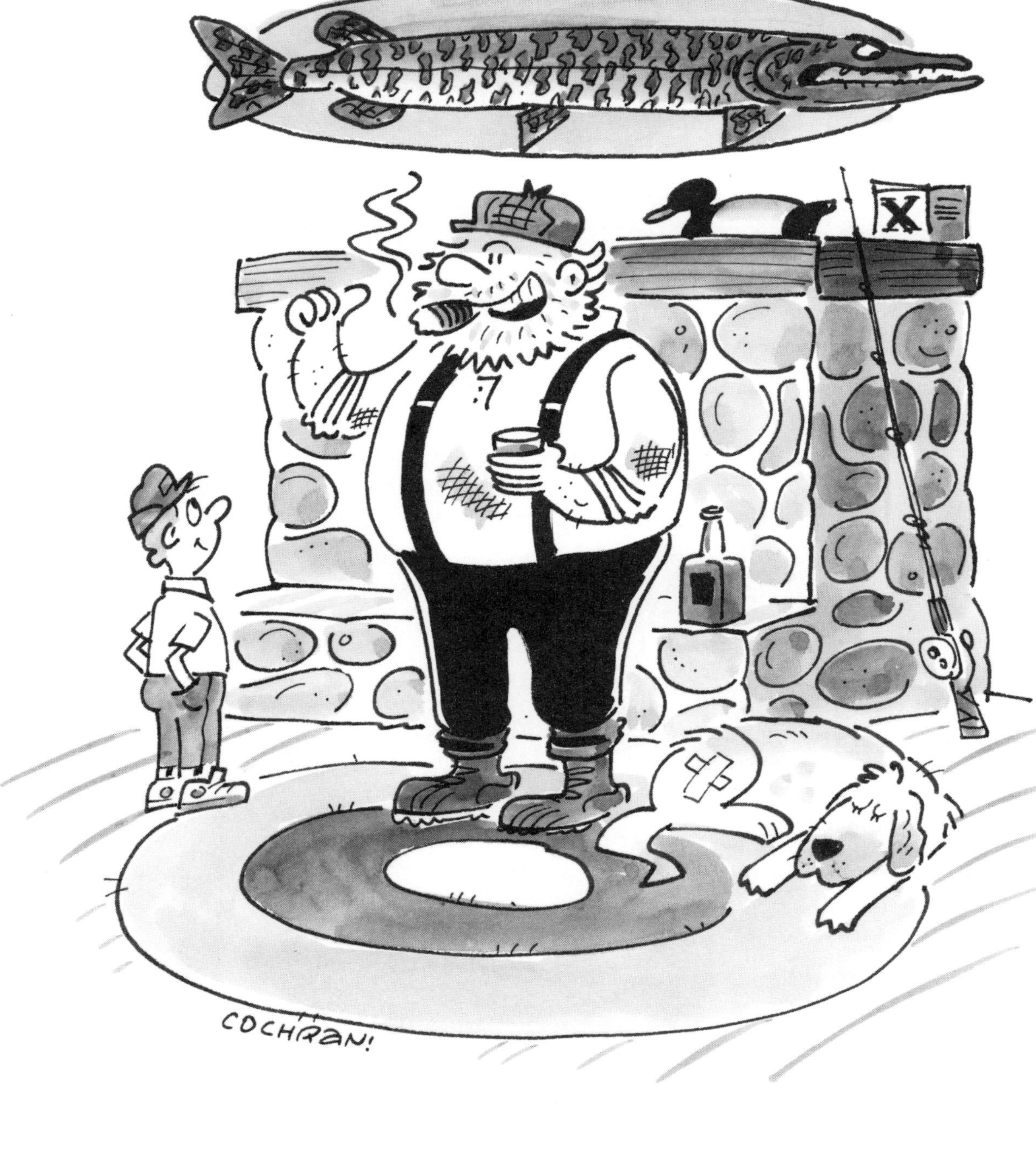
X
COCHRAN!

*"It ain't the biggest muskie I ever caught, kid.*
*But it's the biggest one I ever caught SOBER."*

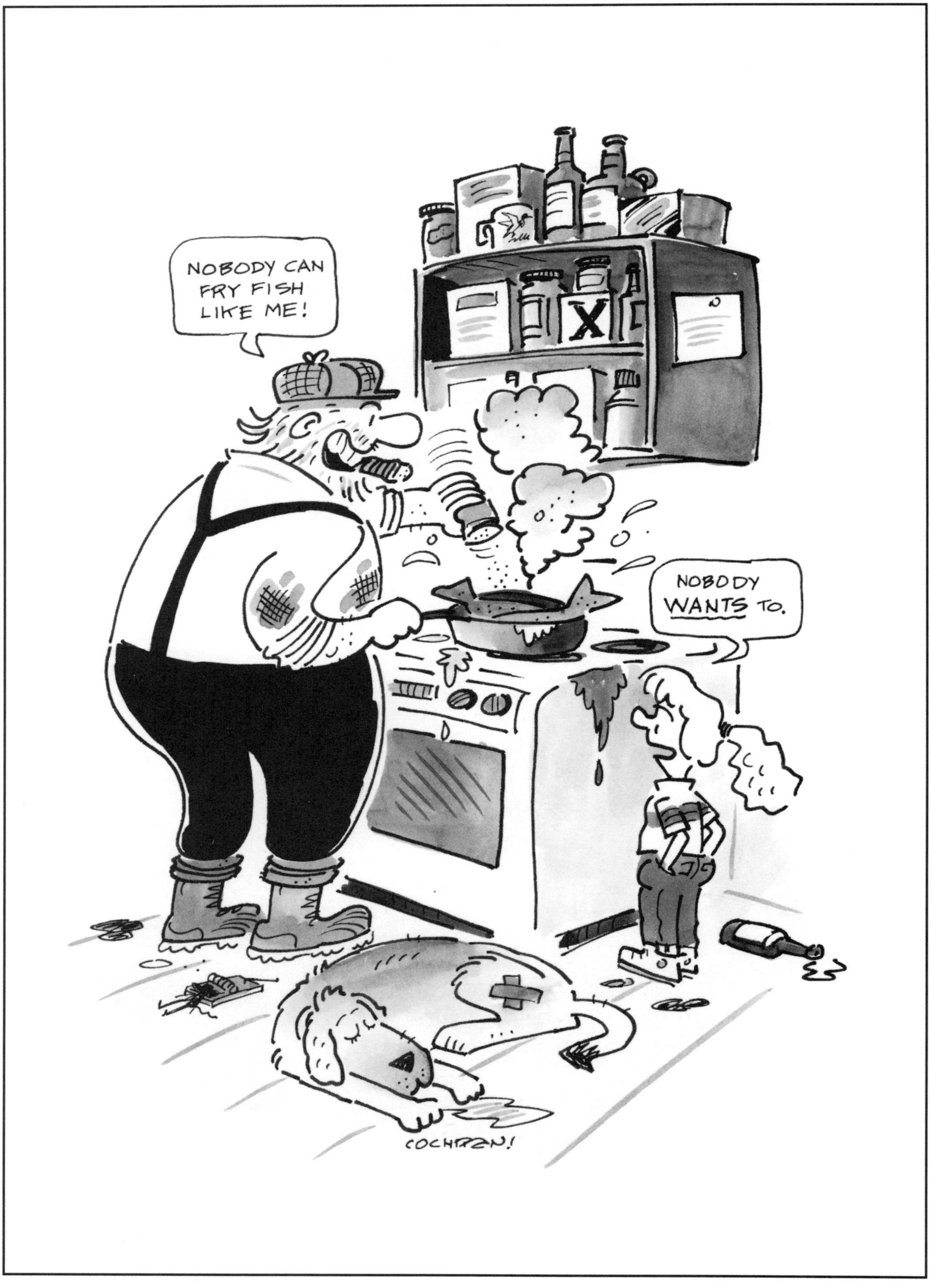
NOBODY CAN FRY FISH LIKE ME!
NOBODY WANTS TO.
COCHRAN!

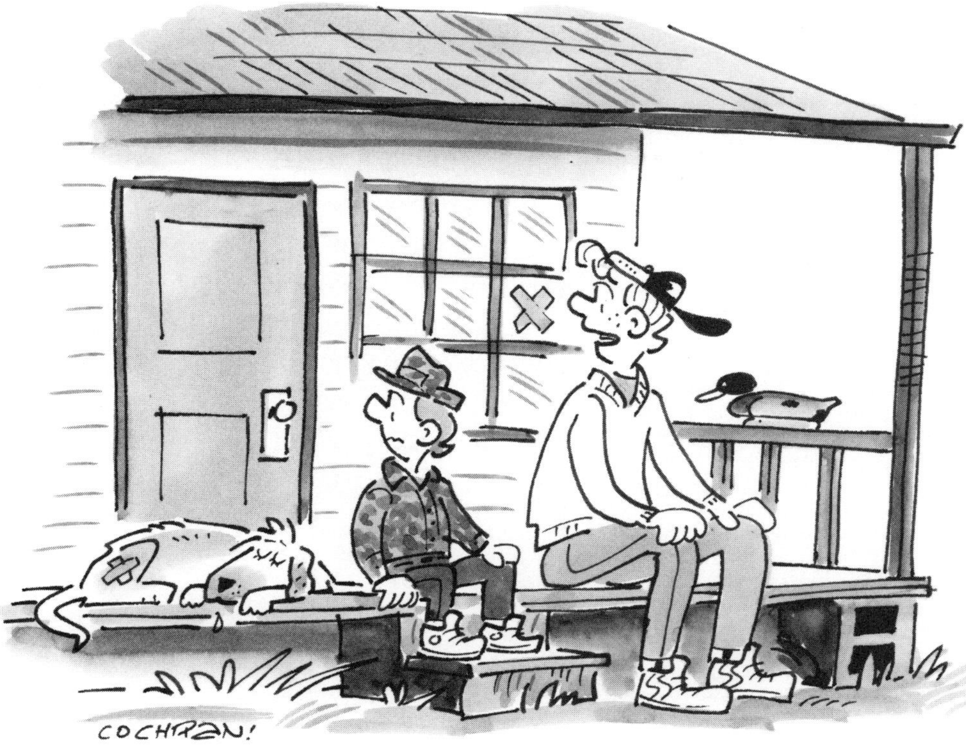
COCHRAN!

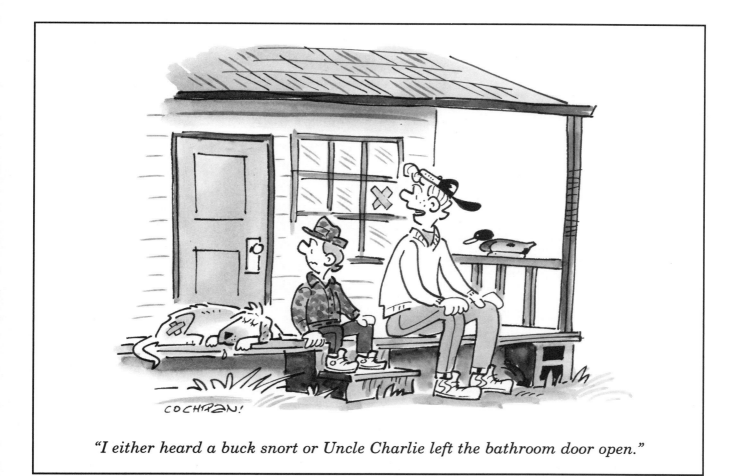

*"I either heard a buck snort or Uncle Charlie left the bathroom door open."*

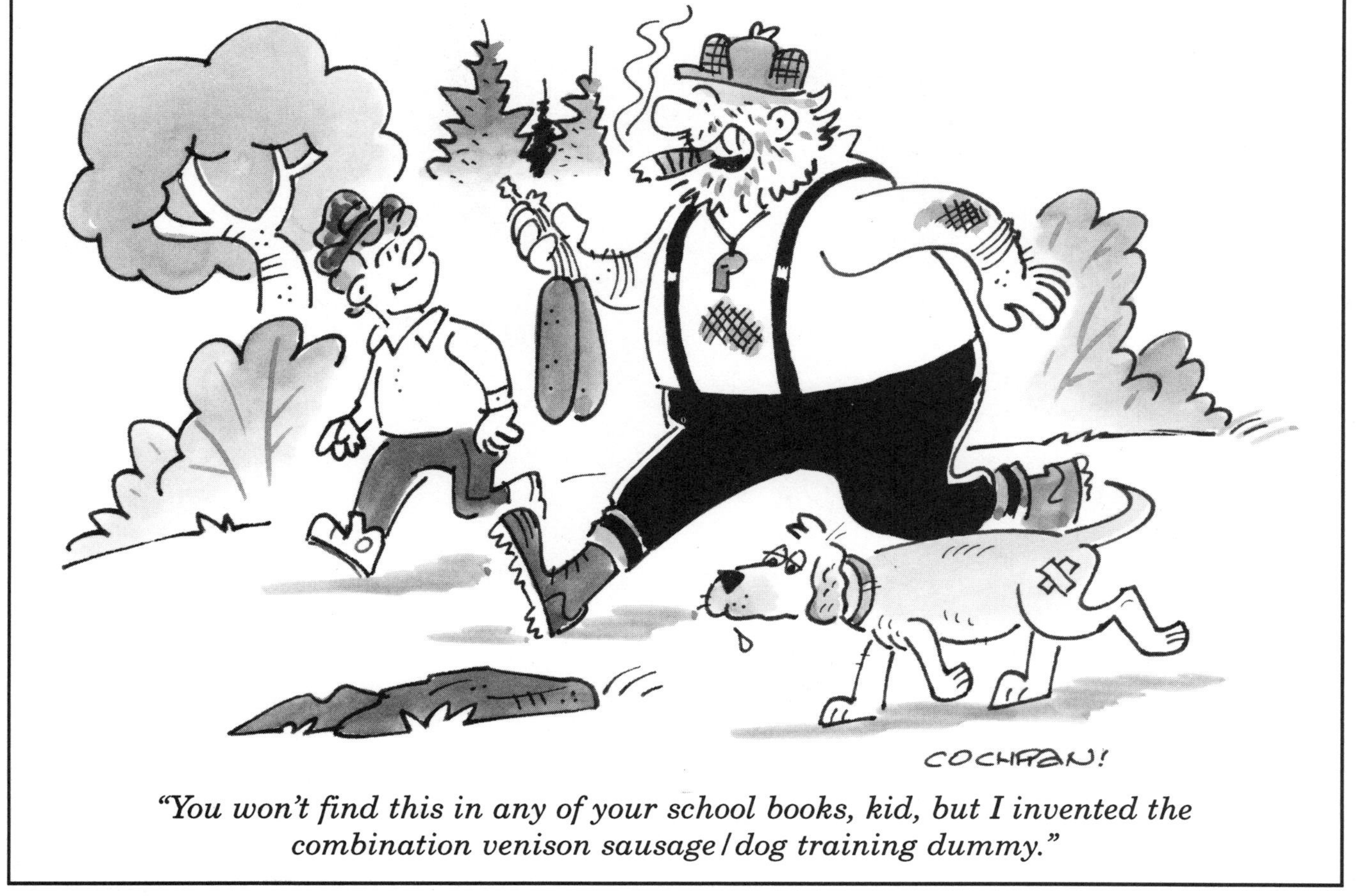
COCHRAN!

*"You won't find this in any of your school books, kid, but I invented the combination venison sausage/dog training dummy."*

# Fall

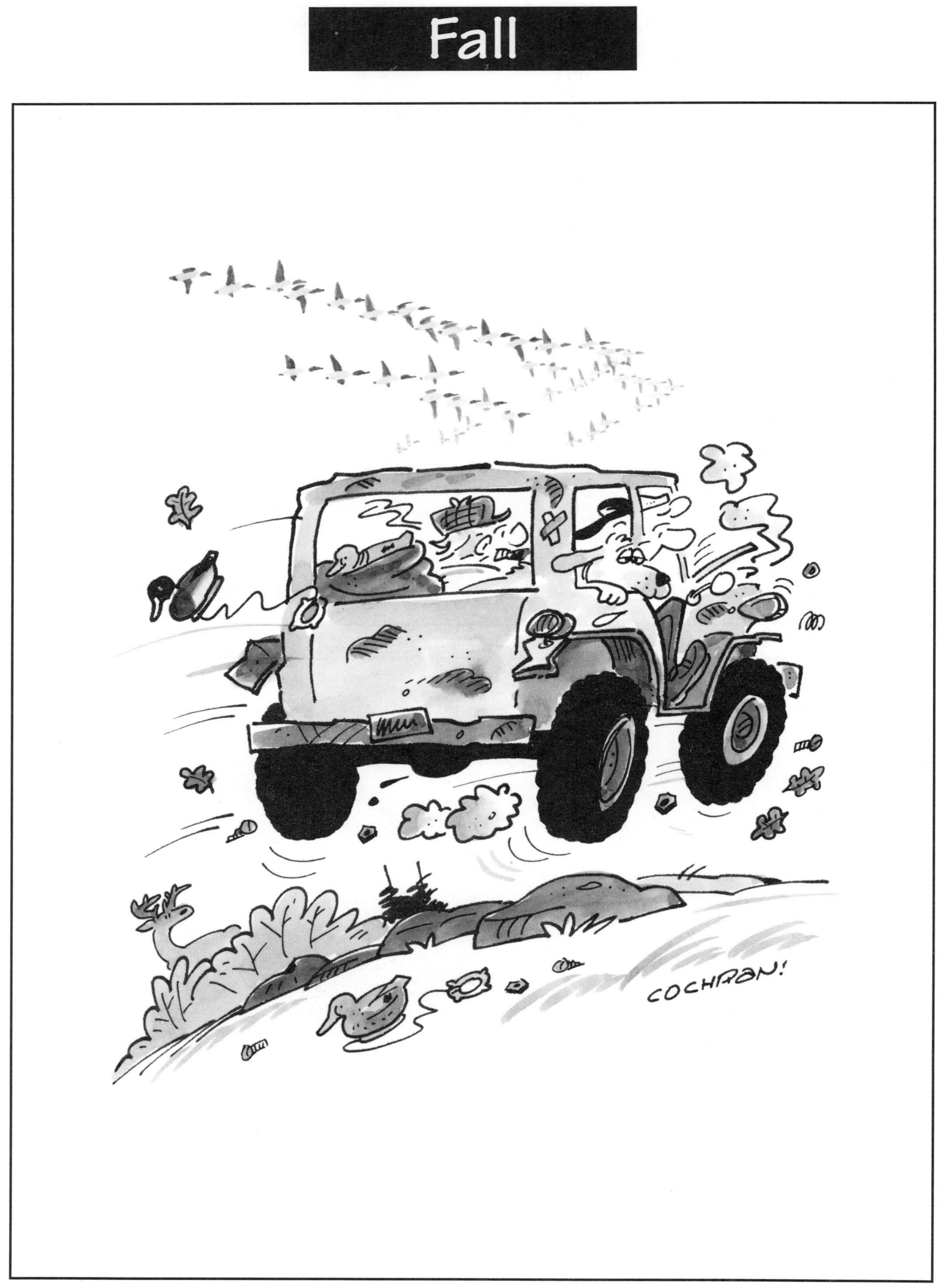
COCHRAN!

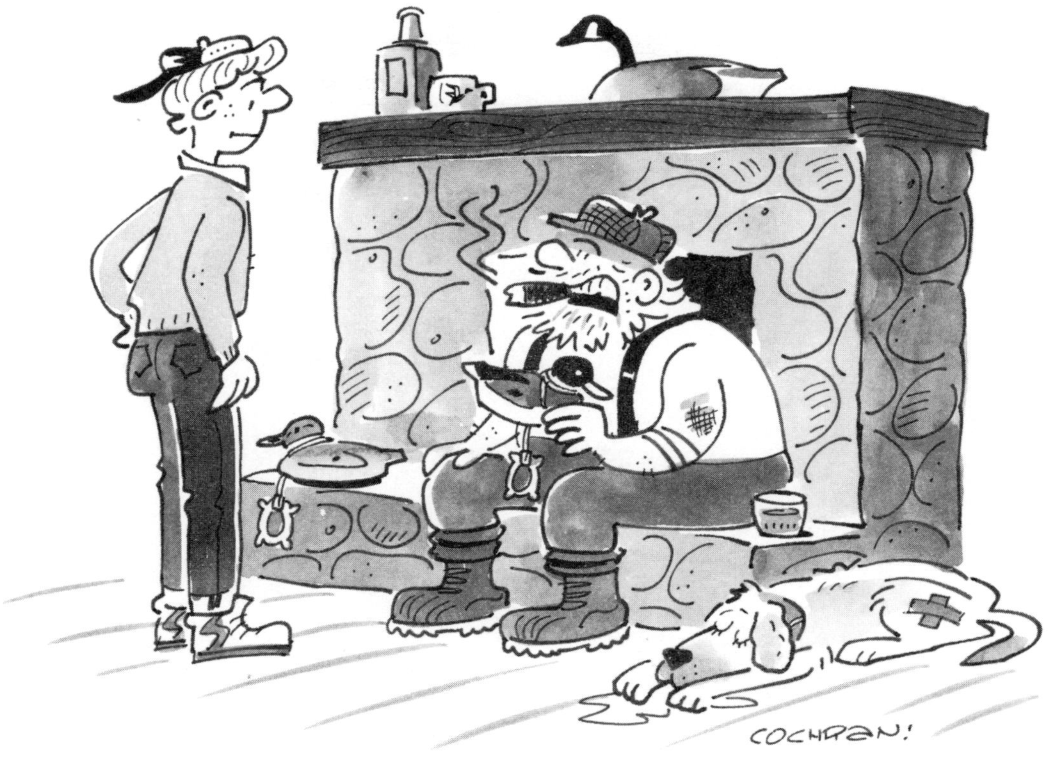
COCHRAN!

*"I'd take you duck huntin', kid, but nowadays you gotta have a law degree."*

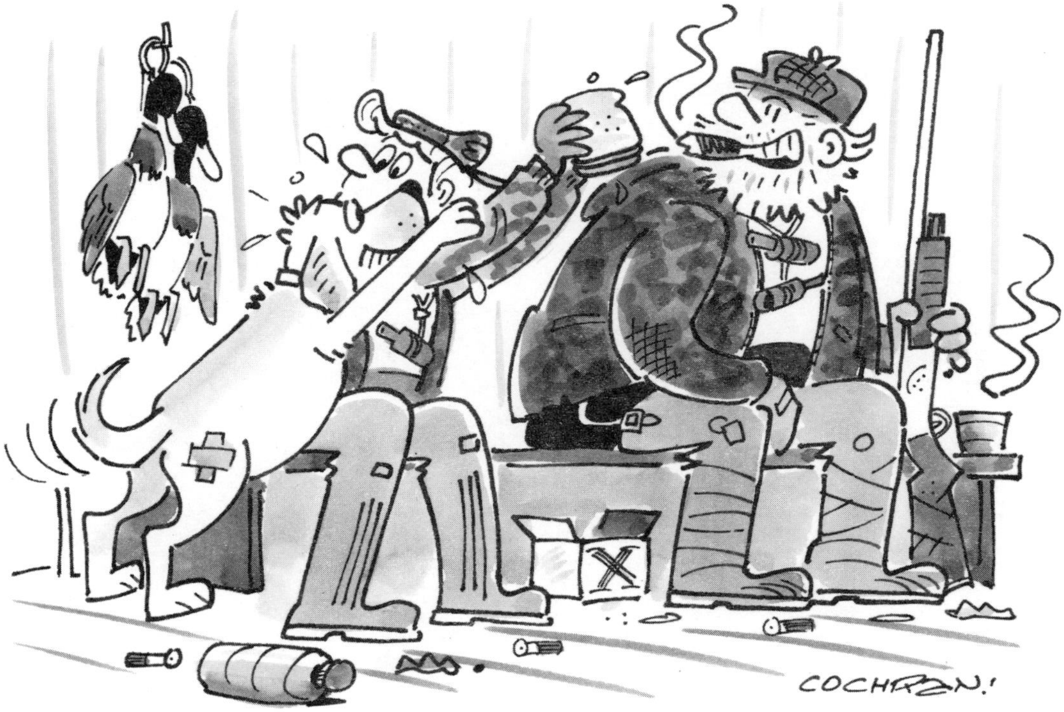
COCHRAN!

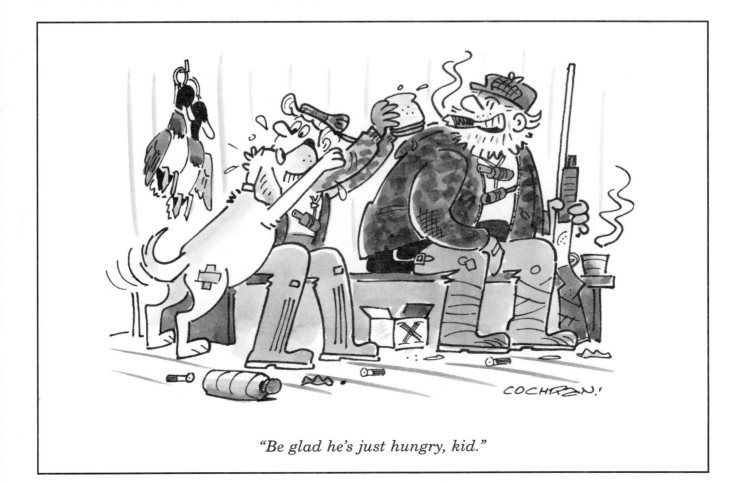

*"Be glad he's just hungry, kid."*

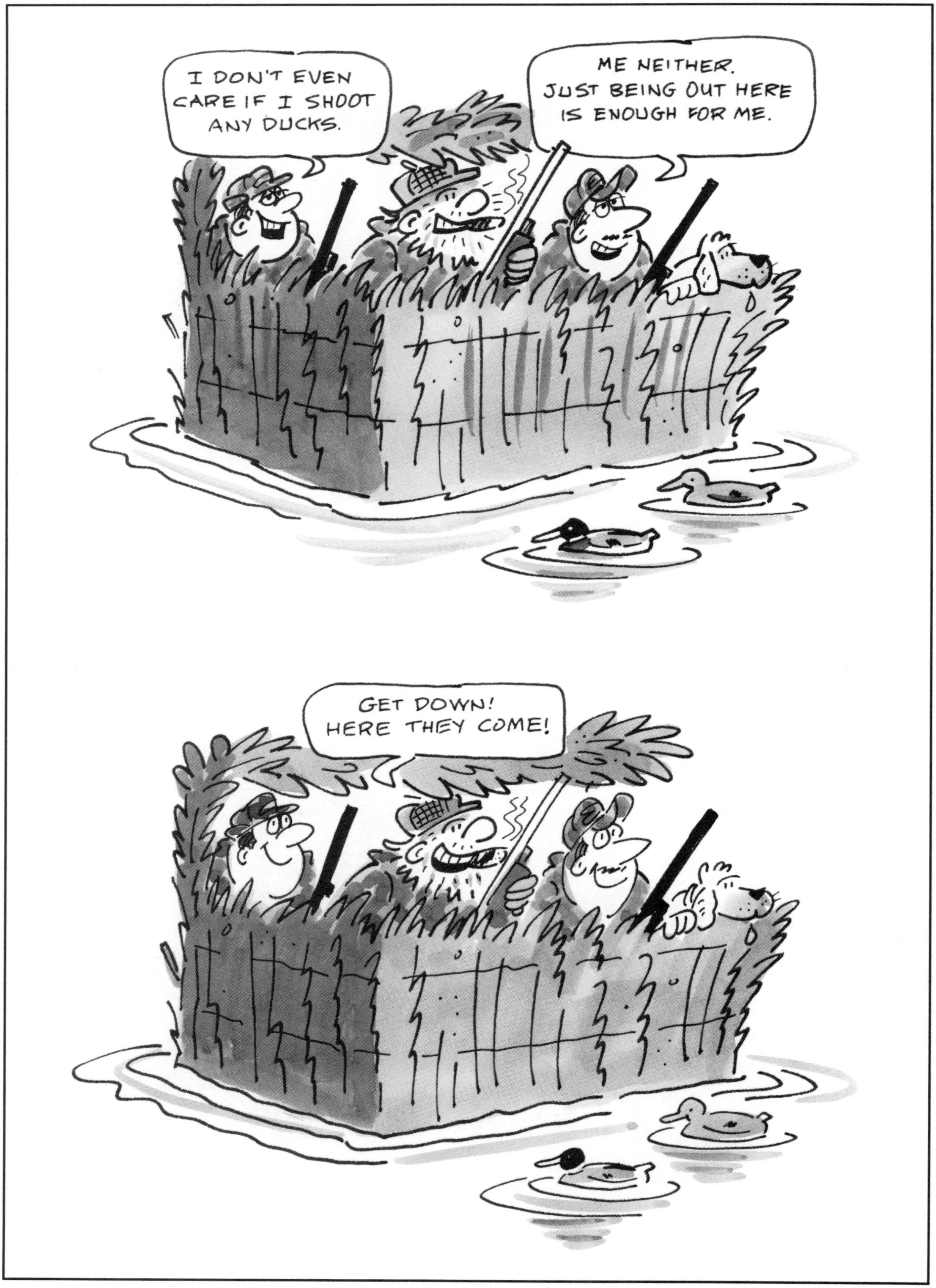
I DON'T EVEN CARE IF I SHOOT ANY DUCKS.
ME NEITHER. JUST BEING OUT HERE IS ENOUGH FOR ME.
GET DOWN! HERE THEY COME!

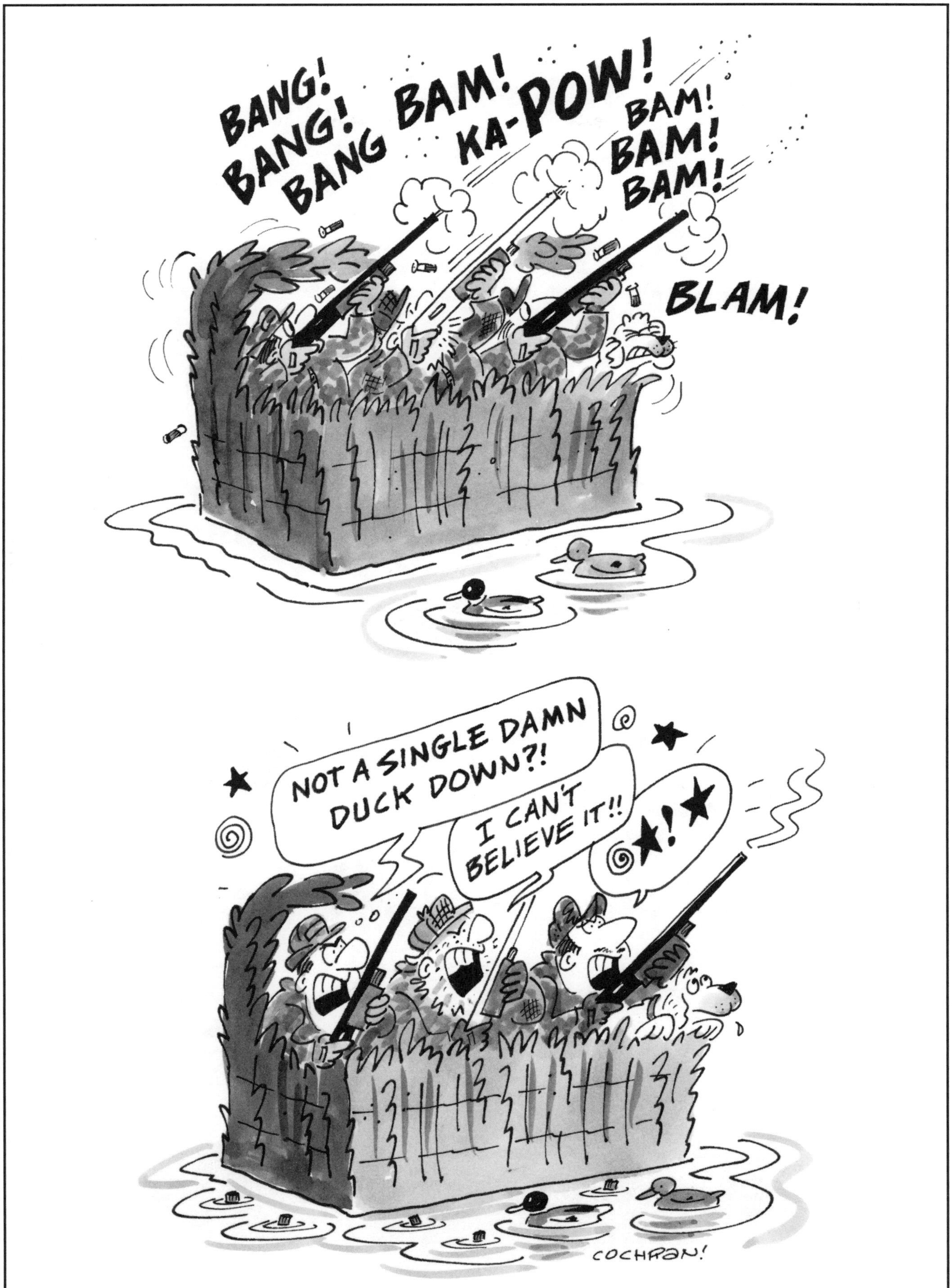
BANG!
BANG!
BANG
BAM!
KA-POW!
BAM!
BAM!
BAM!
BLAM!
NOT A SINGLE DAMN DUCK DOWN?!
I CAN'T BELIEVE IT!!
★!★
COCHRAN!

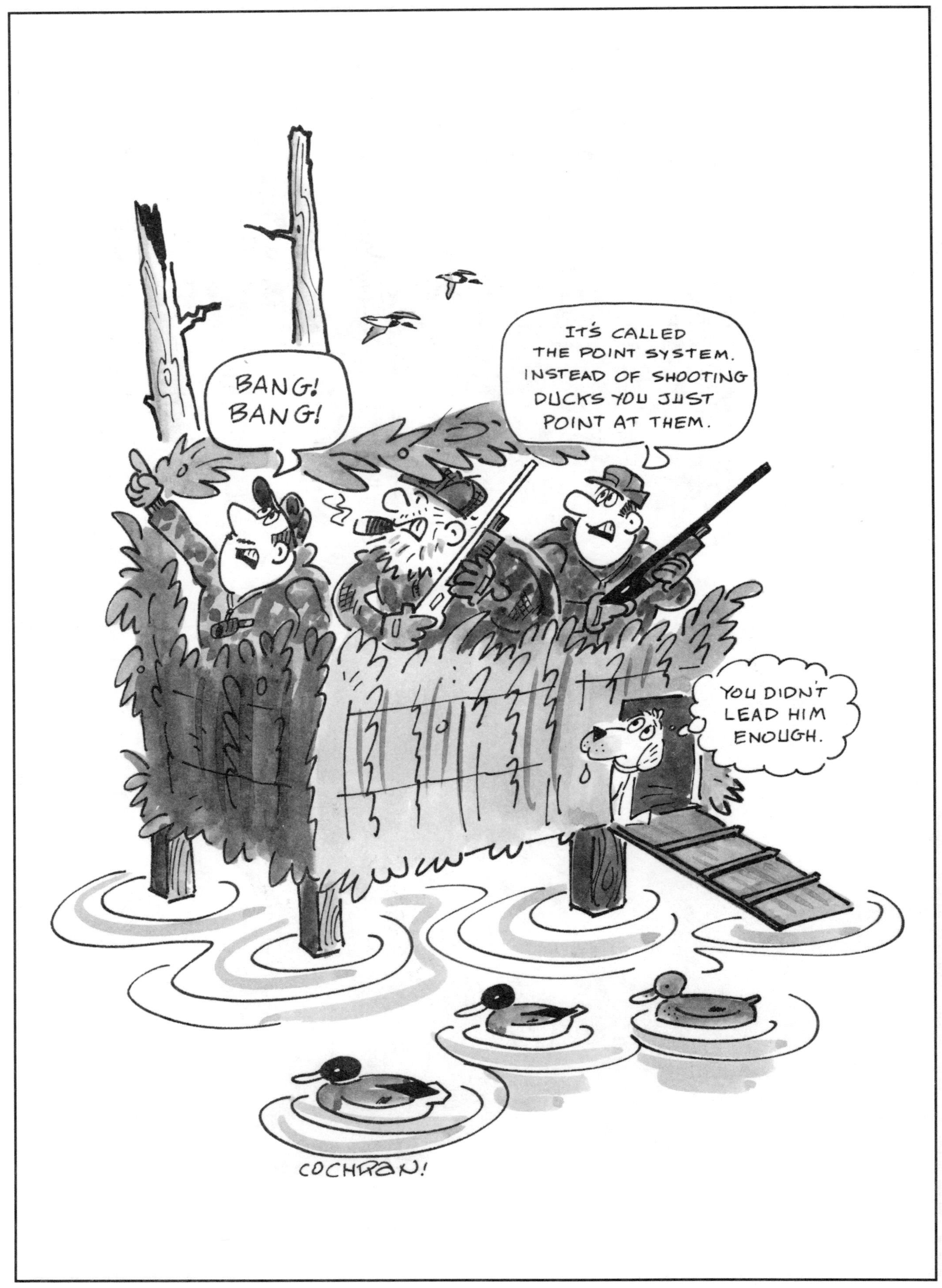
BANG! BANG!
IT'S CALLED THE POINT SYSTEM. INSTEAD OF SHOOTING DUCKS YOU JUST POINT AT THEM.
YOU DIDN'T LEAD HIM ENOUGH.
COCHRAN!

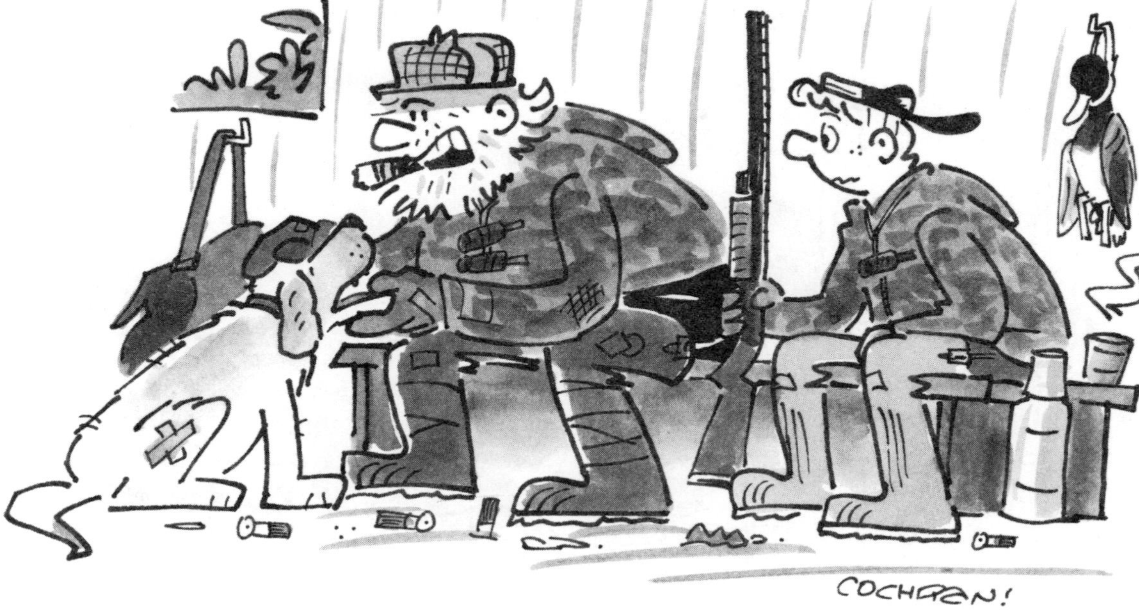
COCHRAN!

*"Last year, after the season was over, we found a teal under his tongue."*

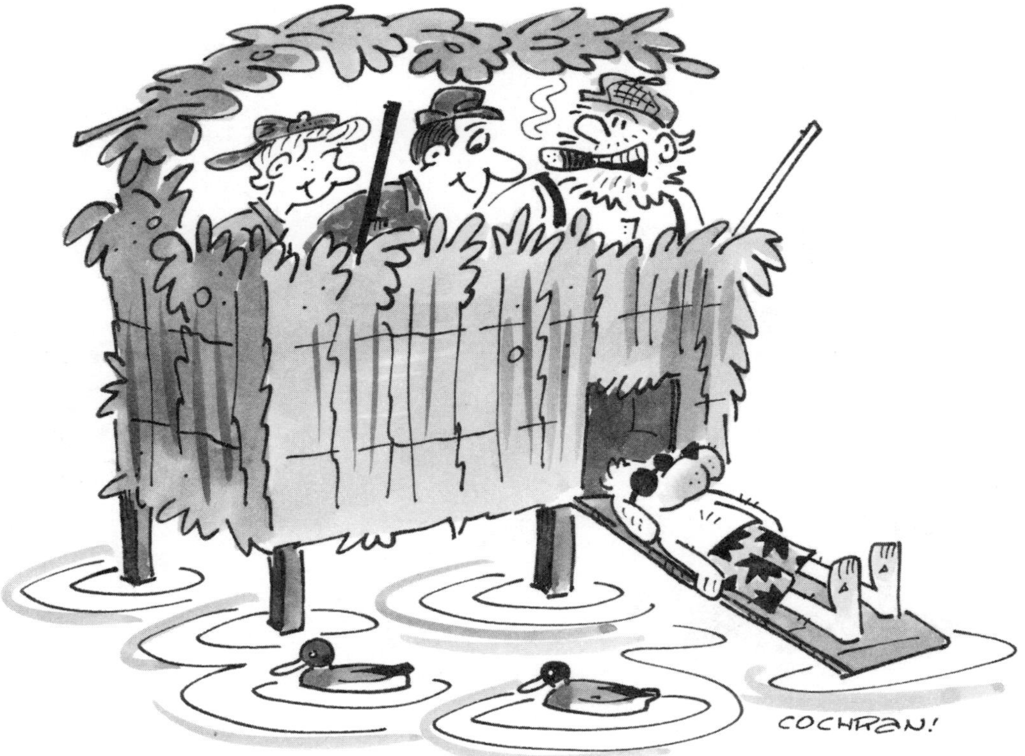
COCHRAN!

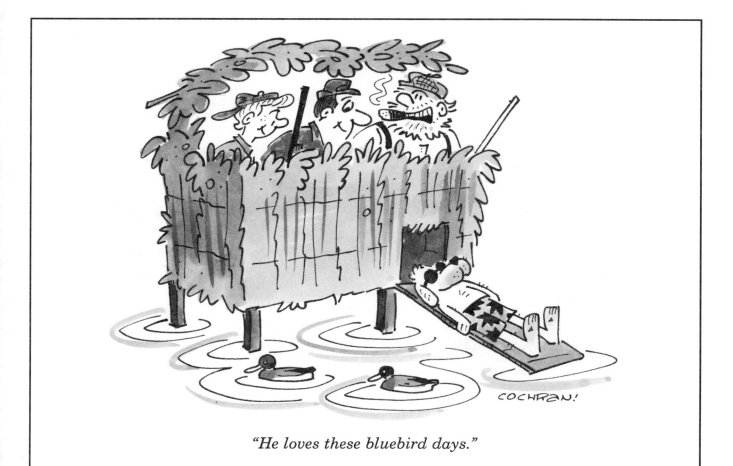

*"He loves these bluebird days."*

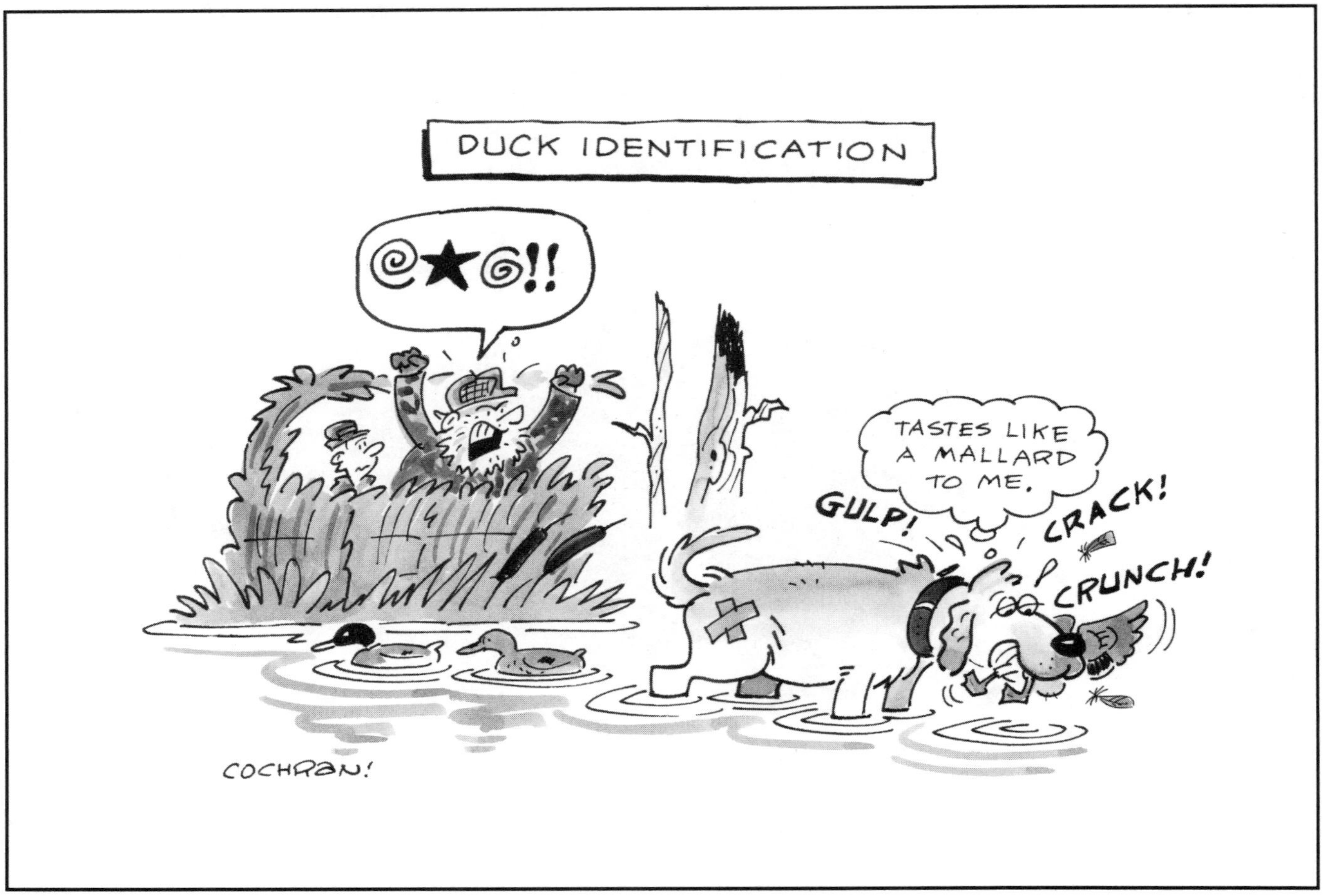
DUCK IDENTIFICATION
@★G!!
TASTES LIKE A MALLARD TO ME.
GULP!
CRACK!
CRUNCH!
COCHRAN!

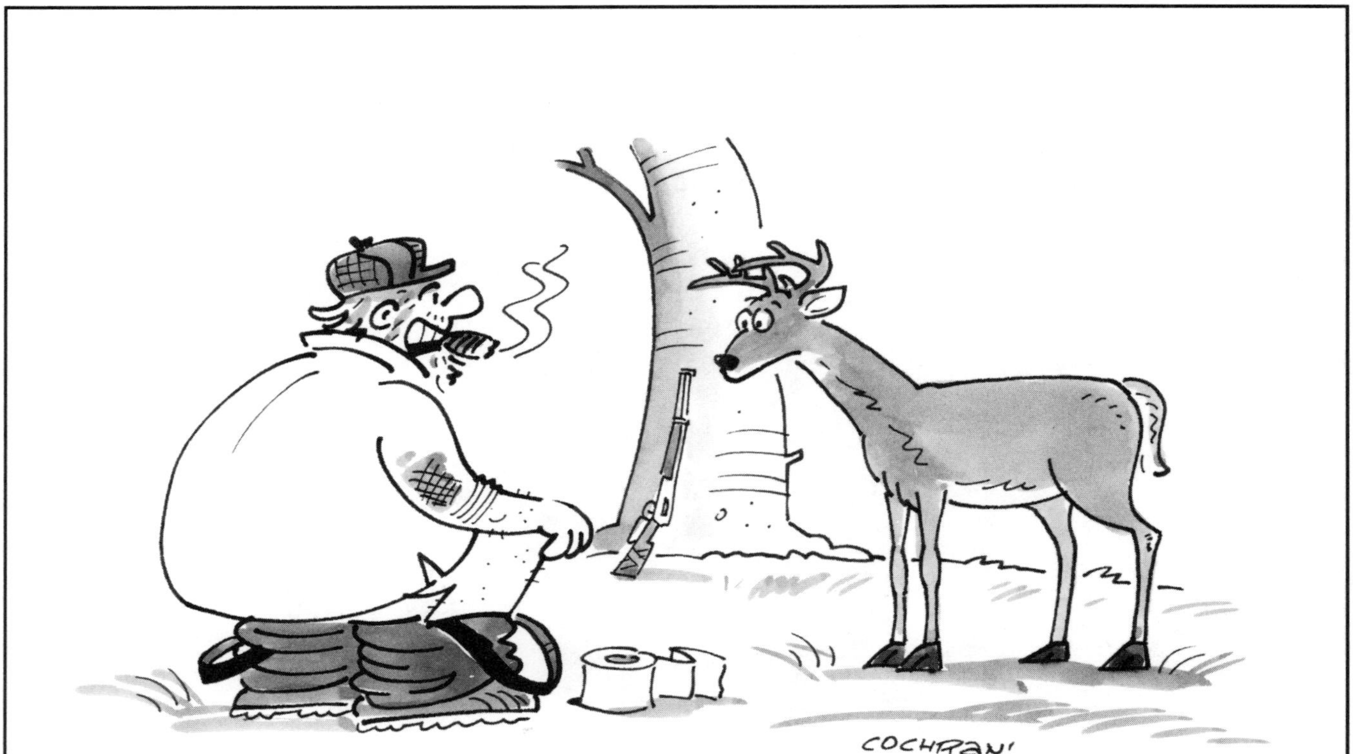
COCHRAN!

*"Time out!"*

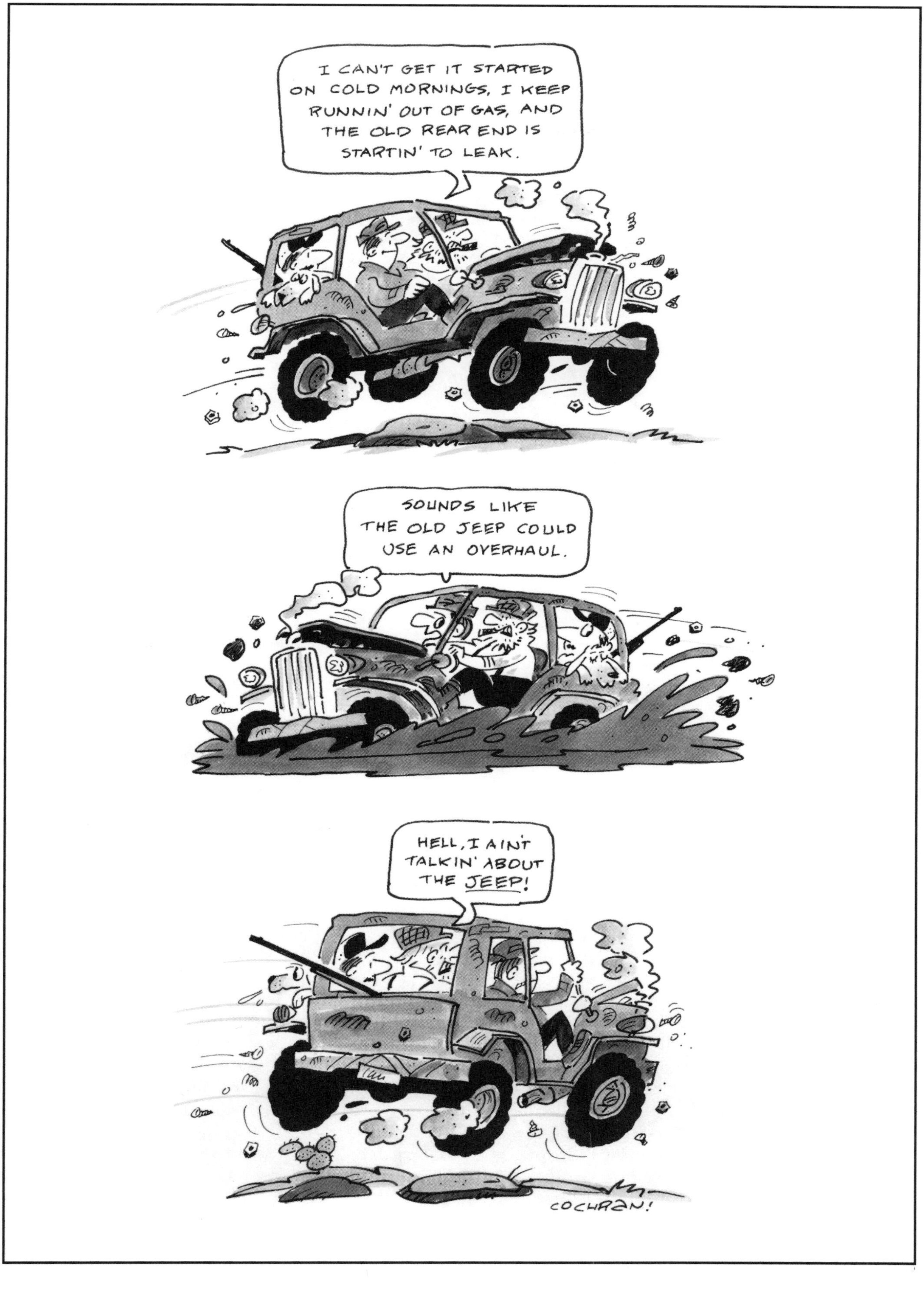
I CAN'T GET IT STARTED ON COLD MORNINGS, I KEEP RUNNIN' OUT OF GAS, AND THE OLD REAR END IS STARTIN' TO LEAK.
SOUNDS LIKE THE OLD JEEP COULD USE AN OVERHAUL.
HELL, I AIN'T TALKIN' ABOUT THE JEEP!
COCHRAN!

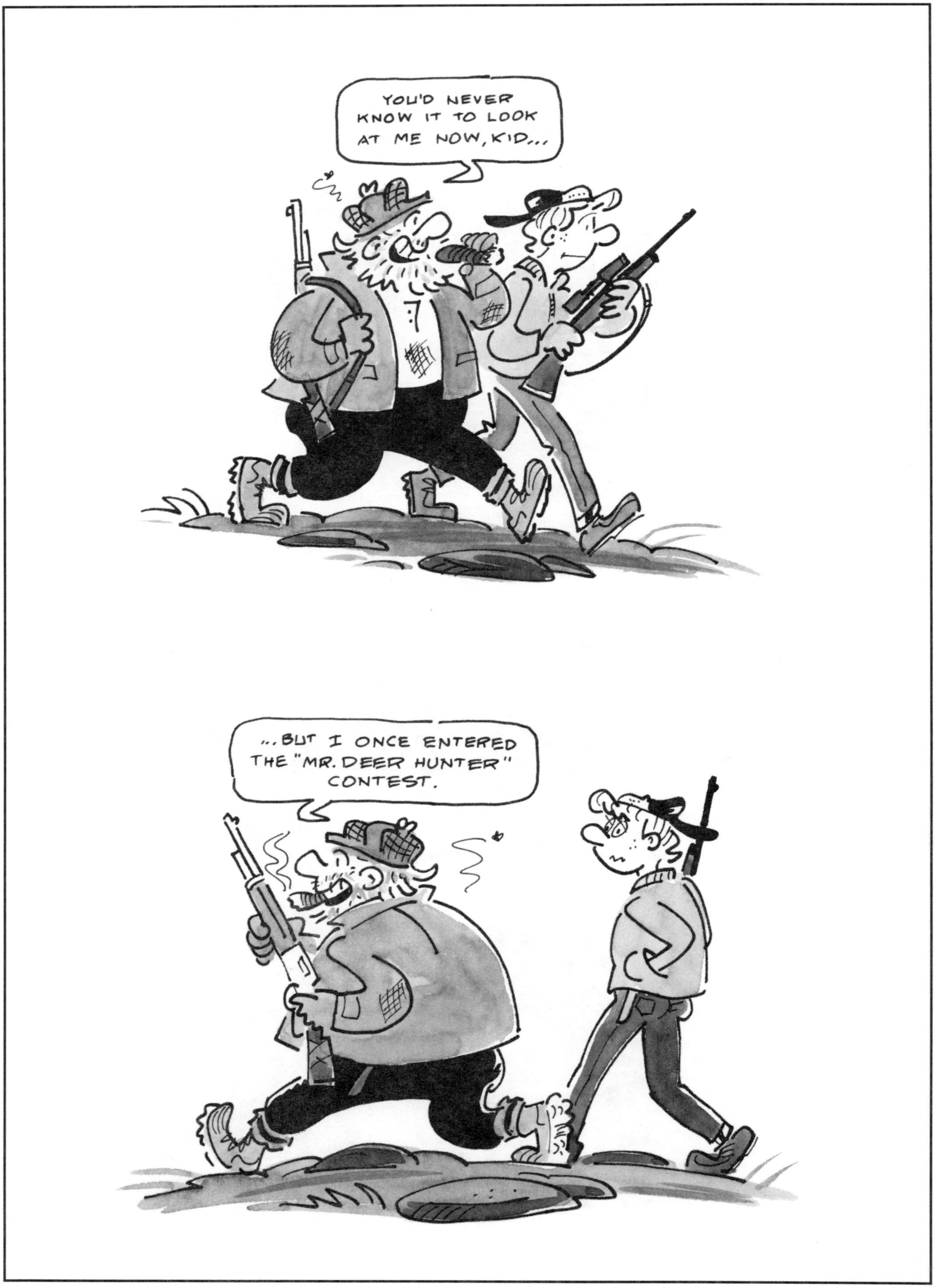
YOU'D NEVER KNOW IT TO LOOK AT ME NOW, KID...
...BUT I ONCE ENTERED THE "MR. DEER HUNTER" CONTEST.

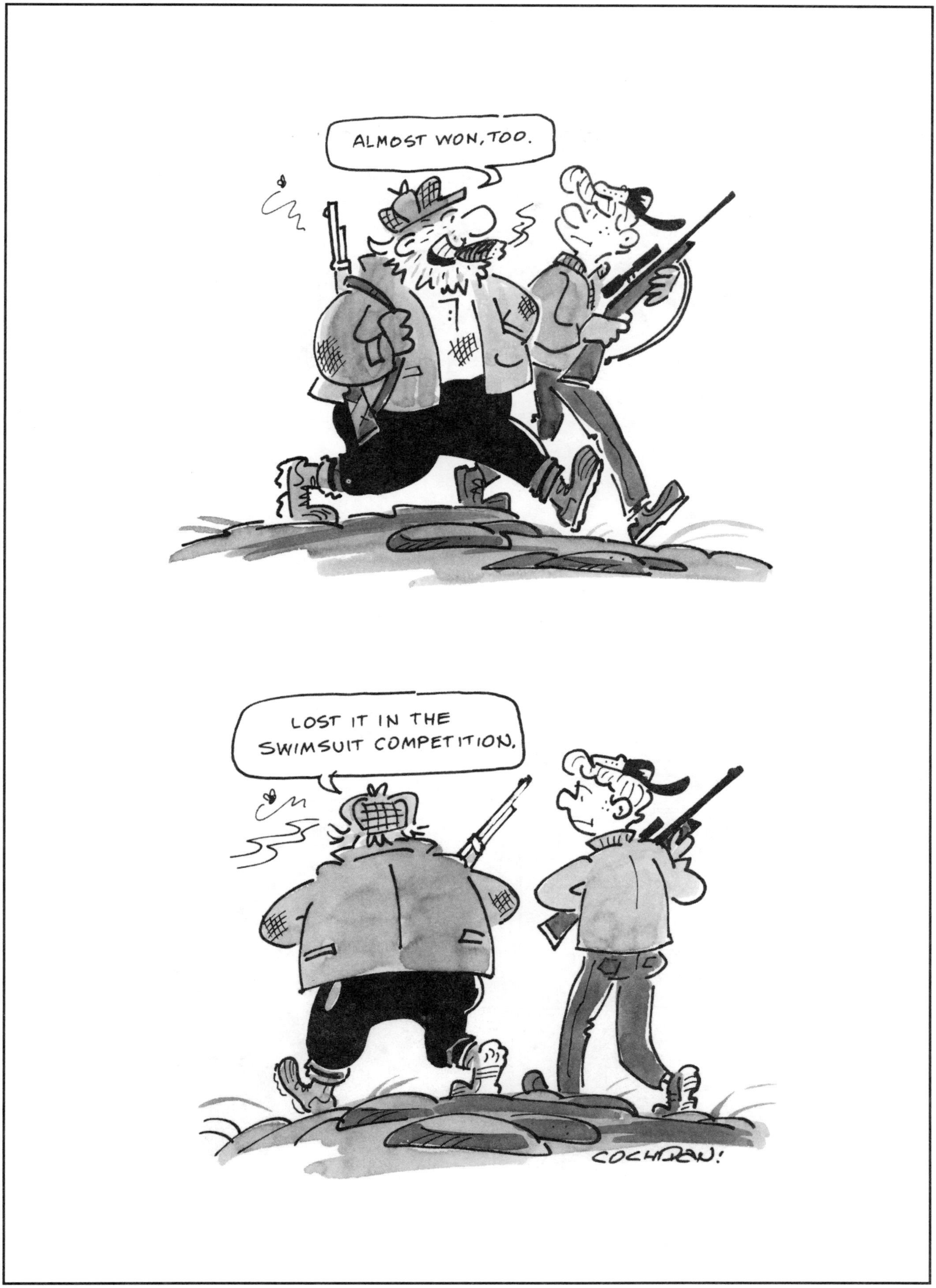
ALMOST WON, TOO.
LOST IT IN THE SWIMSUIT COMPETITION.
COCHRAN!

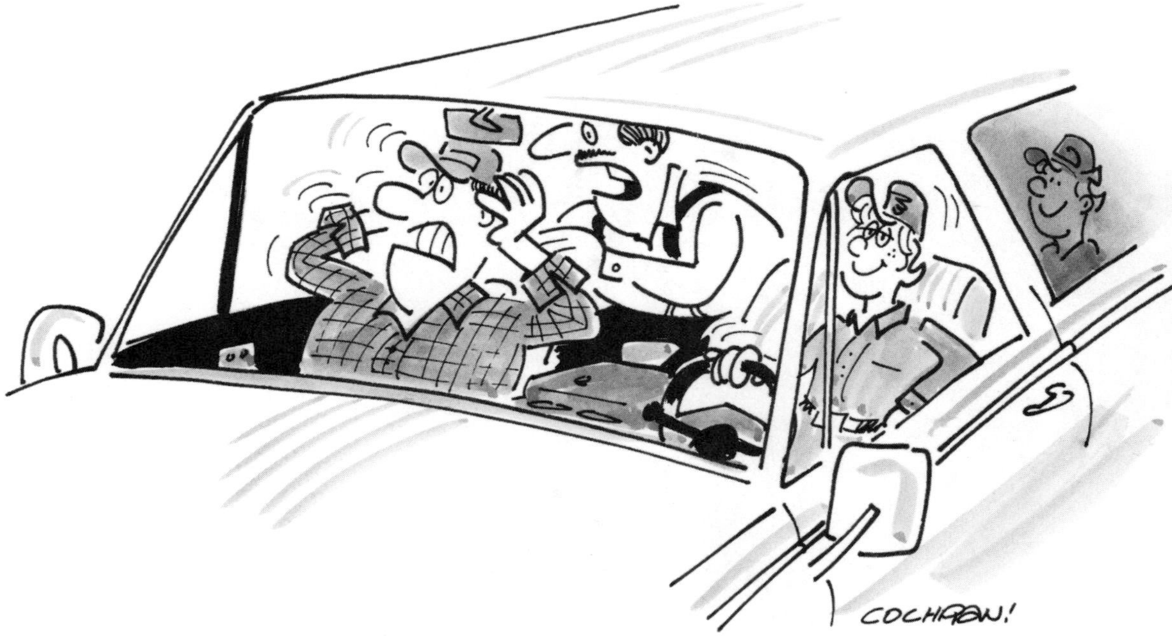
COCHRAN!

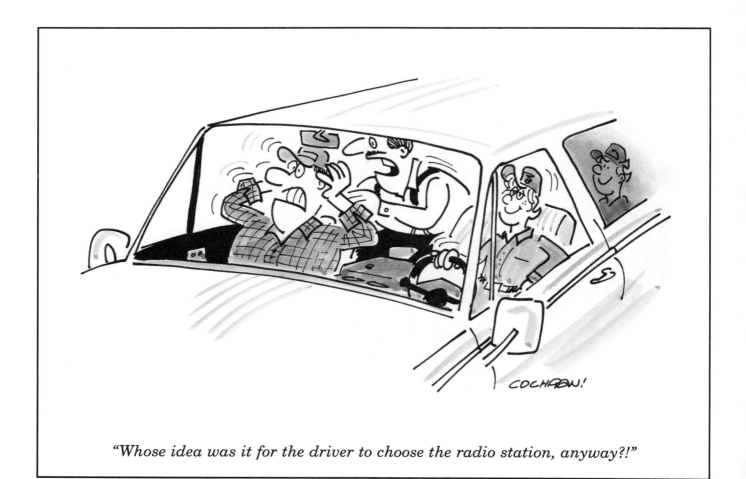

"Whose idea was it for the driver to choose the radio station, anyway?!"

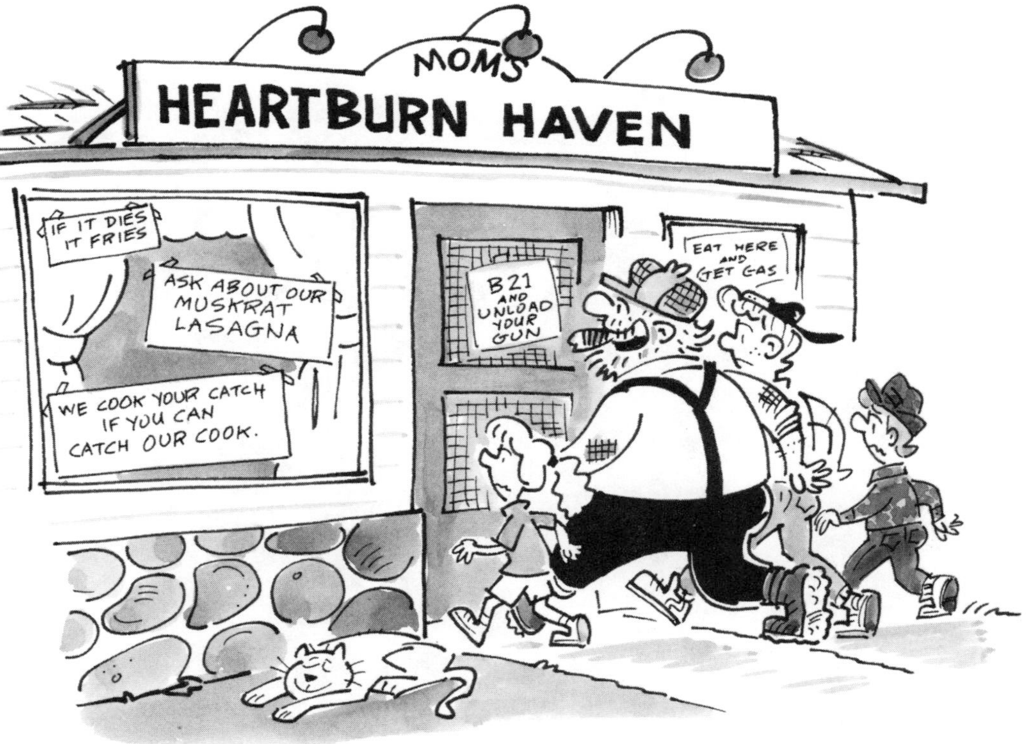
MOM'S
HEARTBURN HAVEN
IF IT DIES IT FRIES
ASK ABOUT OUR MUSKRAT LASAGNA
WE COOK YOUR CATCH IF YOU CAN CATCH OUR COOK.
B21 AND UNLOAD YOUR GUN
EAT HERE AND GET GAS
COCHRAN!

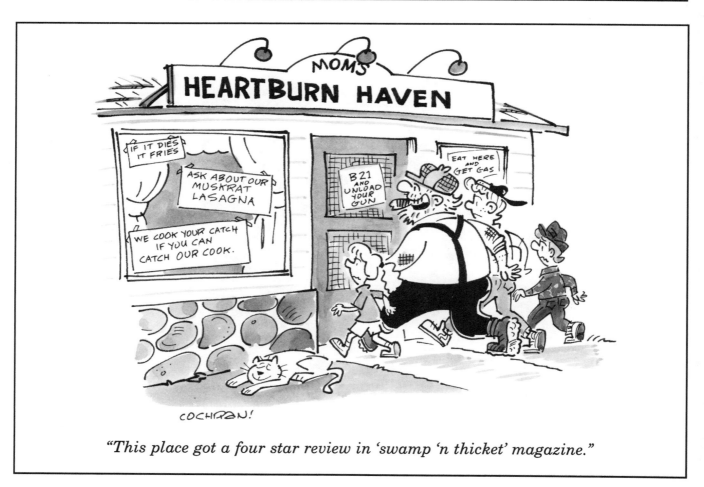

"This place got a four star review in 'swamp 'n thicket' magazine."

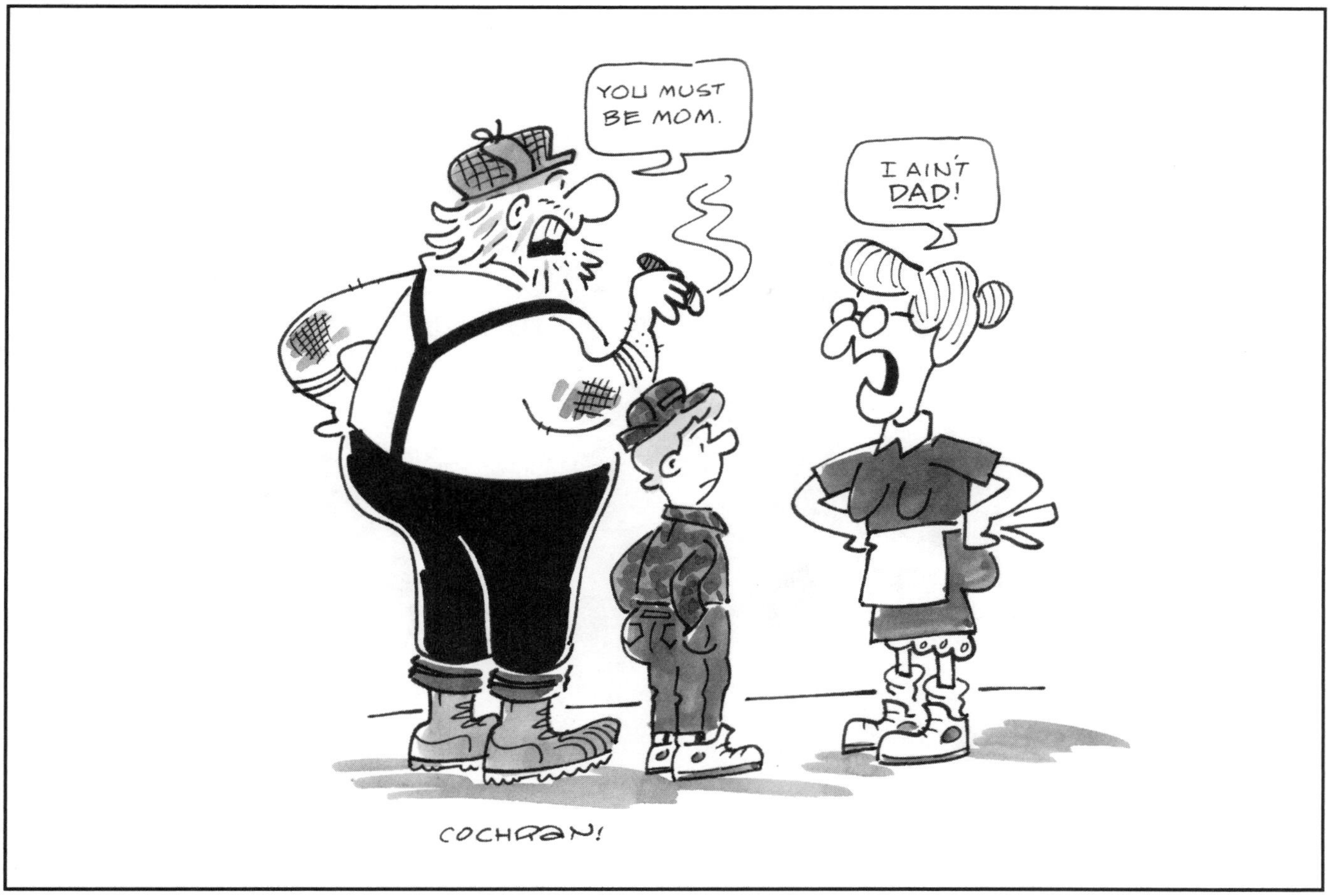
YOU MUST BE MOM.
I AIN'T DAD!
COCHRAN!

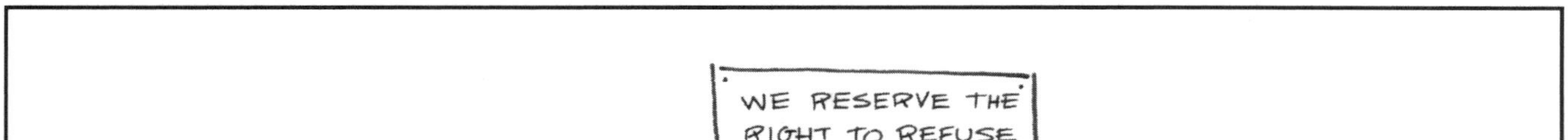
WE RESERVE THE RIGHT TO REFUSE SERVICE TO EVERYONE
COCHRAN!

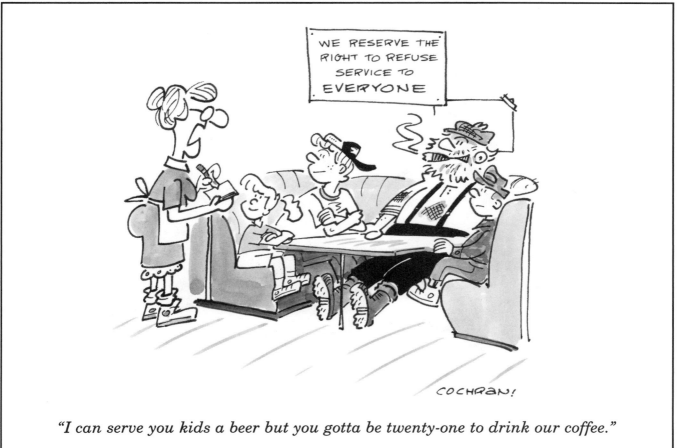

*"I can serve you kids a beer but you gotta be twenty-one to drink our coffee."*

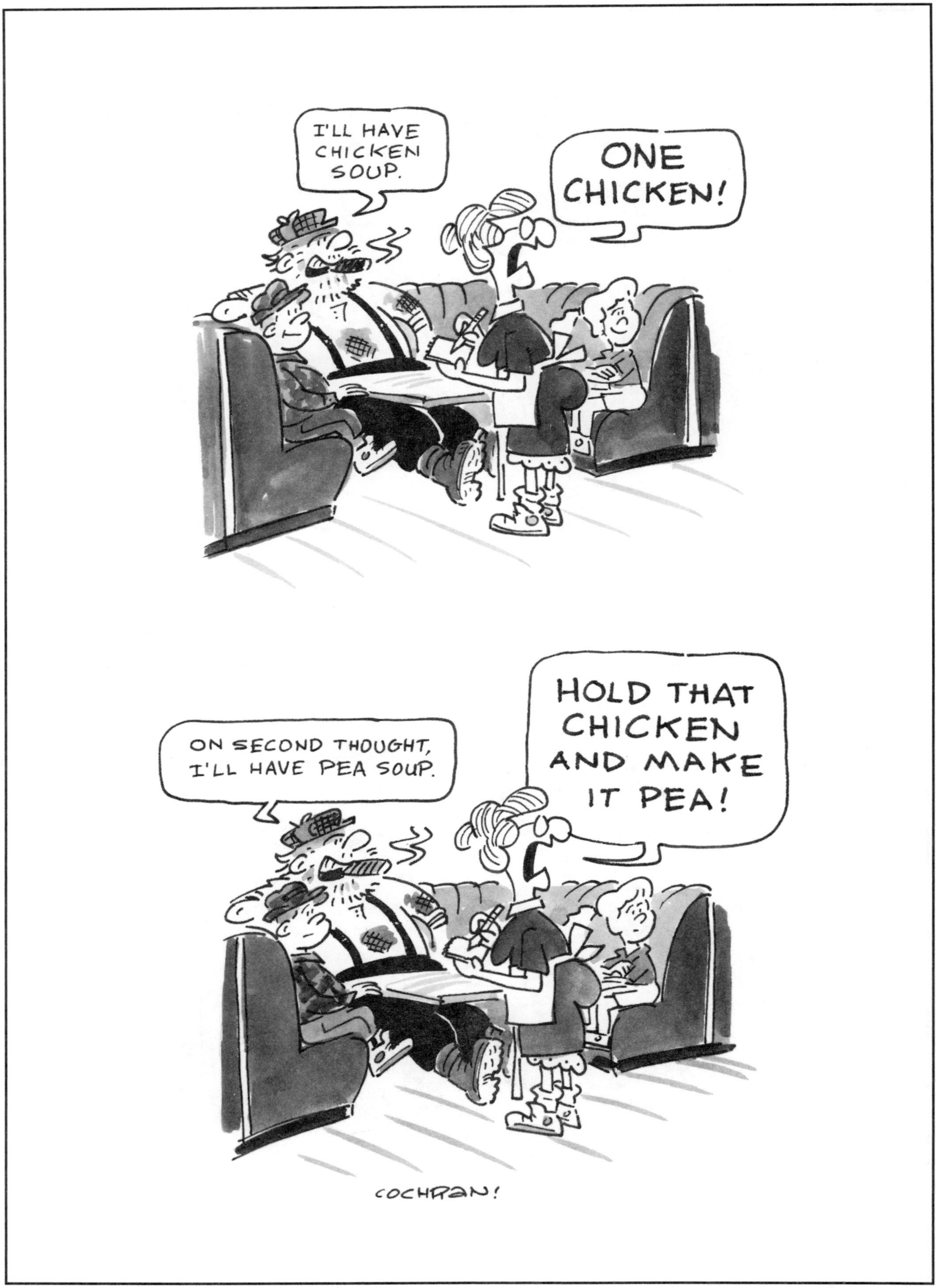
I'LL HAVE CHICKEN SOUP.
ONE CHICKEN!
ON SECOND THOUGHT, I'LL HAVE PEA SOUP.
HOLD THAT CHICKEN AND MAKE IT PEA!
COCHRAN!

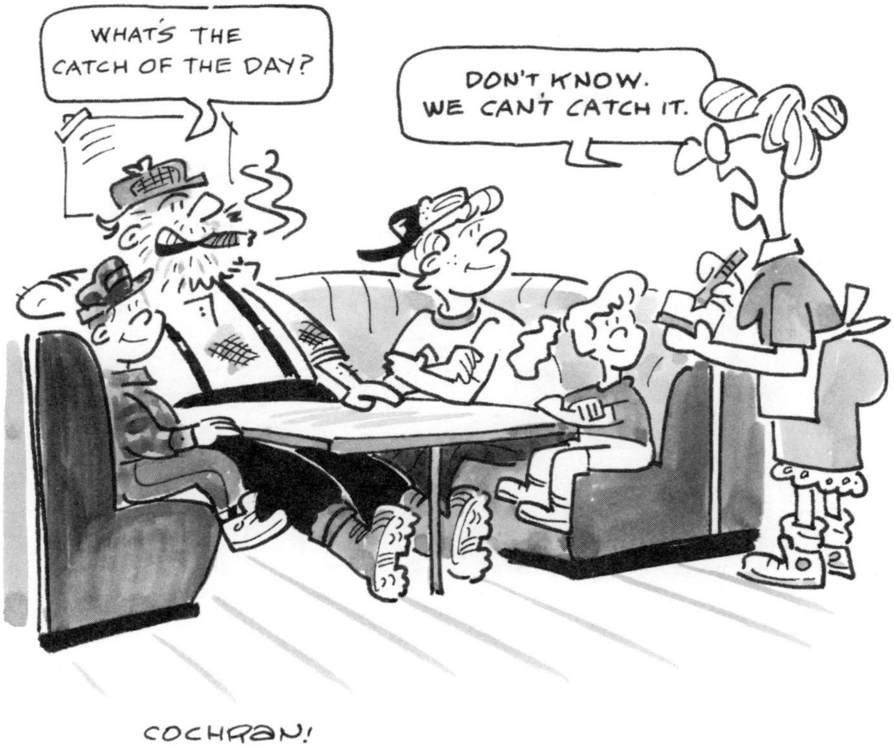
WHAT'S THE CATCH OF THE DAY?
DON'T KNOW. WE CAN'T CATCH IT.
COCHRAN!

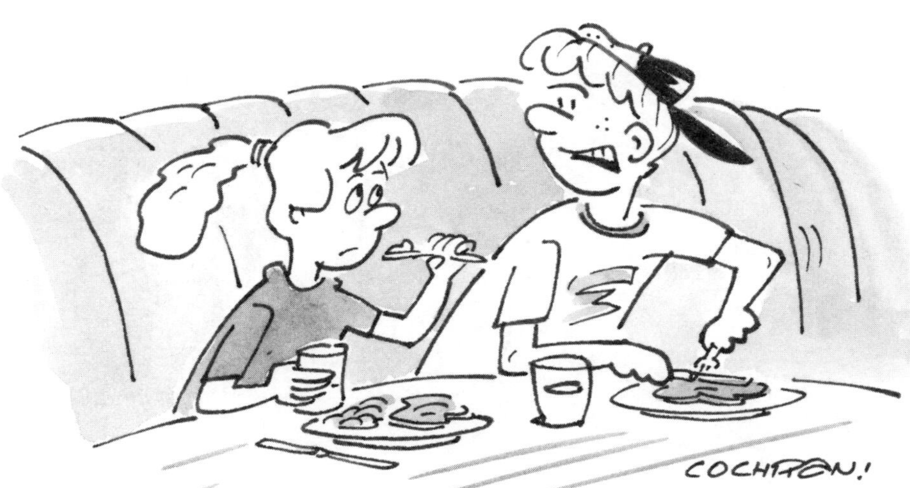
COCHRAN!

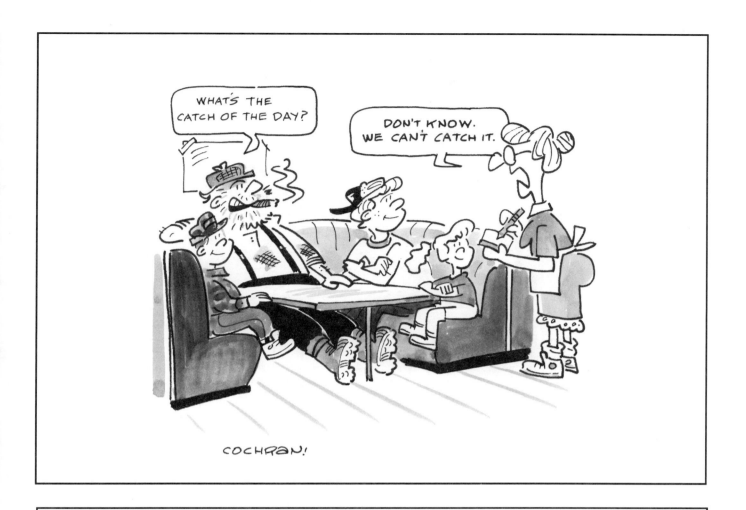

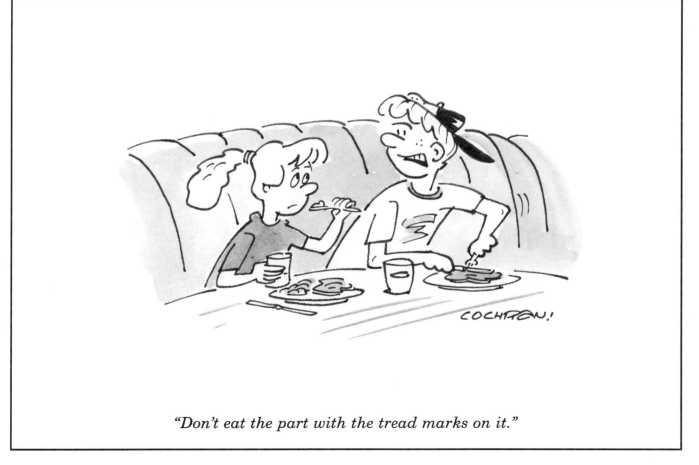

*"Don't eat the part with the tread marks on it."*

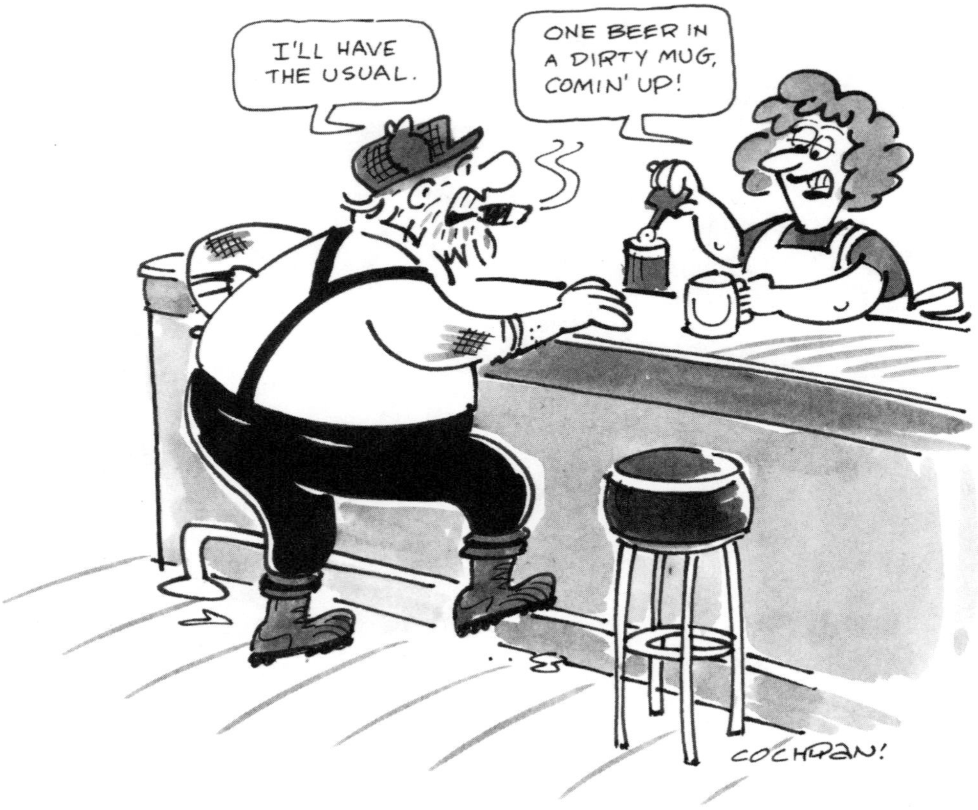
I'LL HAVE THE USUAL.
ONE BEER IN A DIRTY MUG, COMIN' UP!
COCHRAN!

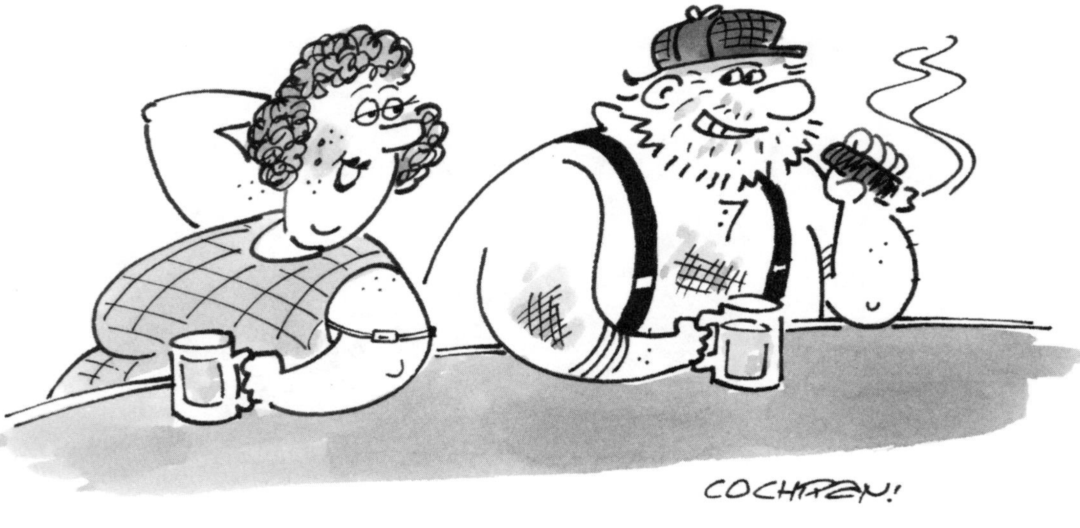
COCHRAN!

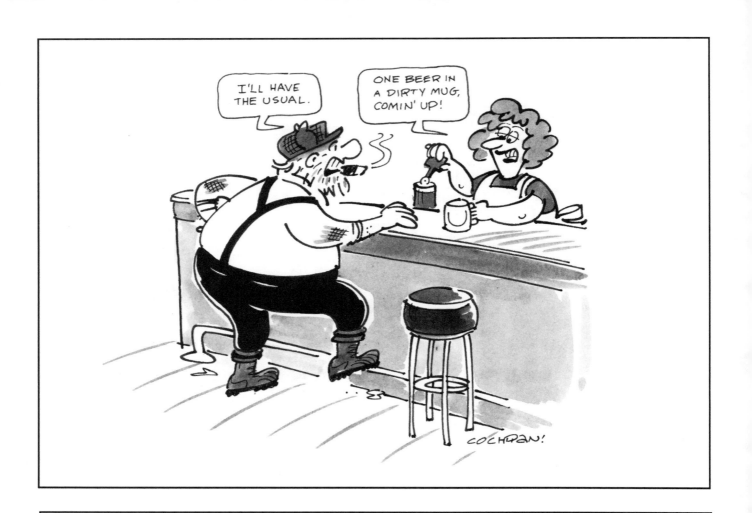

*"You have B.O. I like that in a man."*

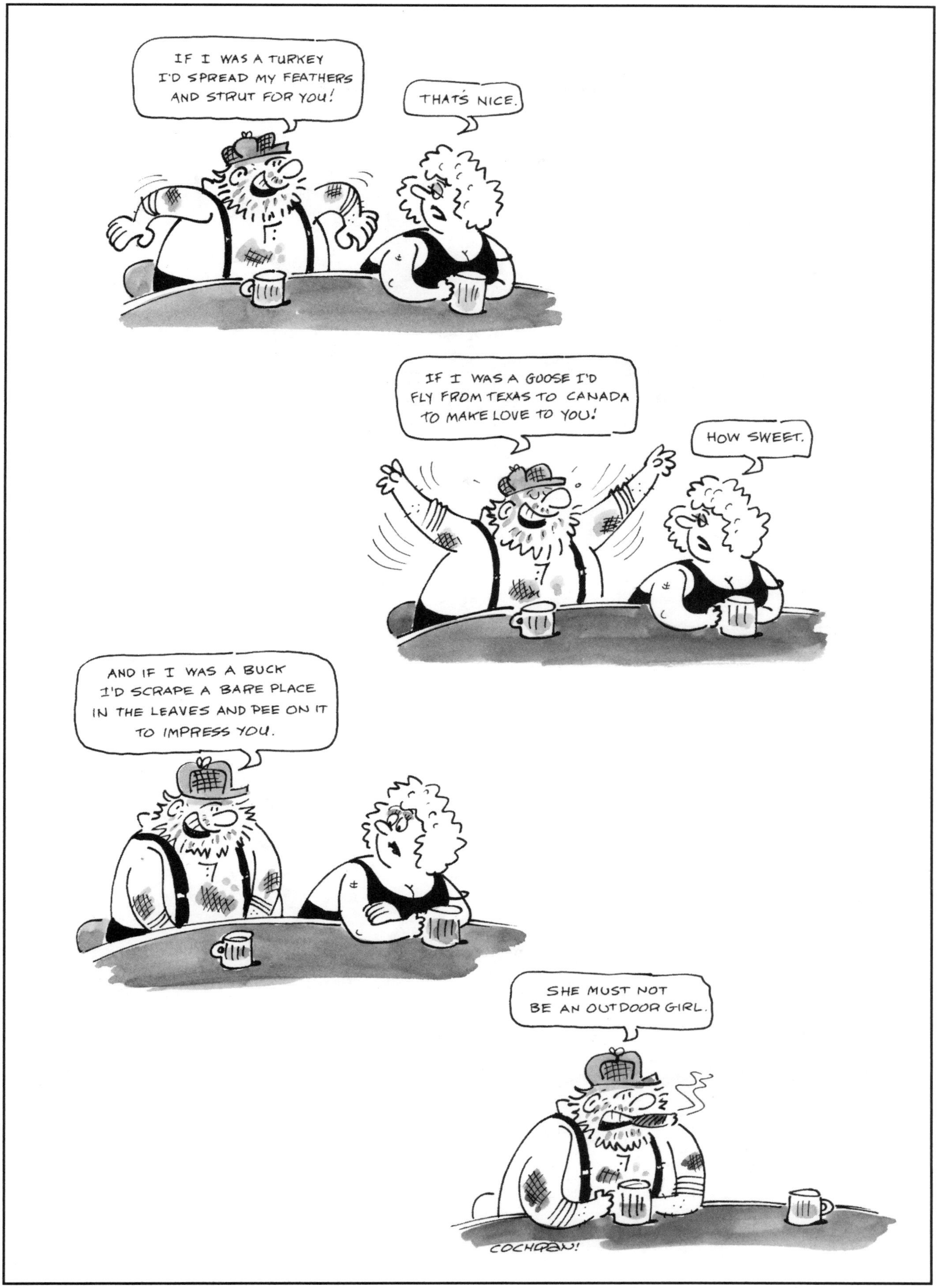
IF I WAS A TURKEY I'D SPREAD MY FEATHERS AND STRUT FOR YOU!
THAT'S NICE.
IF I WAS A GOOSE I'D FLY FROM TEXAS TO CANADA TO MAKE LOVE TO YOU!
HOW SWEET.
AND IF I WAS A BUCK I'D SCRAPE A BARE PLACE IN THE LEAVES AND PEE ON IT TO IMPRESS YOU.
SHE MUST NOT BE AN OUTDOOR GIRL.
COCHRAN!

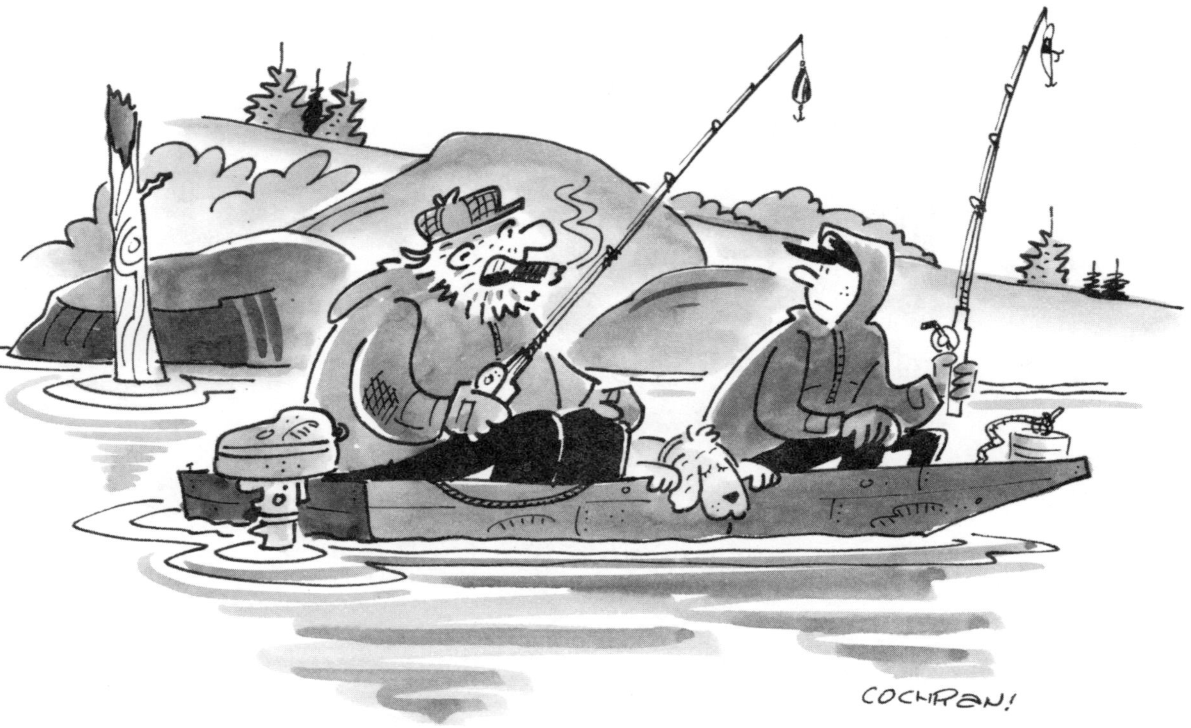
COCHRAN!

*"I've caught lots of things in this old boat, kid. Colds, pneumonia, dysentery . . ."*

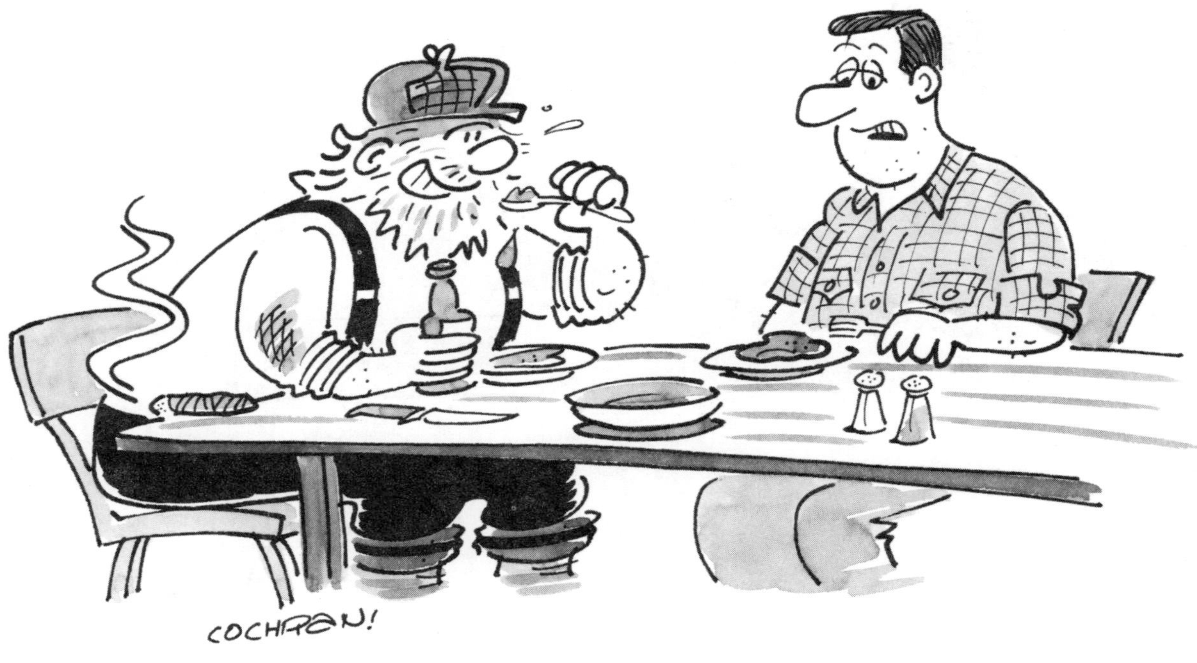
COCHRAN!

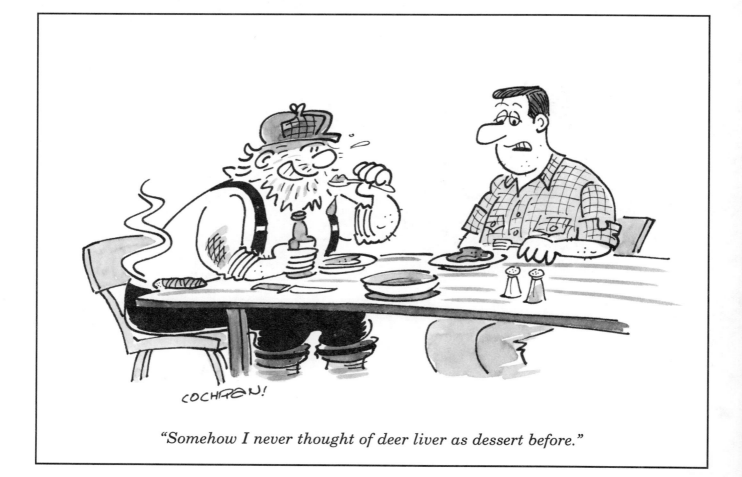

*"Somehow I never thought of deer liver as dessert before."*

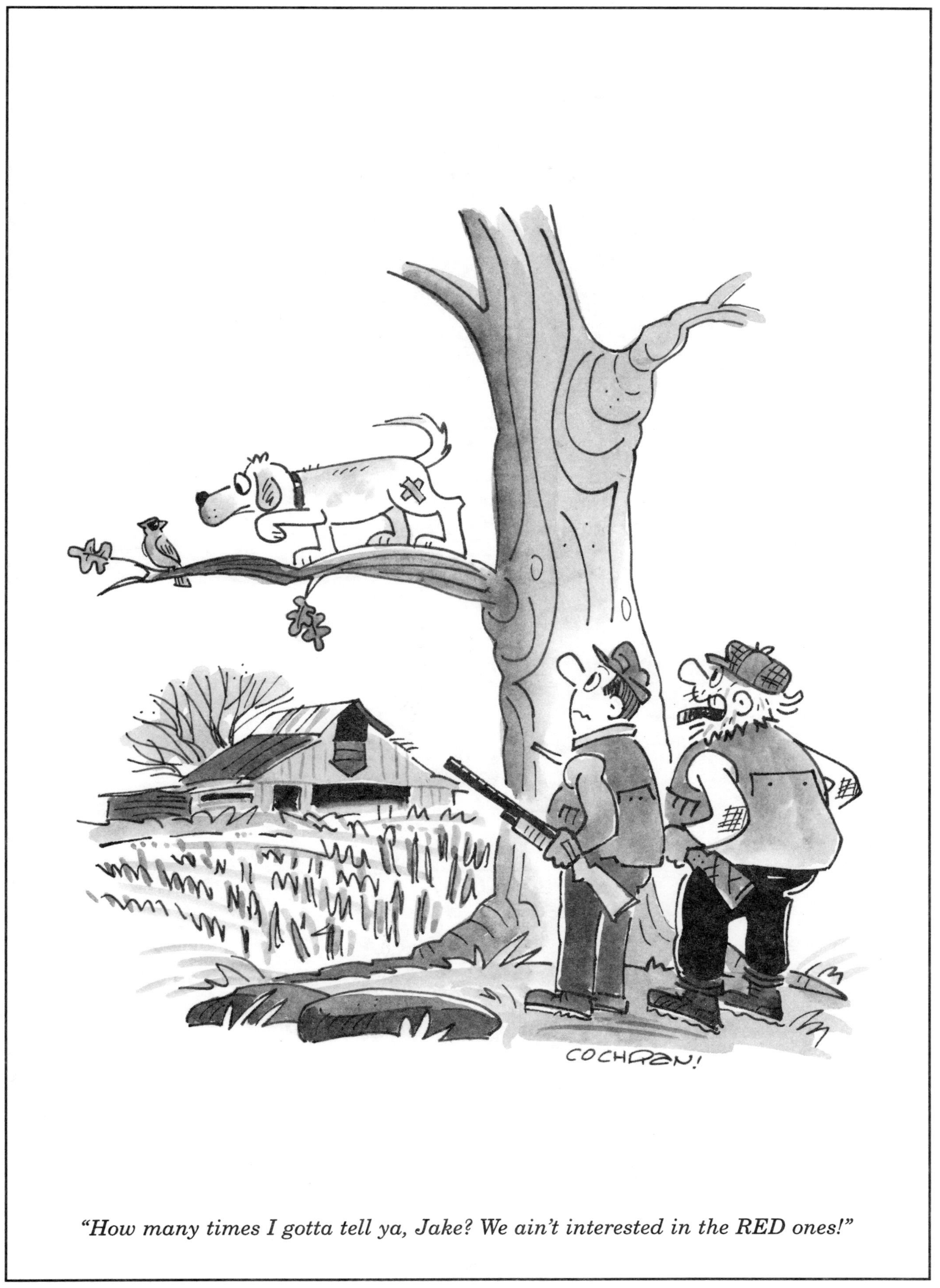
COCHRAN!

*"How many times I gotta tell ya, Jake? We ain't interested in the RED ones!"*

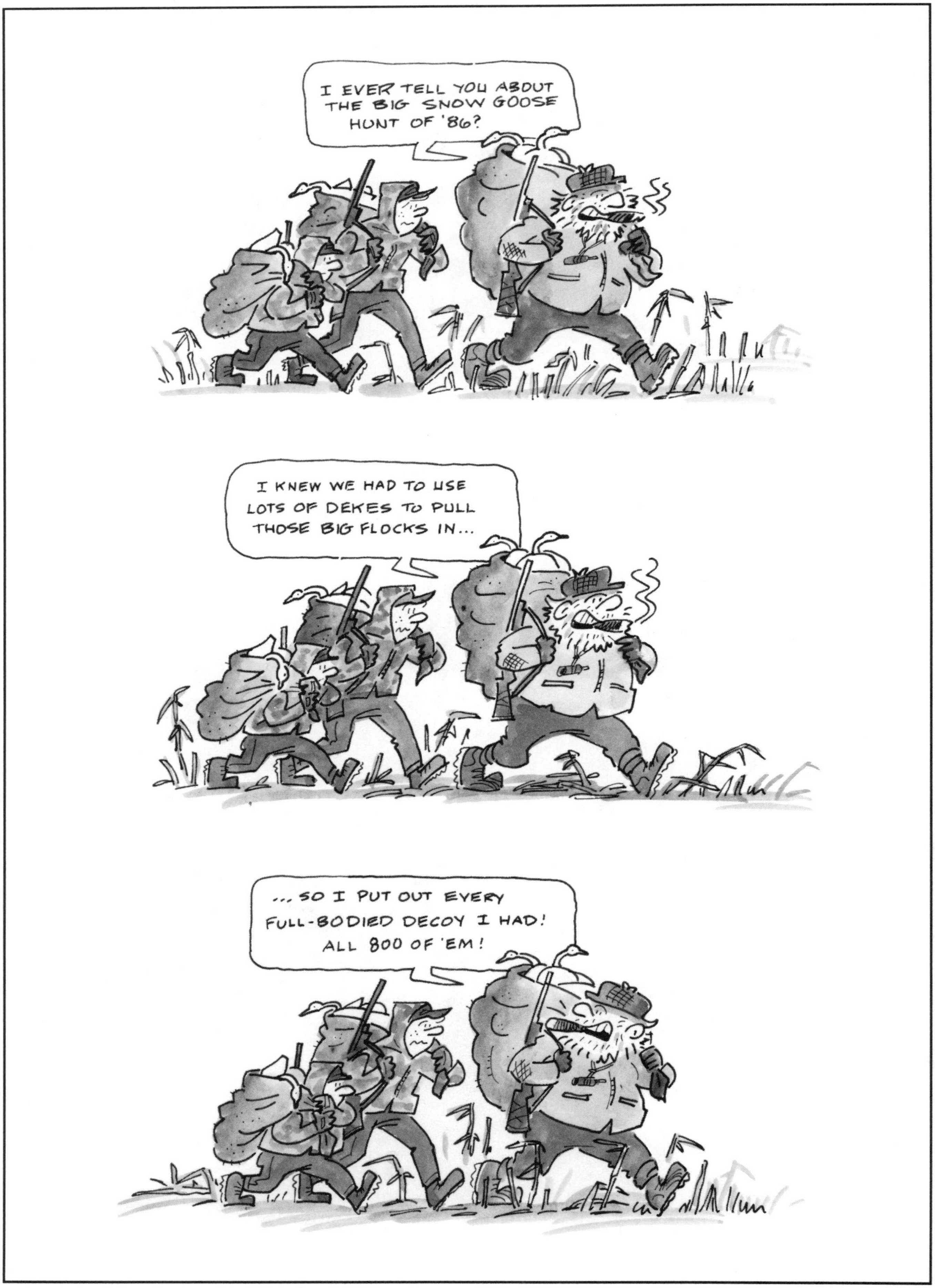
I EVER TELL YOU ABOUT THE BIG SNOW GOOSE HUNT OF '86?
I KNEW WE HAD TO USE LOTS OF DEKES TO PULL THOSE BIG FLOCKS IN...
...SO I PUT OUT EVERY FULL-BODIED DECOY I HAD! ALL 800 OF 'EM!

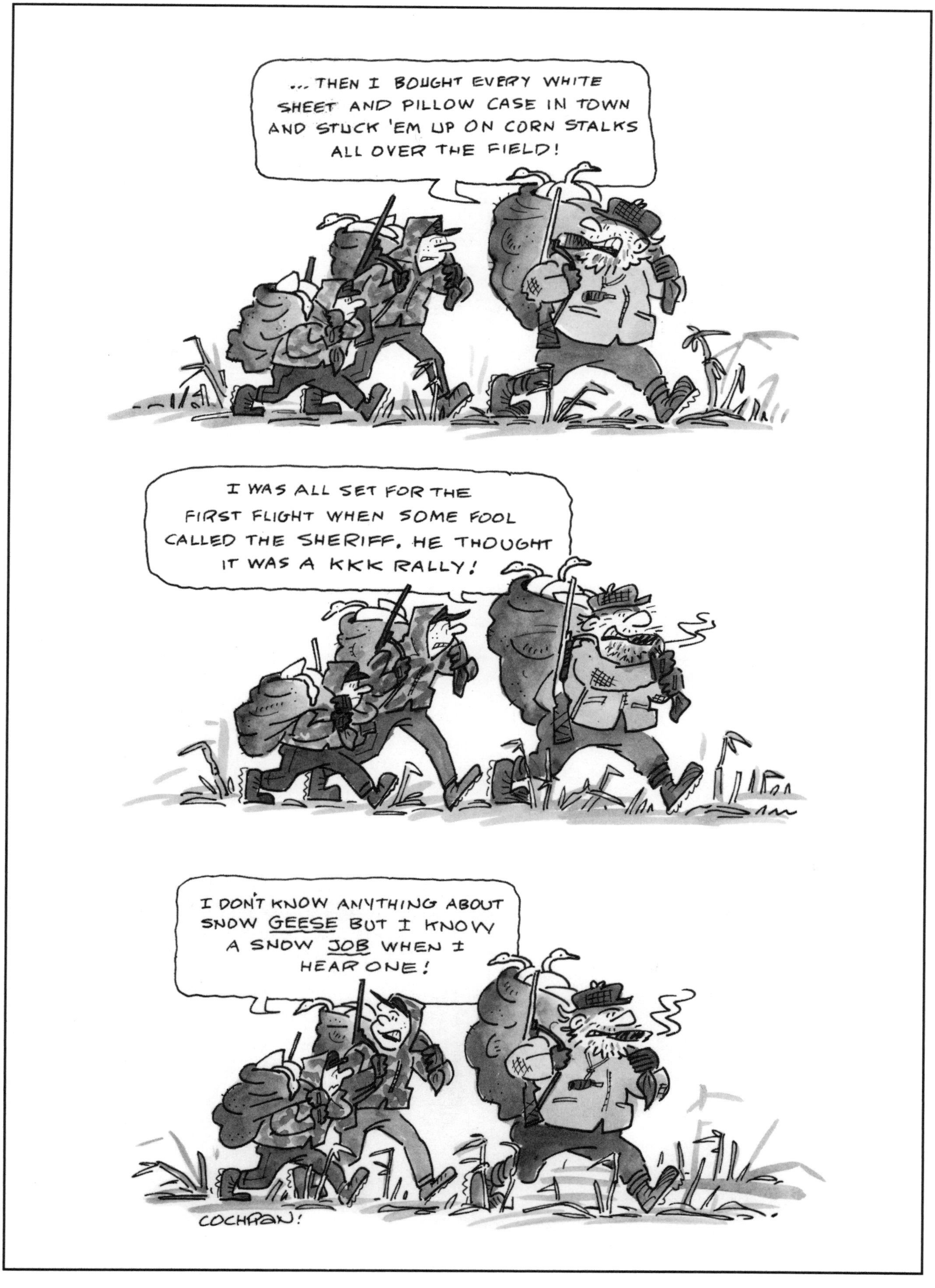
... THEN I BOUGHT EVERY WHITE SHEET AND PILLOW CASE IN TOWN AND STUCK 'EM UP ON CORN STALKS ALL OVER THE FIELD!
I WAS ALL SET FOR THE FIRST FLIGHT WHEN SOME FOOL CALLED THE SHERIFF. HE THOUGHT IT WAS A KKK RALLY!
I DON'T KNOW ANYTHING ABOUT SNOW GEESE BUT I KNOW A SNOW JOB WHEN I HEAR ONE!
COCHRAN!

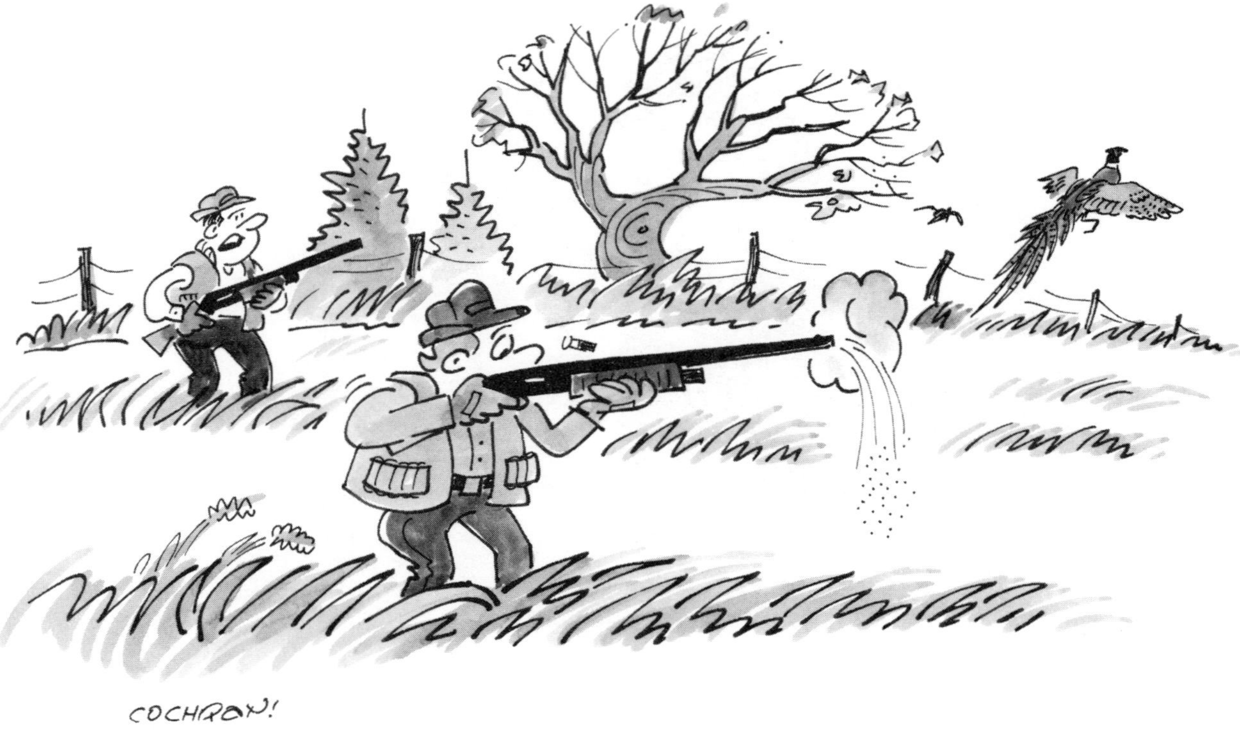
COCHRON!

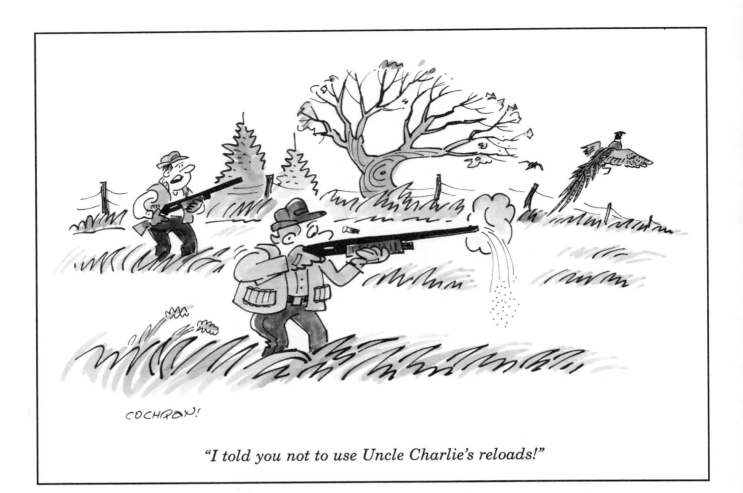

*"I told you not to use Uncle Charlie's reloads!"*

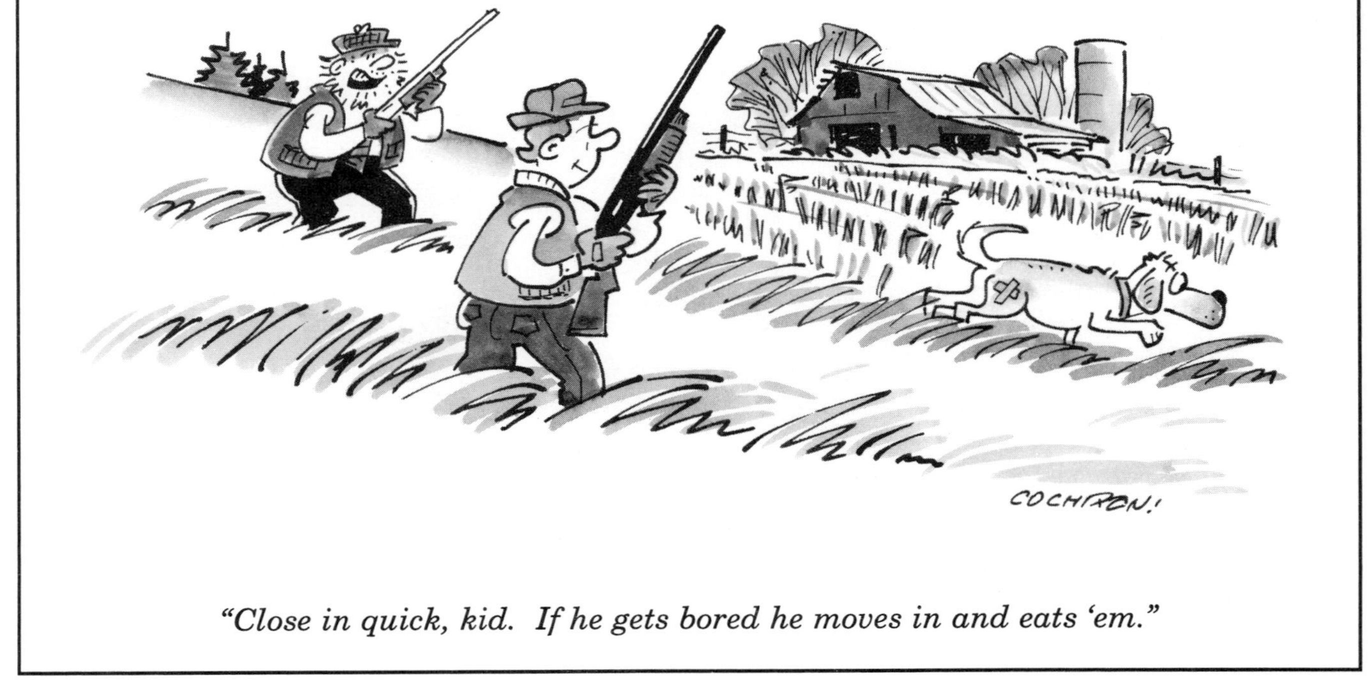
COCHRON!

*"Close in quick, kid. If he gets bored he moves in and eats 'em."*

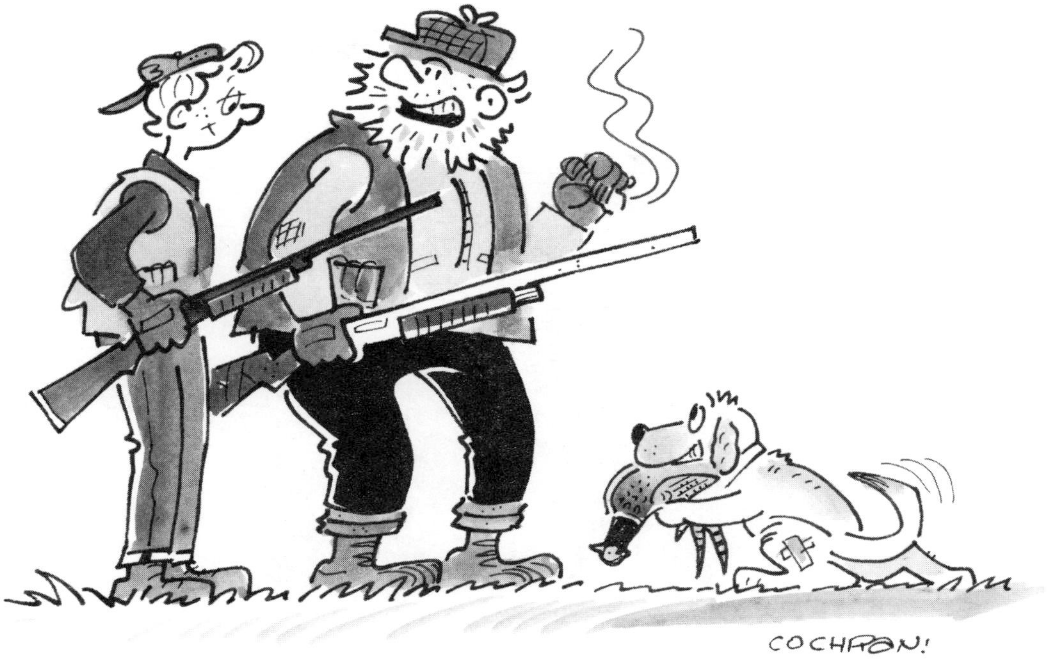
COCHRAN!

*"Eager to please, ain't he?"*

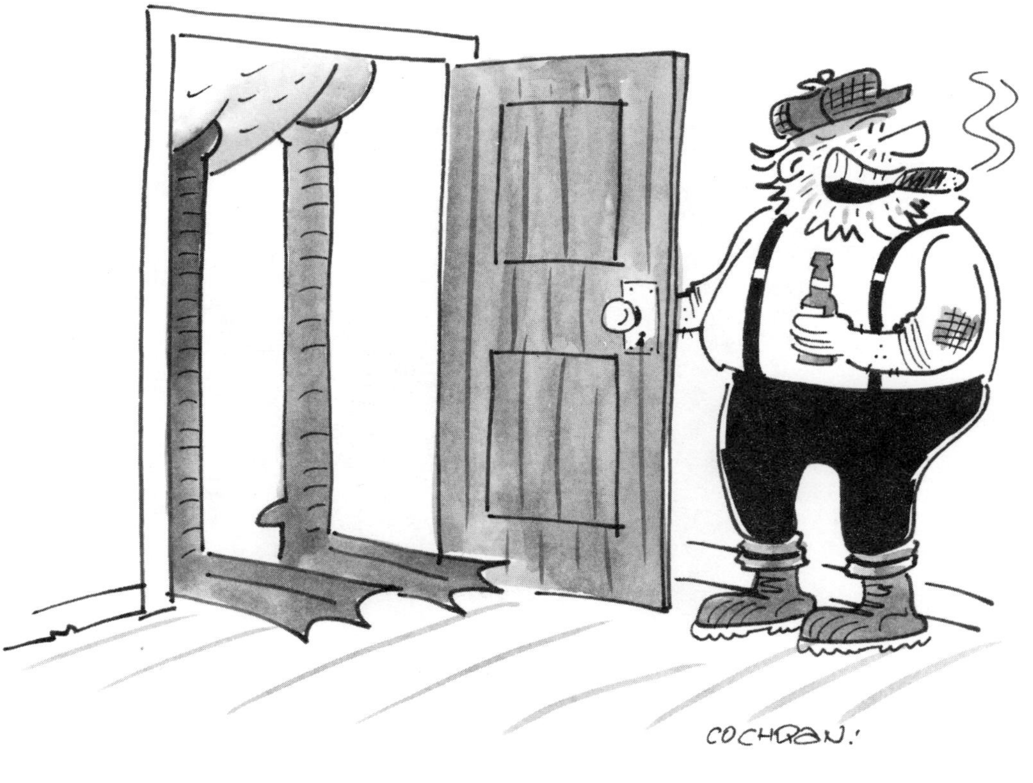
COCHRAN!

*"Guess what, guys! The 'big red legs' have finally come down!"*

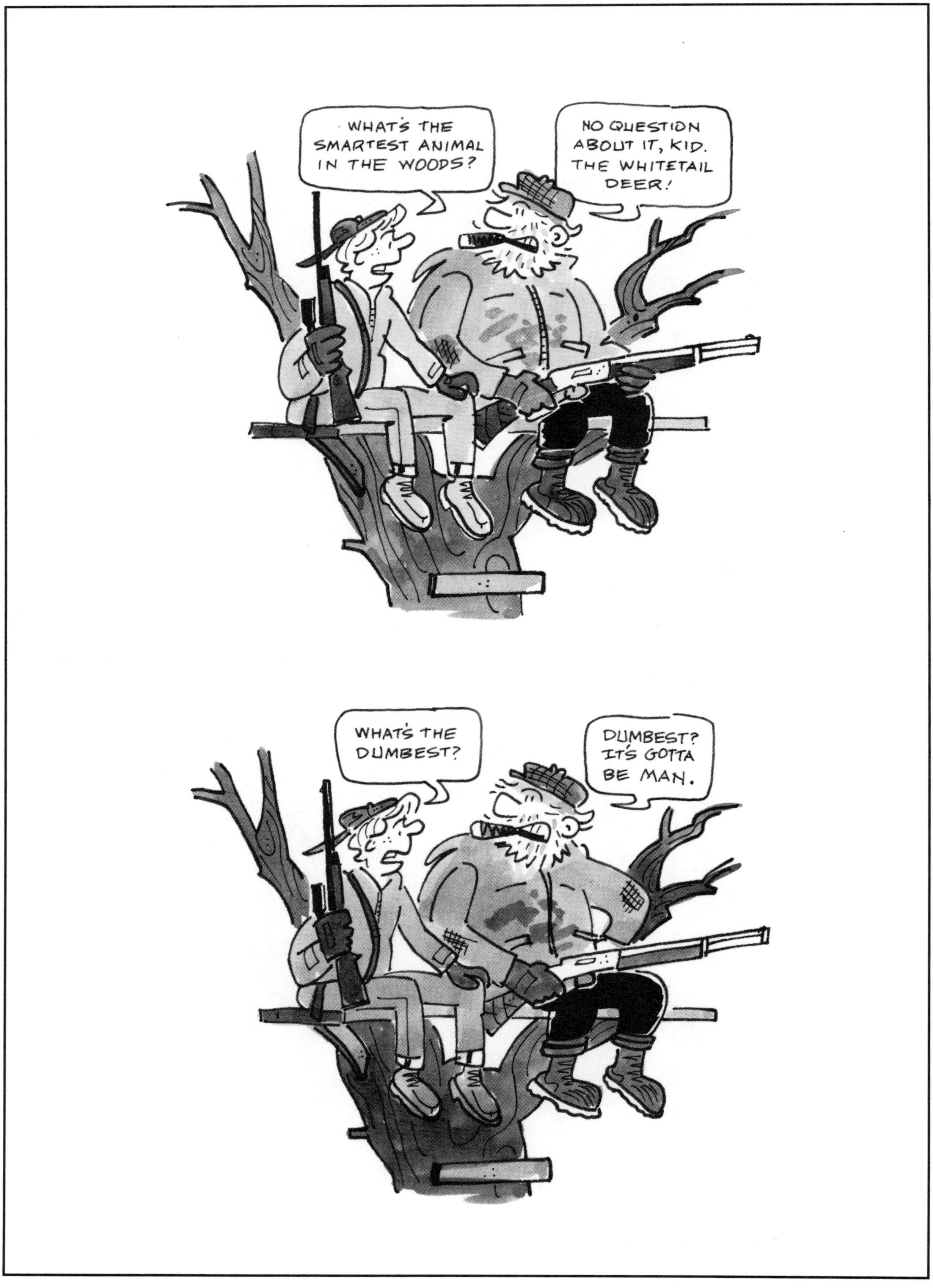
WHAT'S THE SMARTEST ANIMAL IN THE WOODS?
NO QUESTION ABOUT IT, KID. THE WHITETAIL DEER!
WHAT'S THE DUMBEST?
DUMBEST? IT'S GOTTA BE MAN.

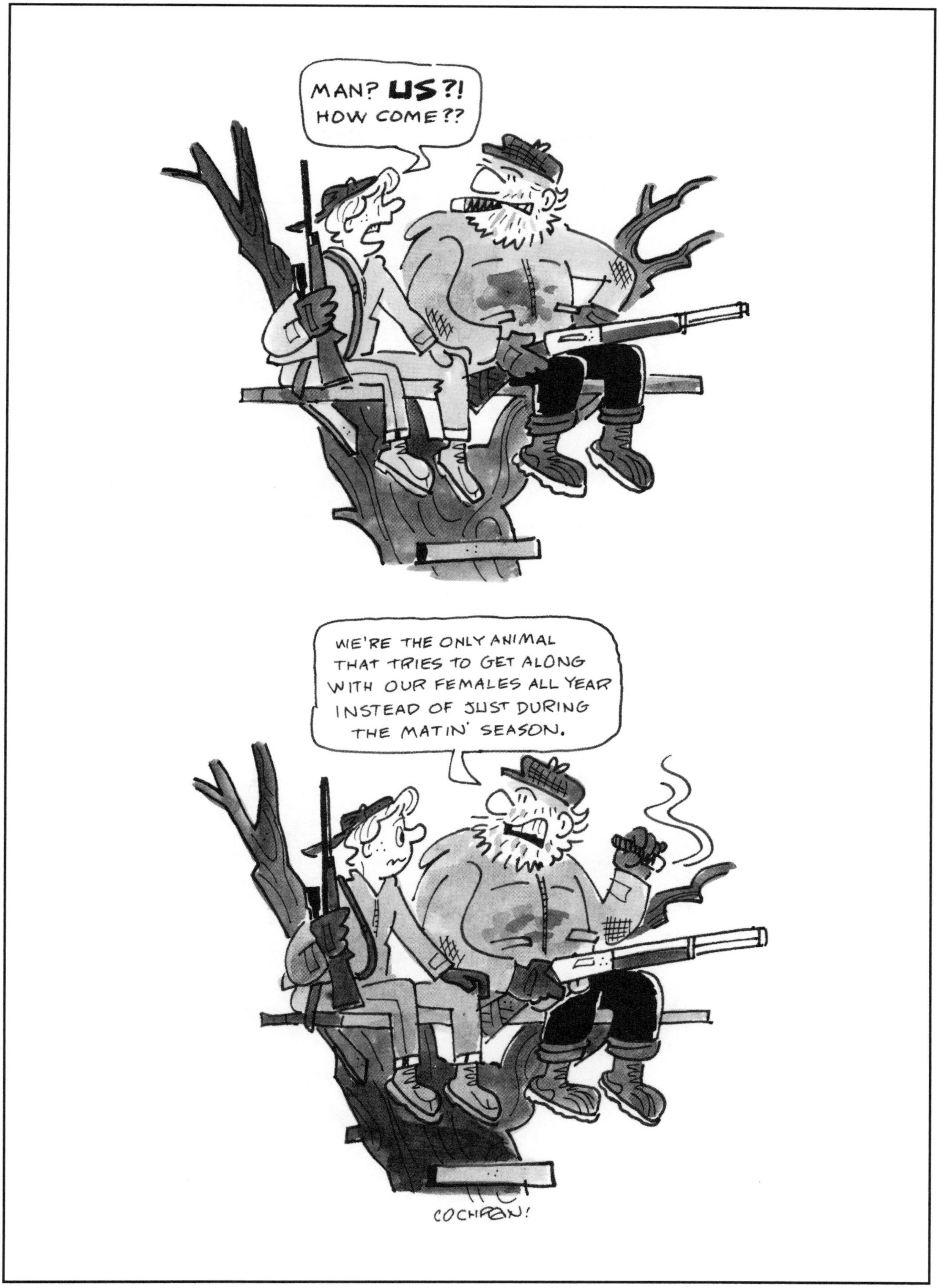
MAN? US?! HOW COME??
WE'RE THE ONLY ANIMAL THAT TRIES TO GET ALONG WITH OUR FEMALES ALL YEAR INSTEAD OF JUST DURING THE MATIN' SEASON.
COCHRAN!

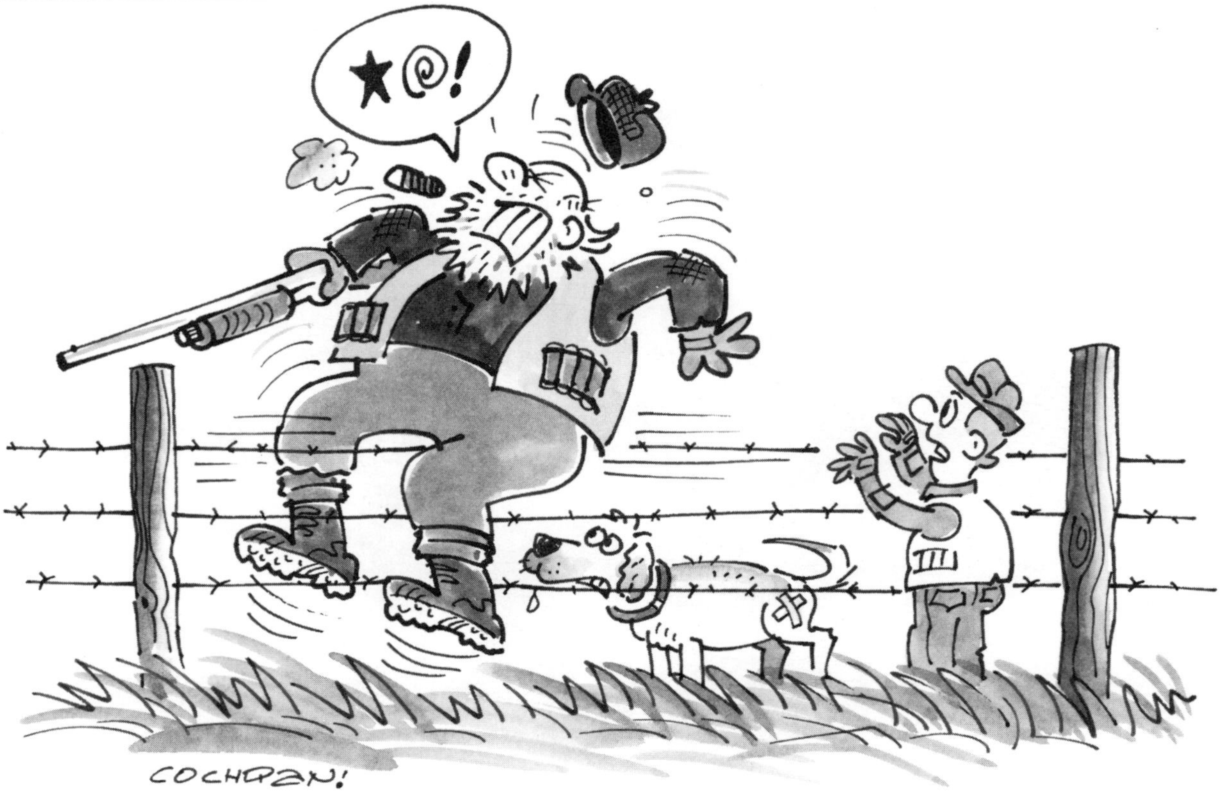
★@!
COCHRAN!

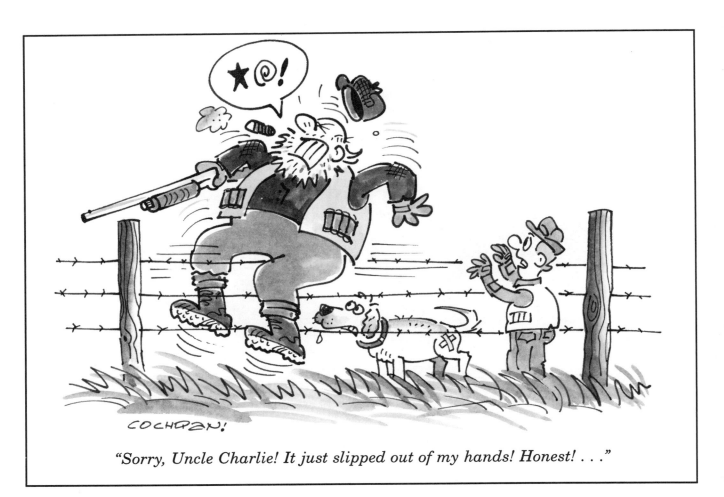

*"Sorry, Uncle Charlie! It just slipped out of my hands! Honest! . . ."*

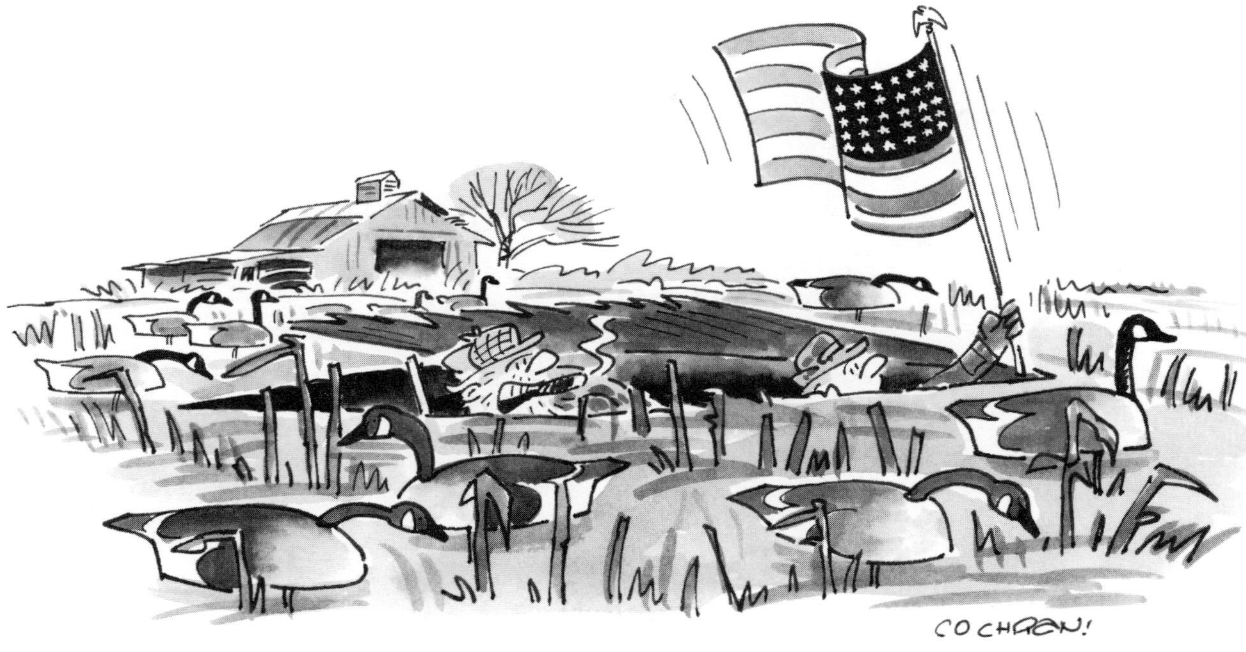
COCHRAN!

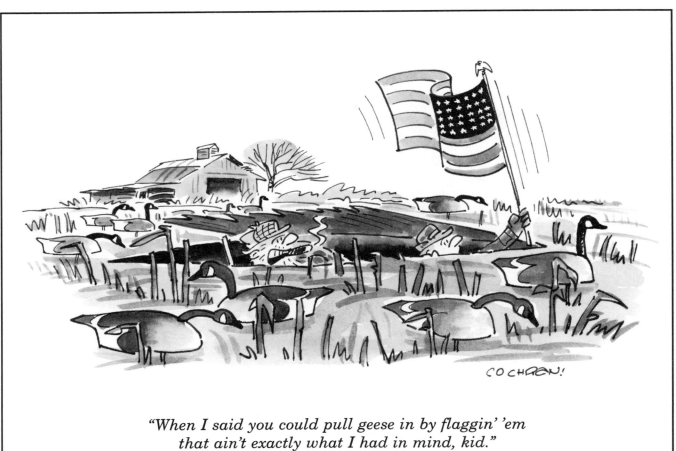

*"When I said you could pull geese in by flaggin' 'em*
*that ain't exactly what I had in mind, kid."*

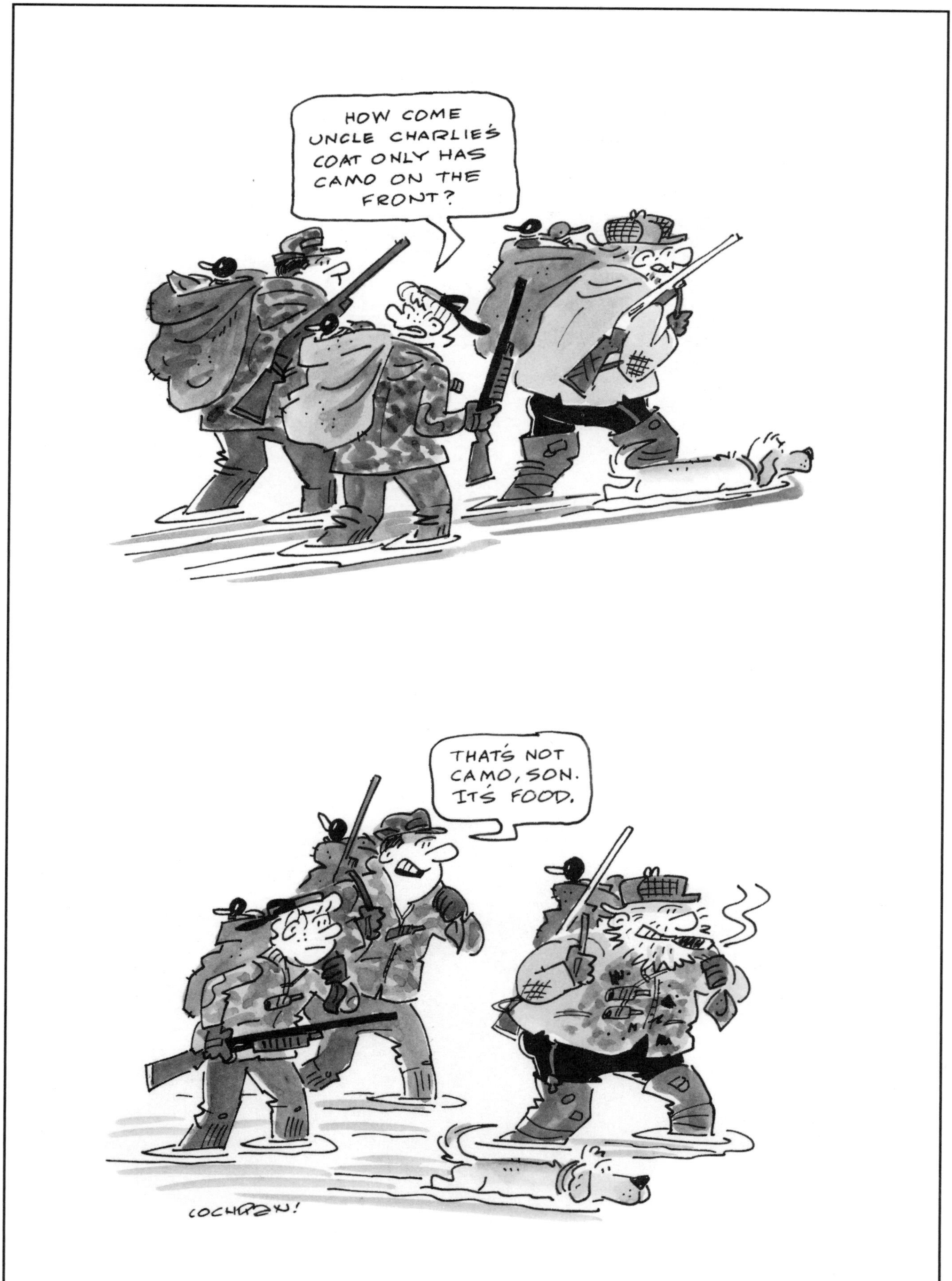
HOW COME UNCLE CHARLIE'S COAT ONLY HAS CAMO ON THE FRONT?
THAT'S NOT CAMO, SON. IT'S FOOD.
COCHRAN!

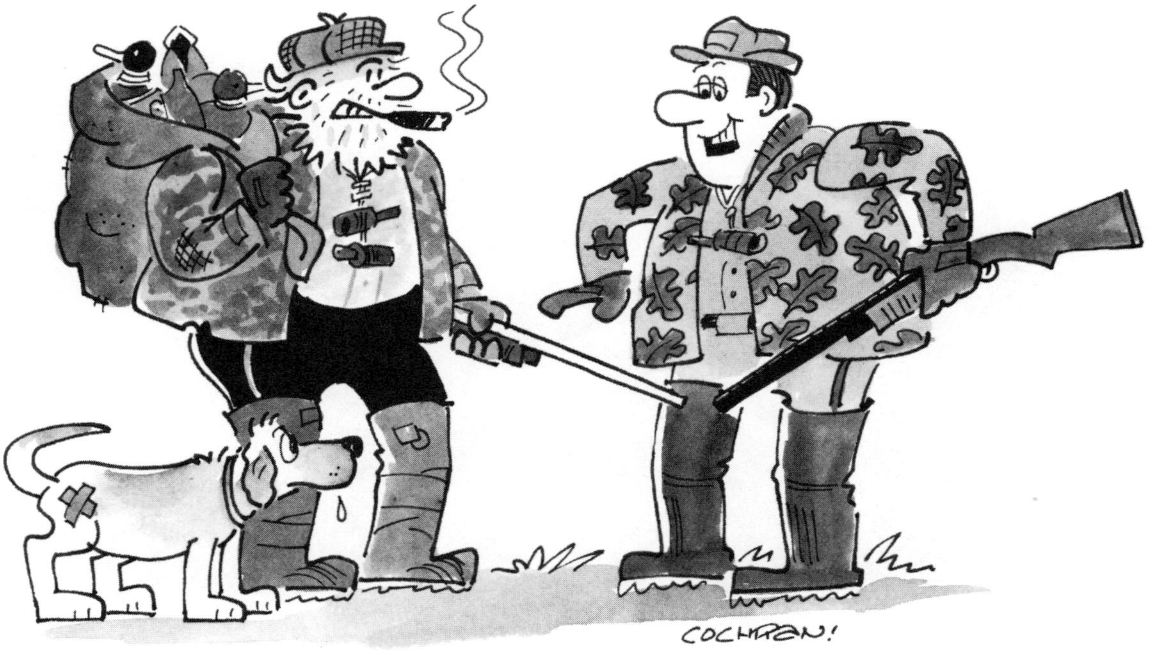
COCHRAN!

*"It's called 'falling leaves camo'! It looks great when I jump out of a tree."*

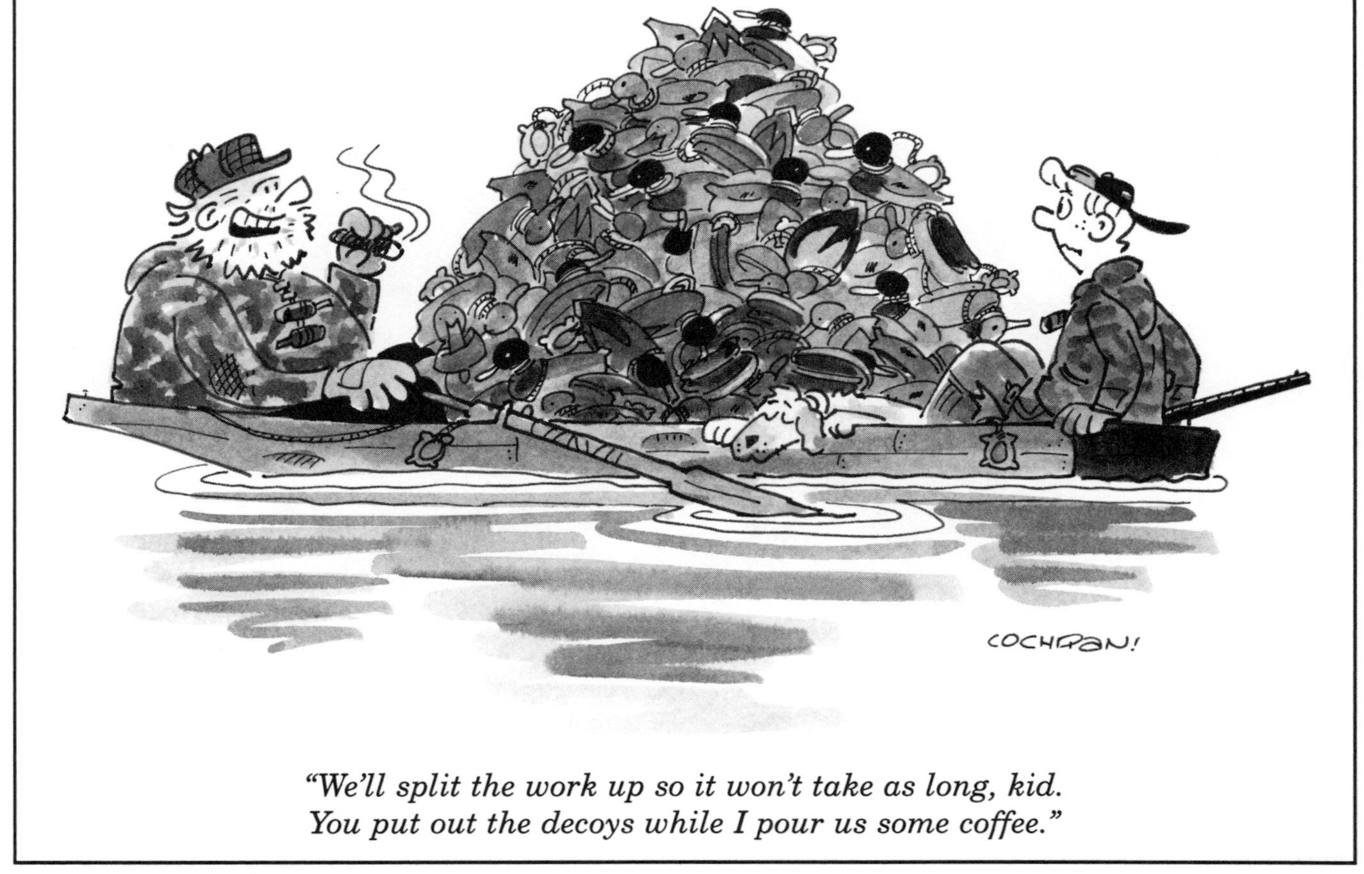
COCHRAN!

*"We'll split the work up so it won't take as long, kid.*
*You put out the decoys while I pour us some coffee."*

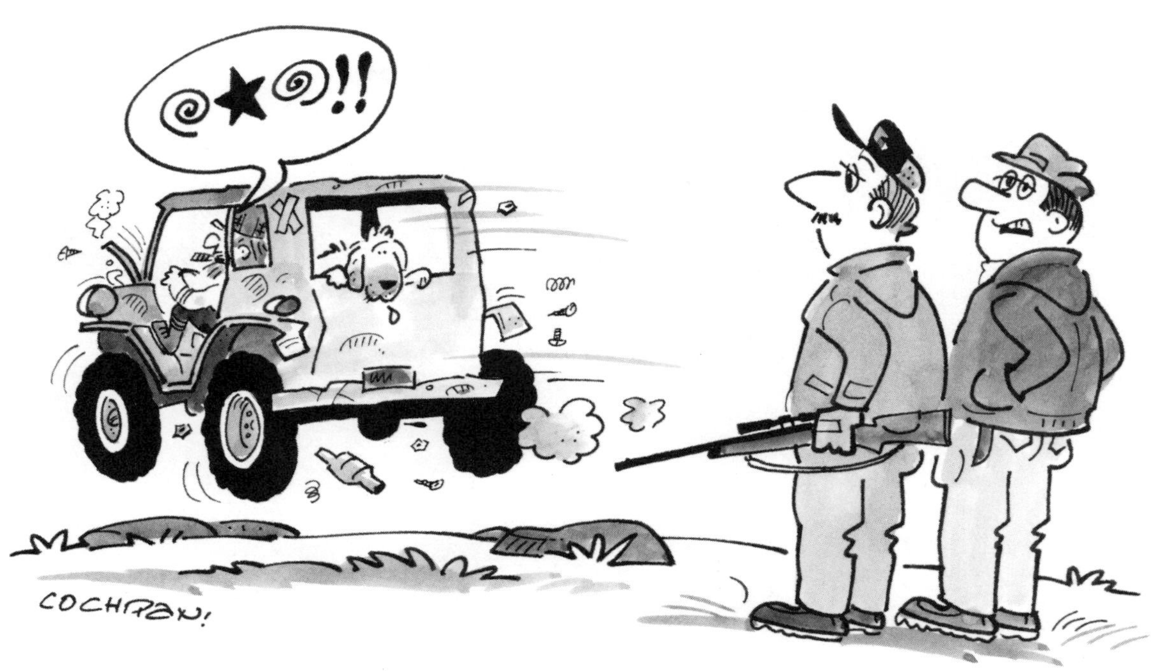

COCHRAN!


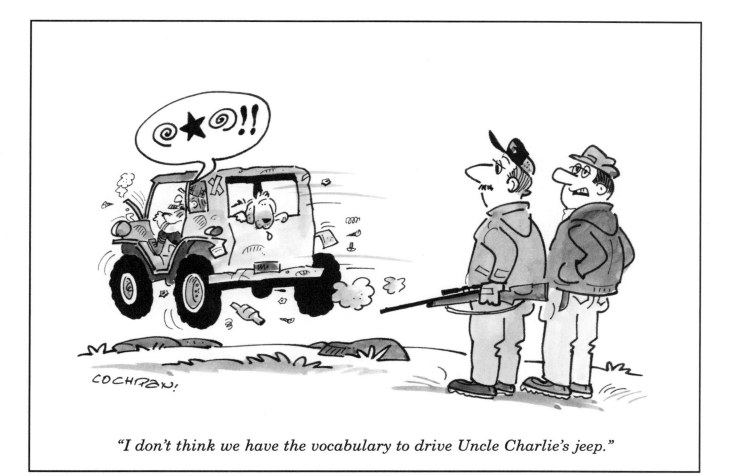

*"I don't think we have the vocabulary to drive Uncle Charlie's jeep."*

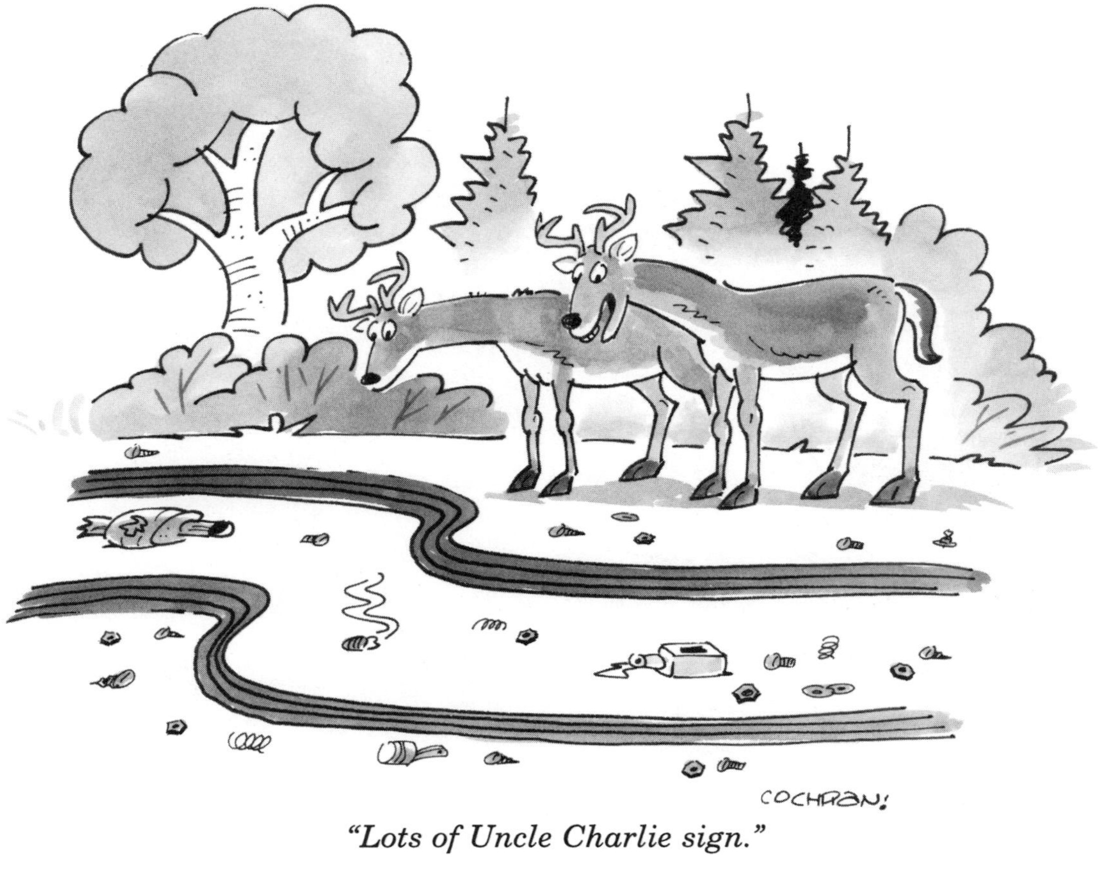

COCHRAN!


*"Lots of Uncle Charlie sign."*

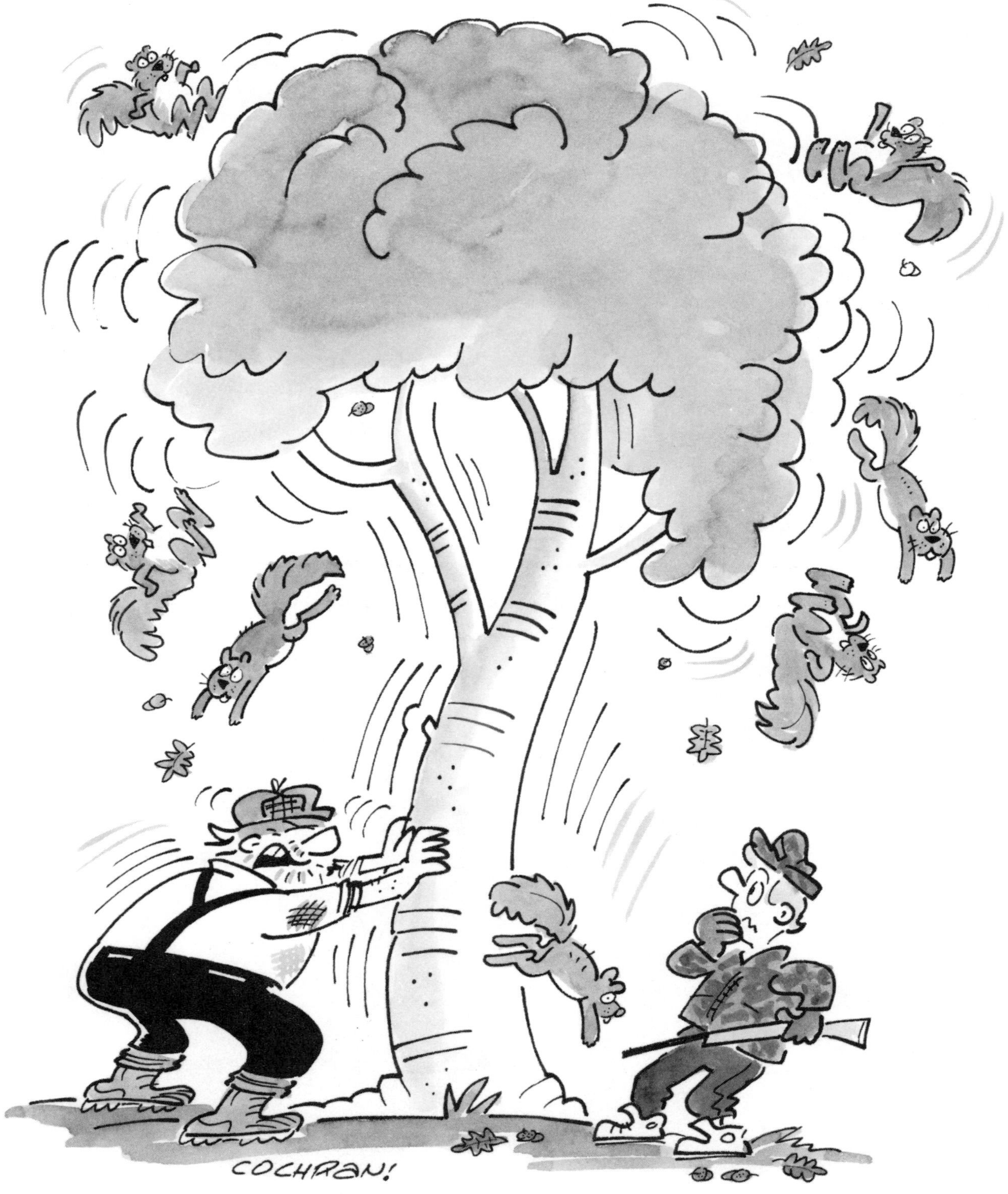
COCHRAN!

*"Nobody but a sissy would hunt squirrels with a gun, kid!"*

# Winter

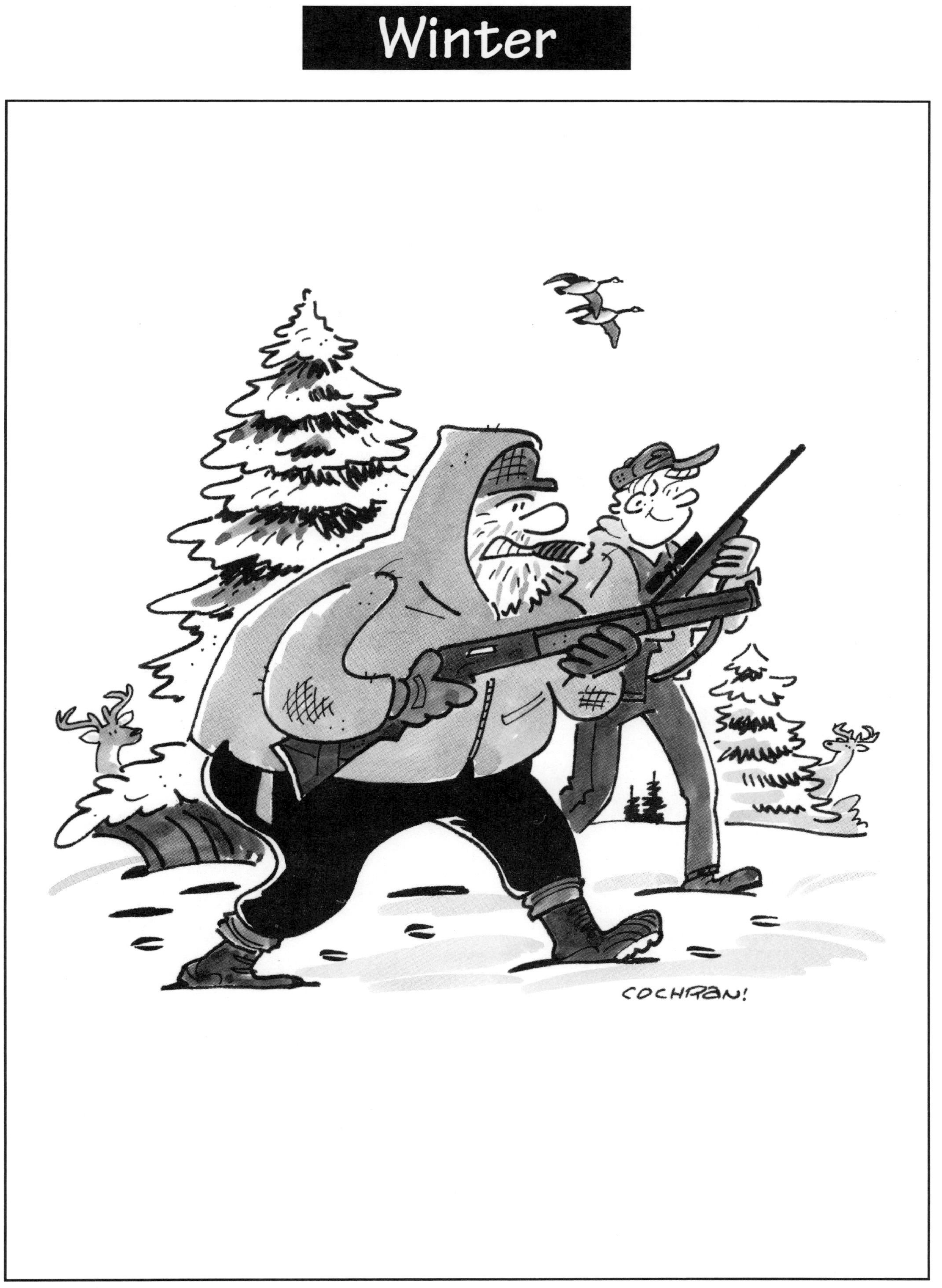
COCHRAN!

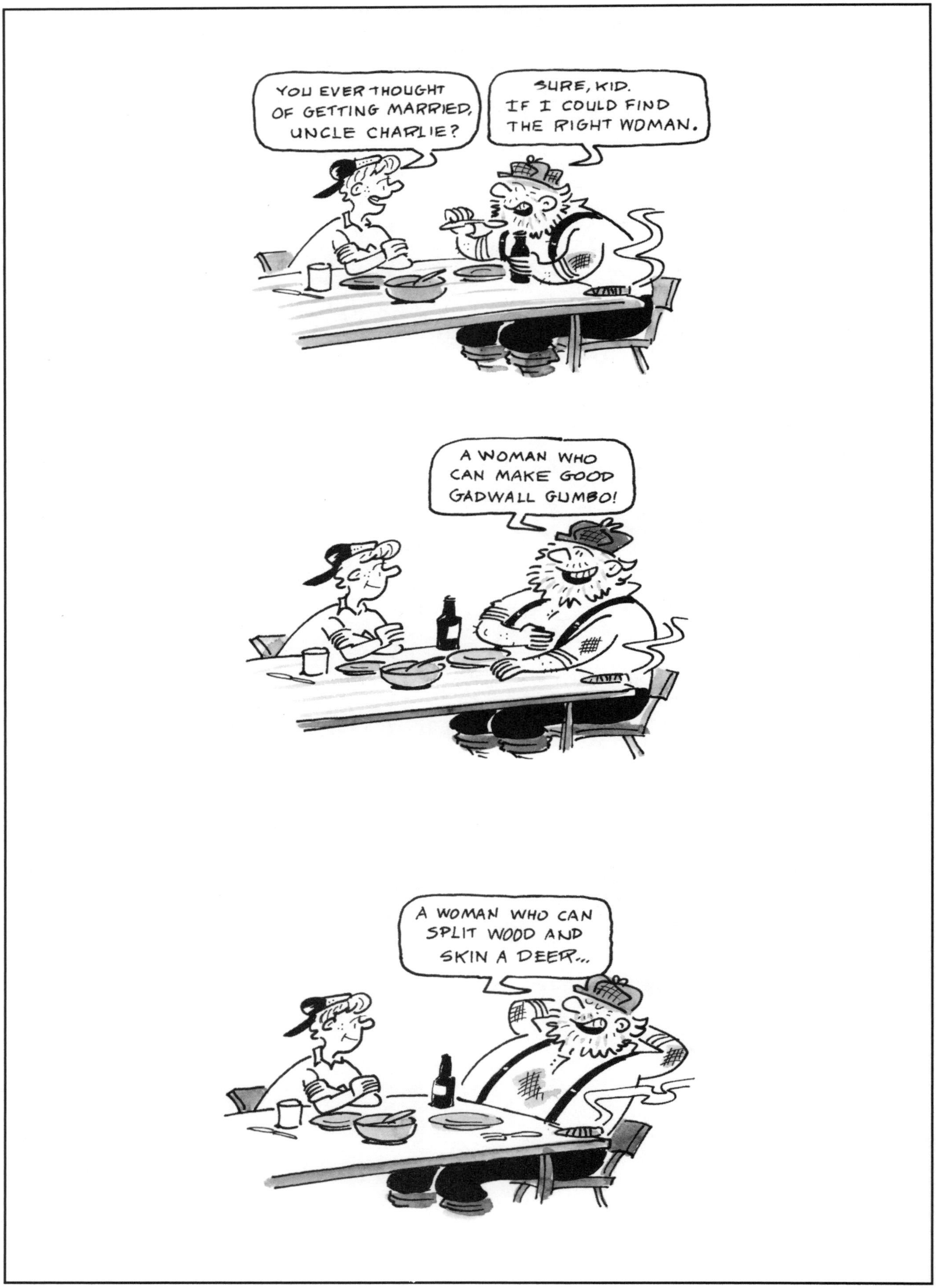
YOU EVER THOUGHT OF GETTING MARRIED, UNCLE CHARLIE?
SURE, KID. IF I COULD FIND THE RIGHT WOMAN.
A WOMAN WHO CAN MAKE GOOD GADWALL GUMBO!
A WOMAN WHO CAN SPLIT WOOD AND SKIN A DEER...

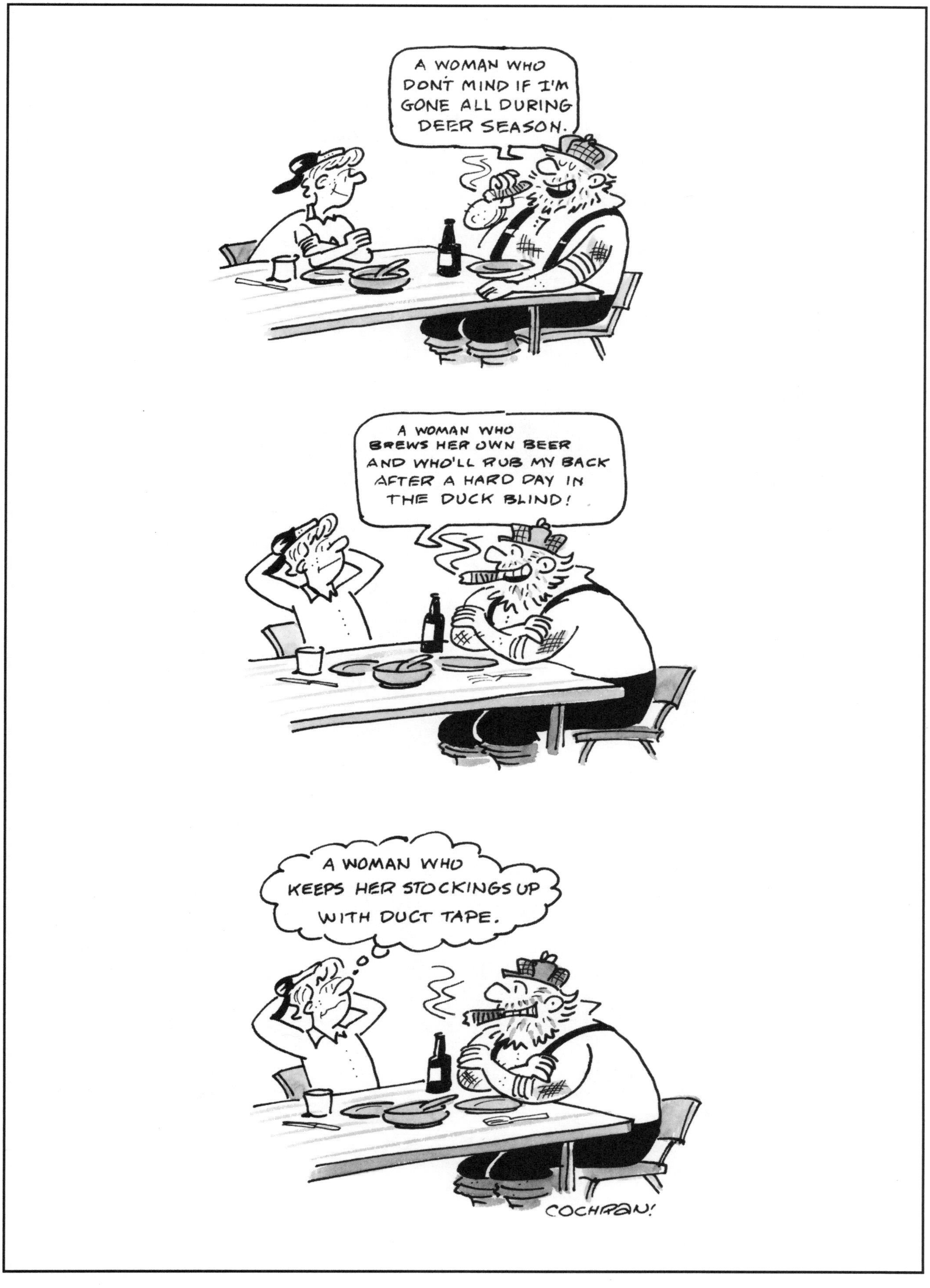
A WOMAN WHO DON'T MIND IF I'M GONE ALL DURING DEER SEASON.
A WOMAN WHO BREWS HER OWN BEER AND WHO'LL RUB MY BACK AFTER A HARD DAY IN THE DUCK BLIND!
A WOMAN WHO KEEPS HER STOCKINGS UP WITH DUCT TAPE.
COCHRAN!

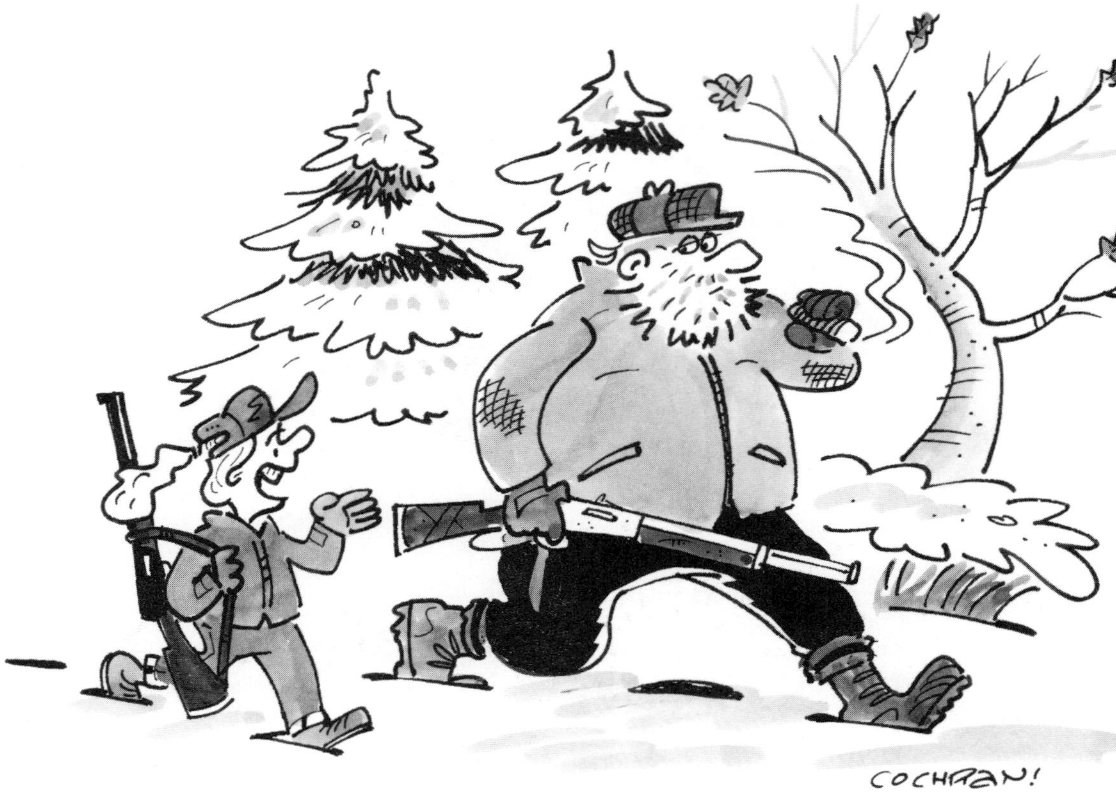
COCHRAN!

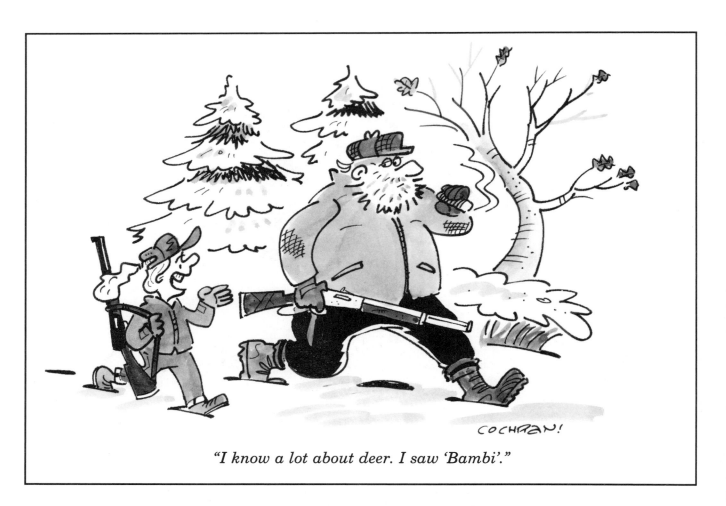

*"I know a lot about deer. I saw 'Bambi'."*

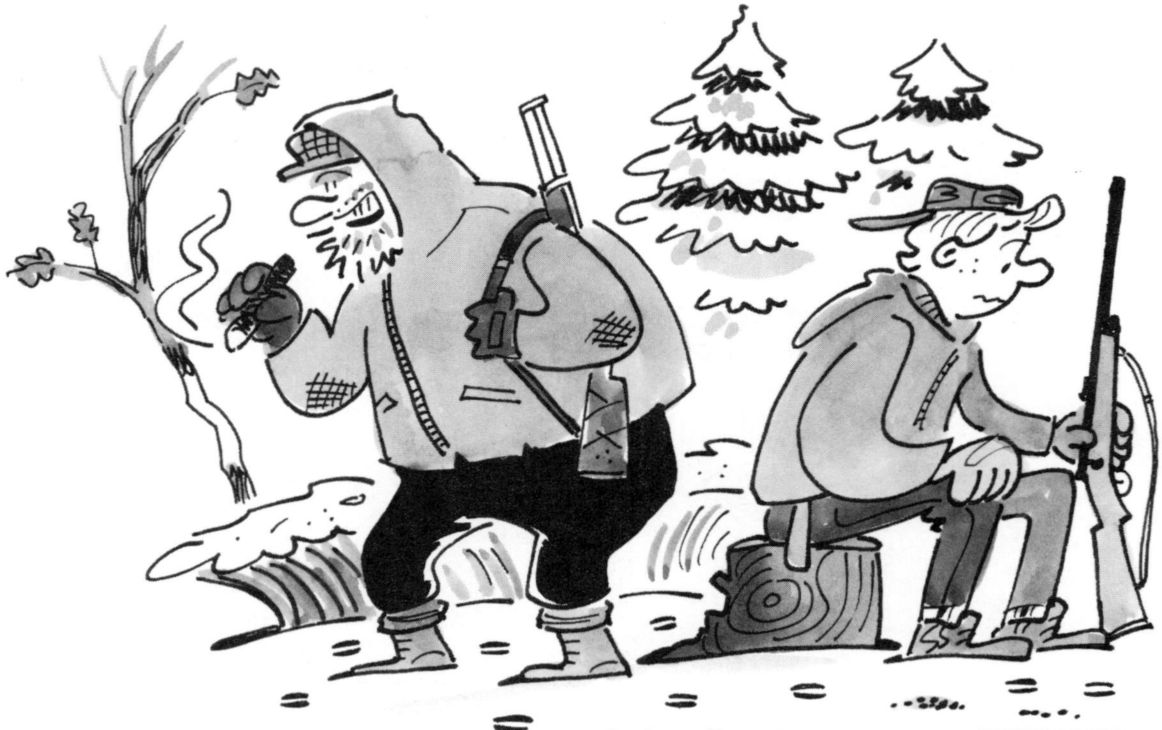
COCHRAN!

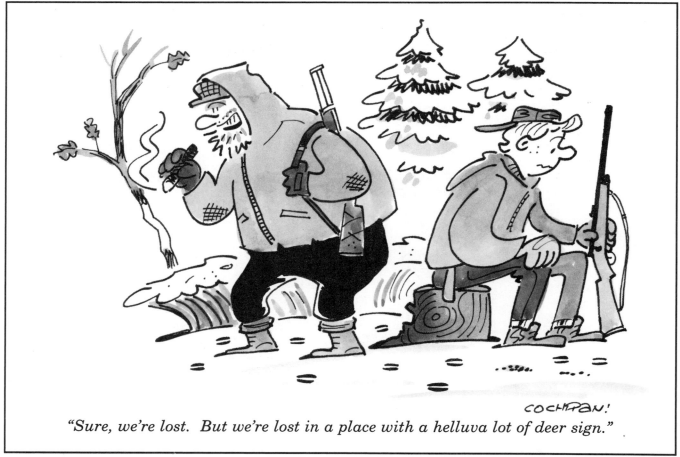

*"Sure, we're lost. But we're lost in a place with a helluva lot of deer sign."*

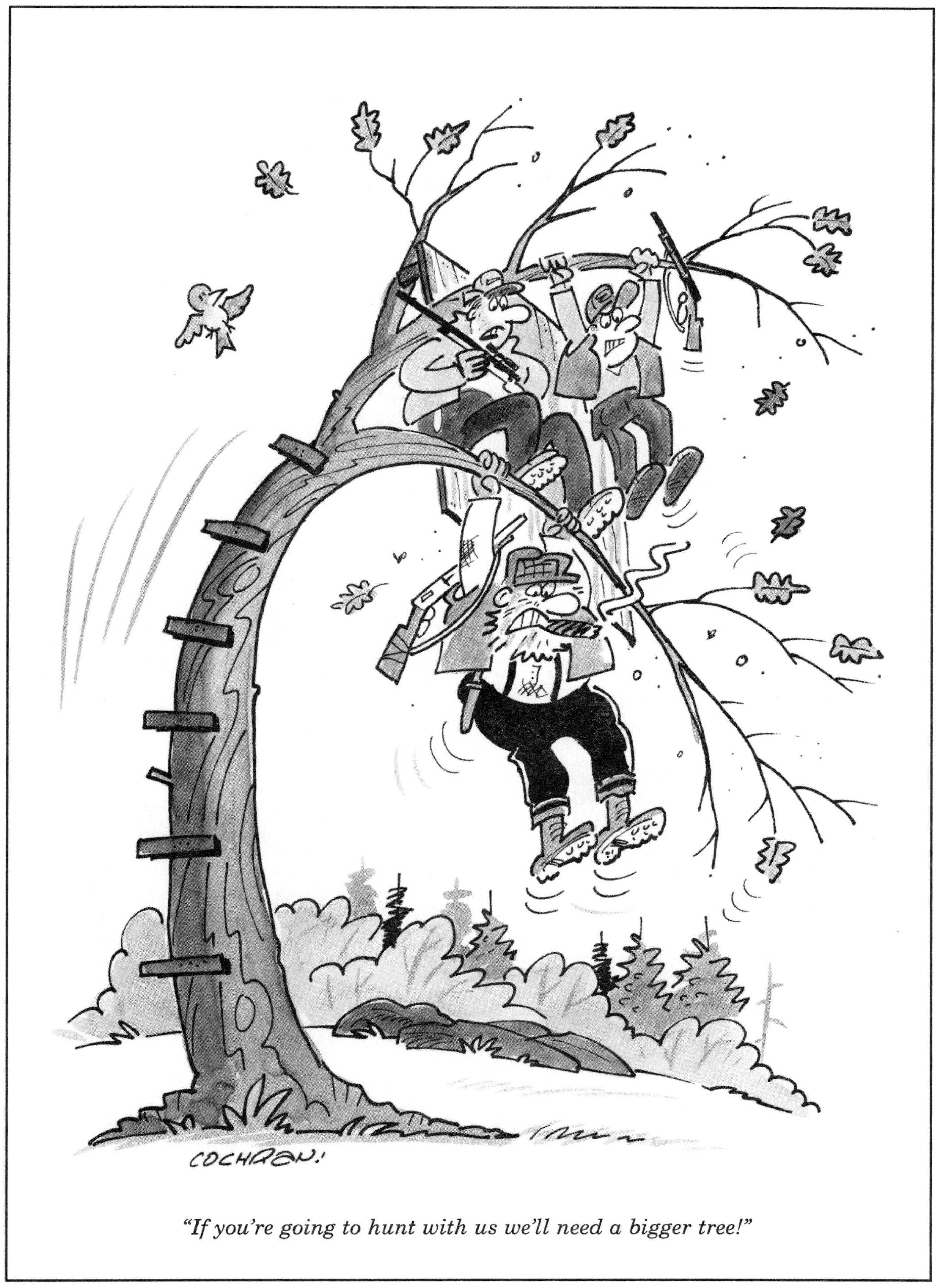
COCHRAN!

*"If you're going to hunt with us we'll need a bigger tree!"*

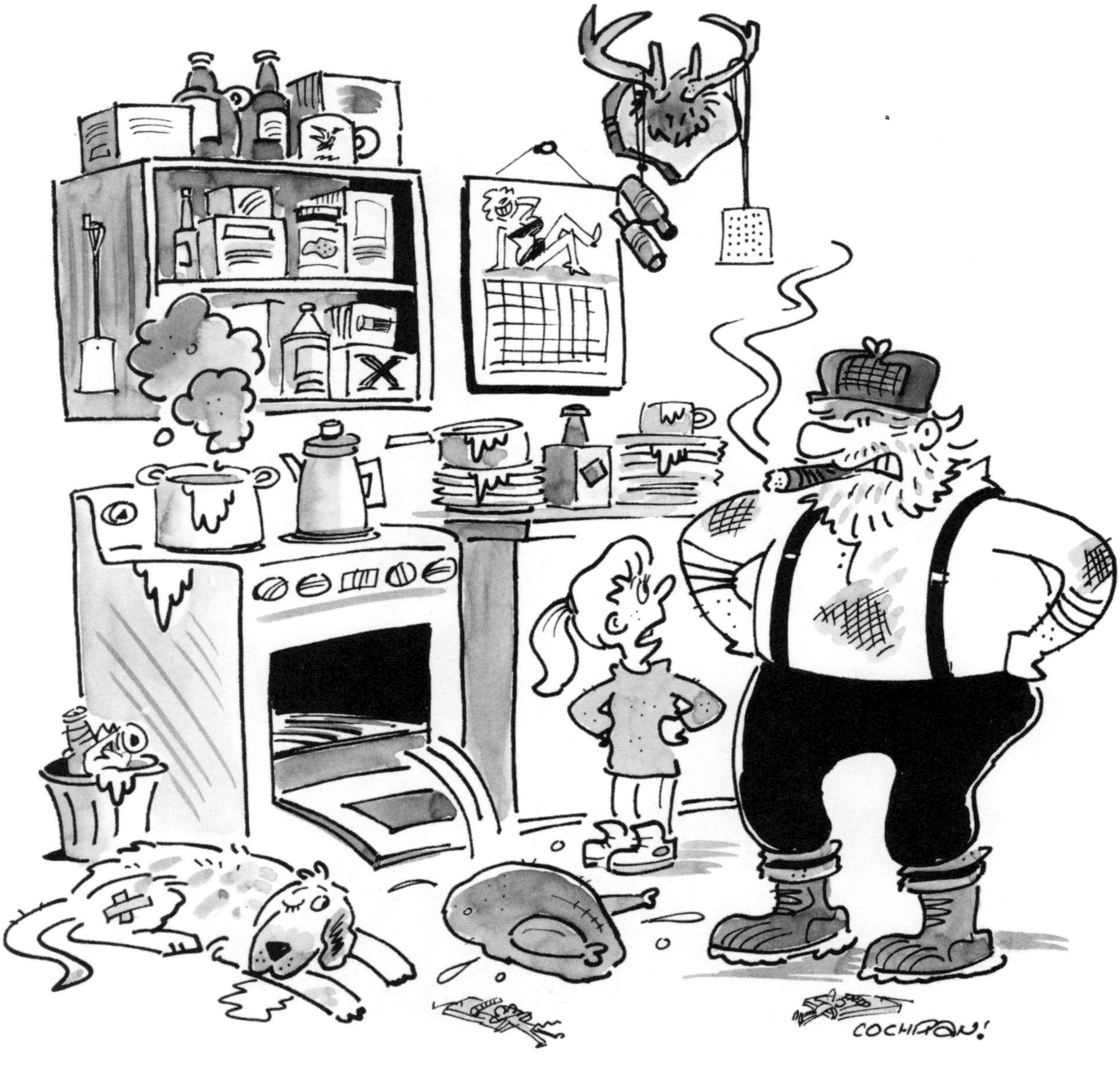
COCHRAN!

*"Of course it keeps sliding out of the oven! You put too much WD-40 on it!"*

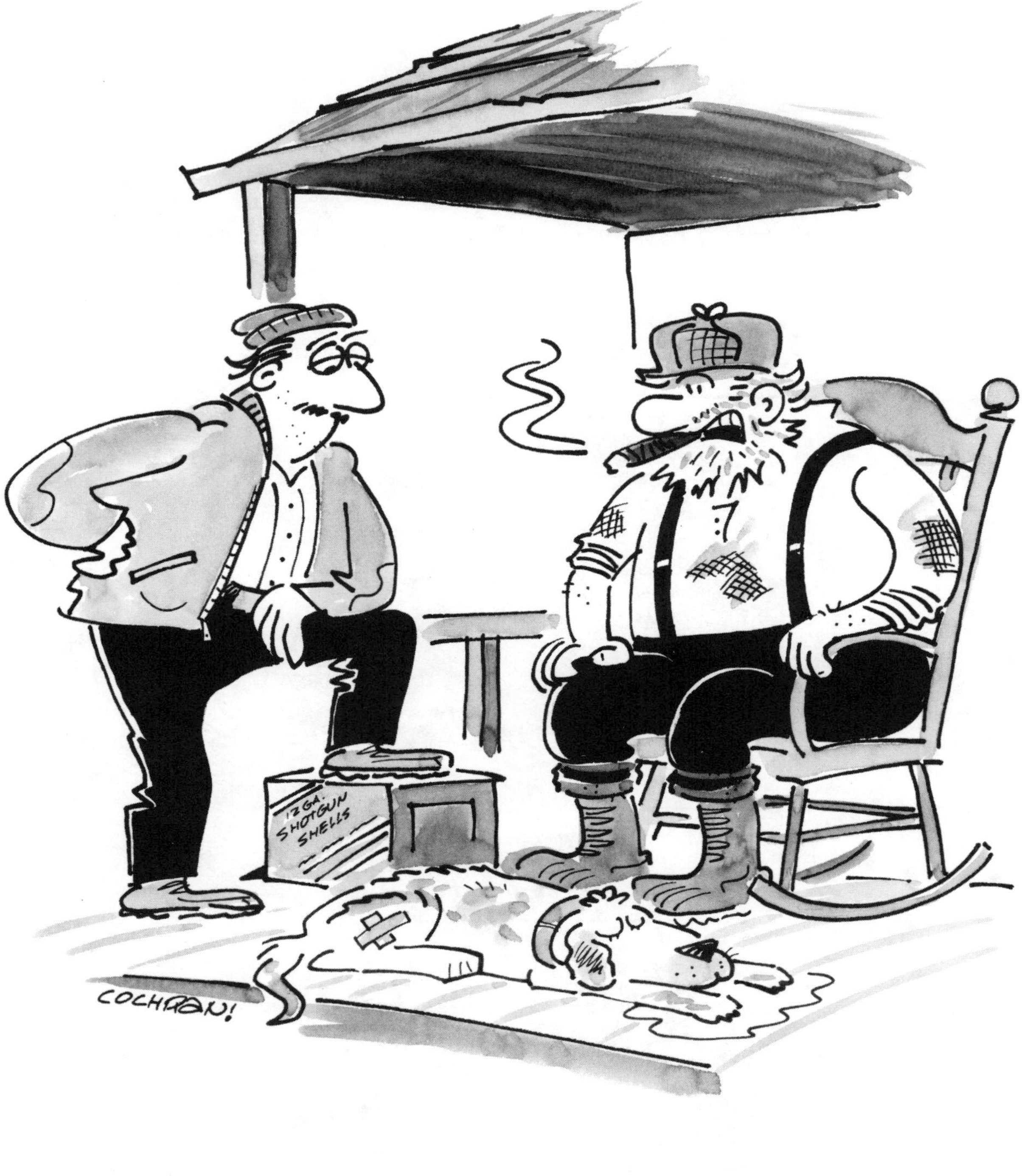
12 GA. SHOTGUN SHELLS
COCHRAN!

*"He don't point or retrieve, but if I teach him to sit I can use him for a door stop."*

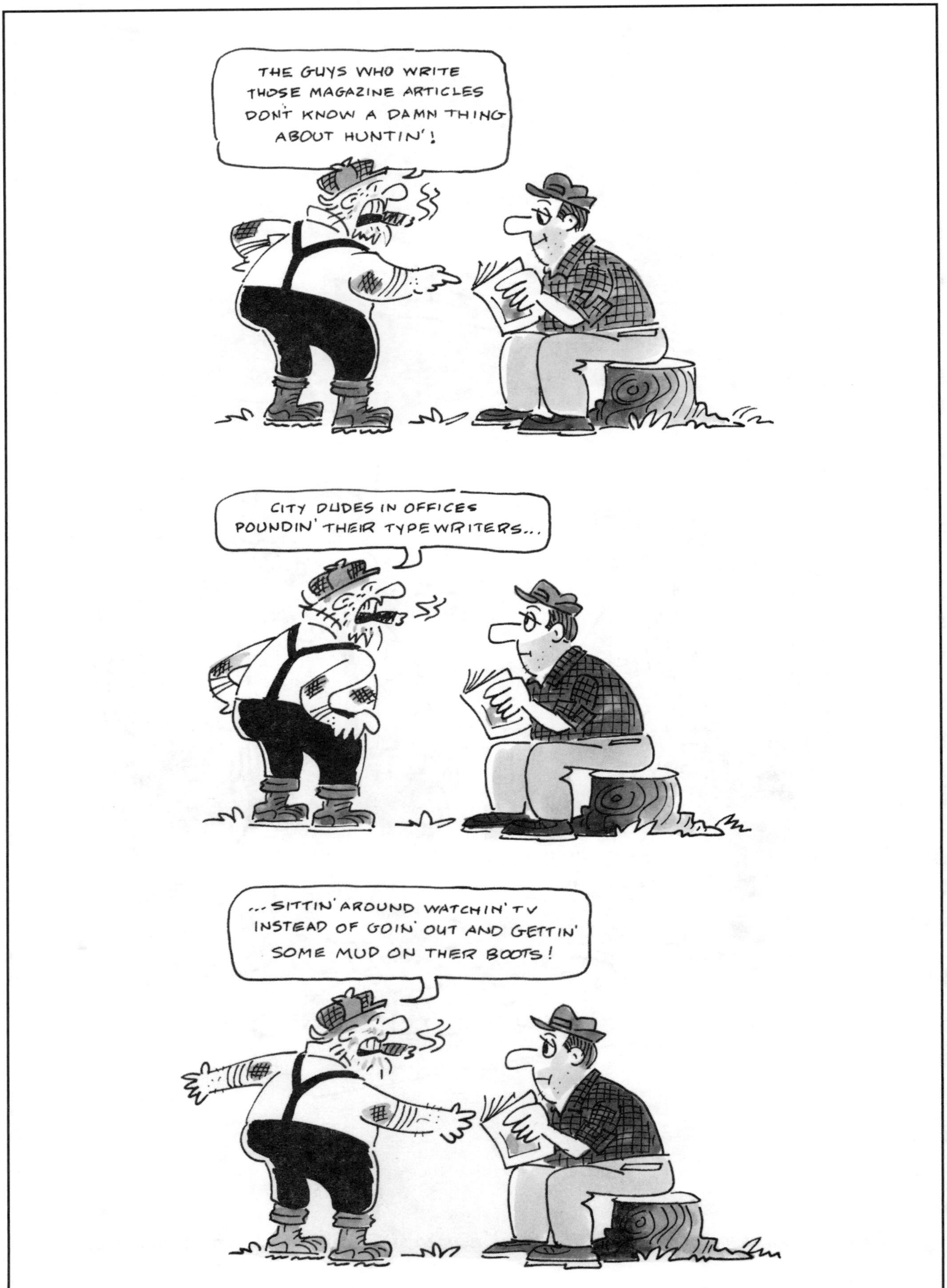
THE GUYS WHO WRITE THOSE MAGAZINE ARTICLES DON'T KNOW A DAMN THING ABOUT HUNTIN'!
CITY DUDES IN OFFICES POUNDIN' THEIR TYPEWRITERS...
...SITTIN' AROUND WATCHIN' TV INSTEAD OF GOIN' OUT AND GETTIN' SOME MUD ON THEIR BOOTS!

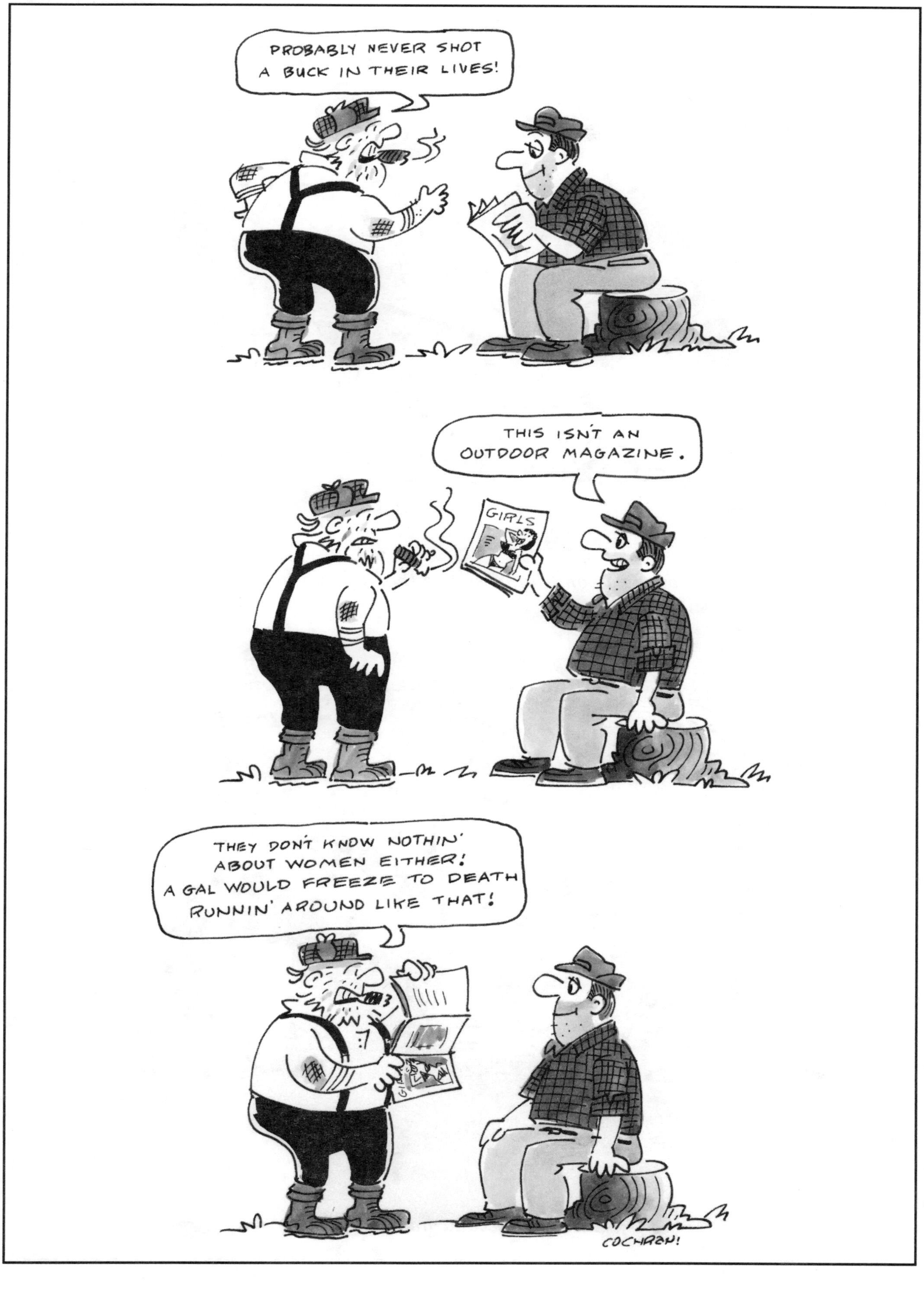
PROBABLY NEVER SHOT A BUCK IN THEIR LIVES!
THIS ISN'T AN OUTDOOR MAGAZINE.
GIRLS
THEY DON'T KNOW NOTHIN' ABOUT WOMEN EITHER! A GAL WOULD FREEZE TO DEATH RUNNIN' AROUND LIKE THAT!
COCHRAN!

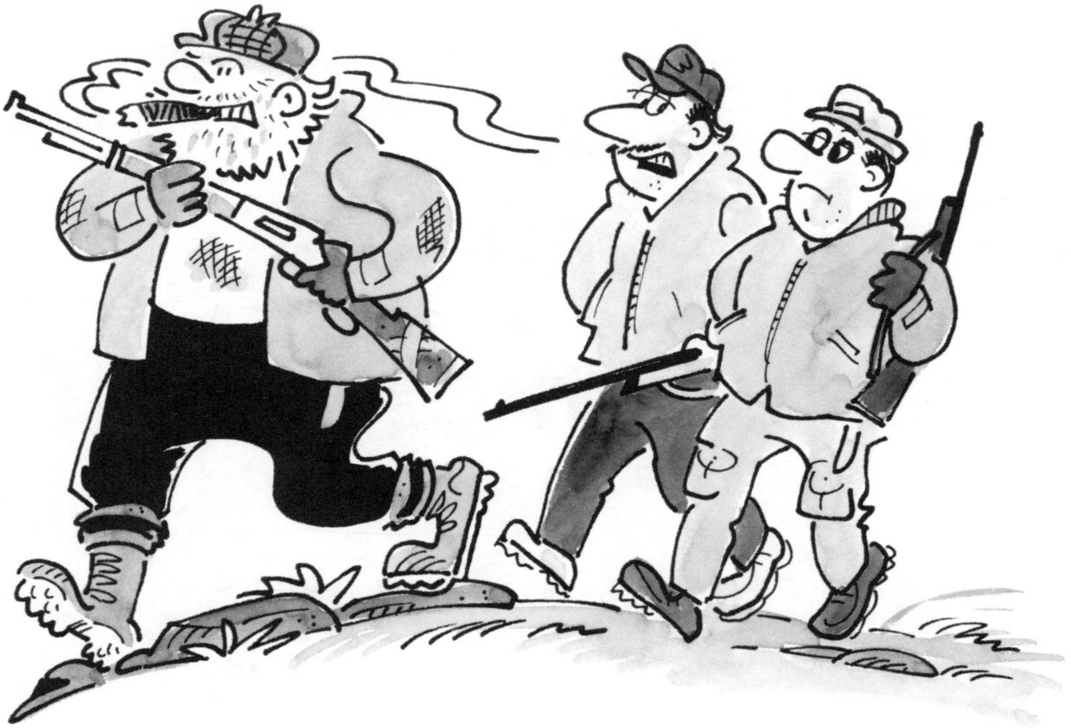

*"It's not the second-hand smoke that's going to get us...*

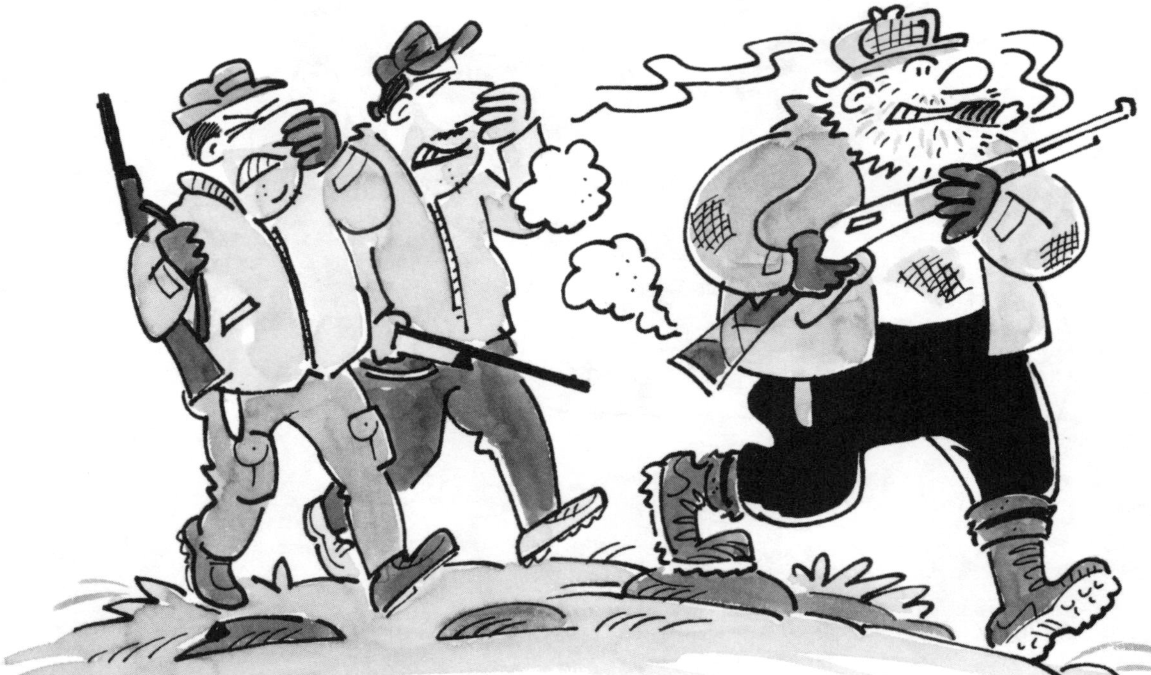
COCHRAN!

*...It's the second-hand gas!"*

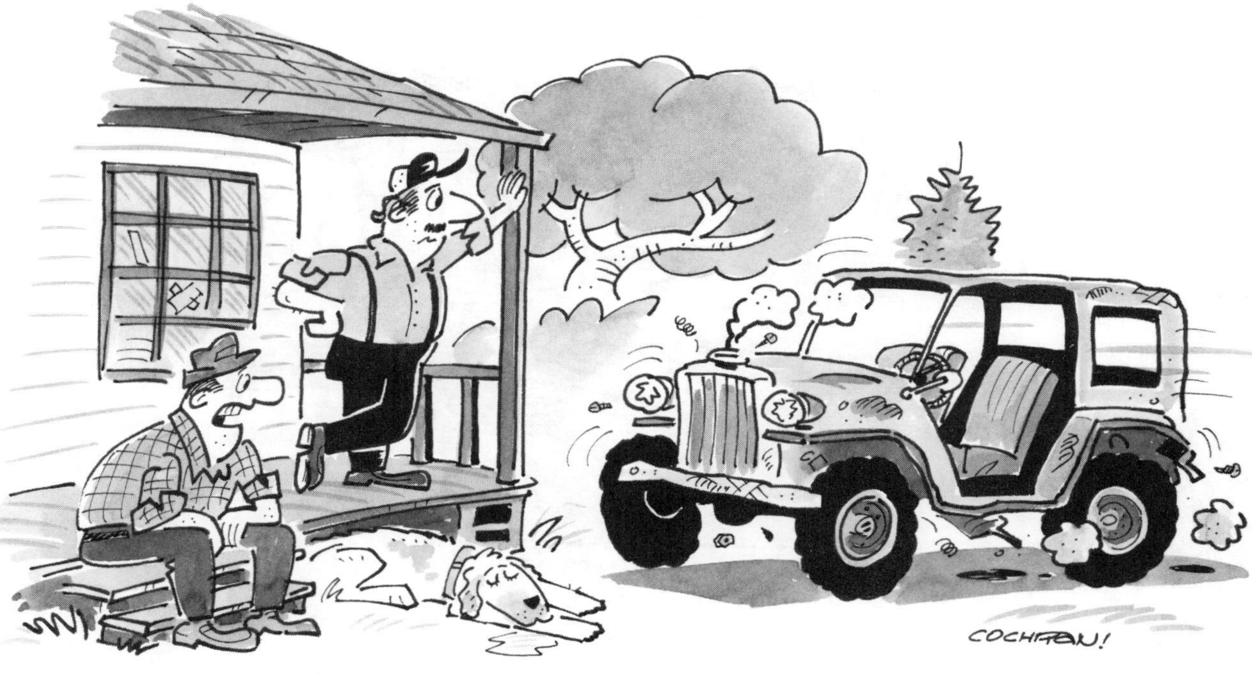
COCHRAN!

*"Something must've happened to Uncle Charlie! His jeep came back without him!"*

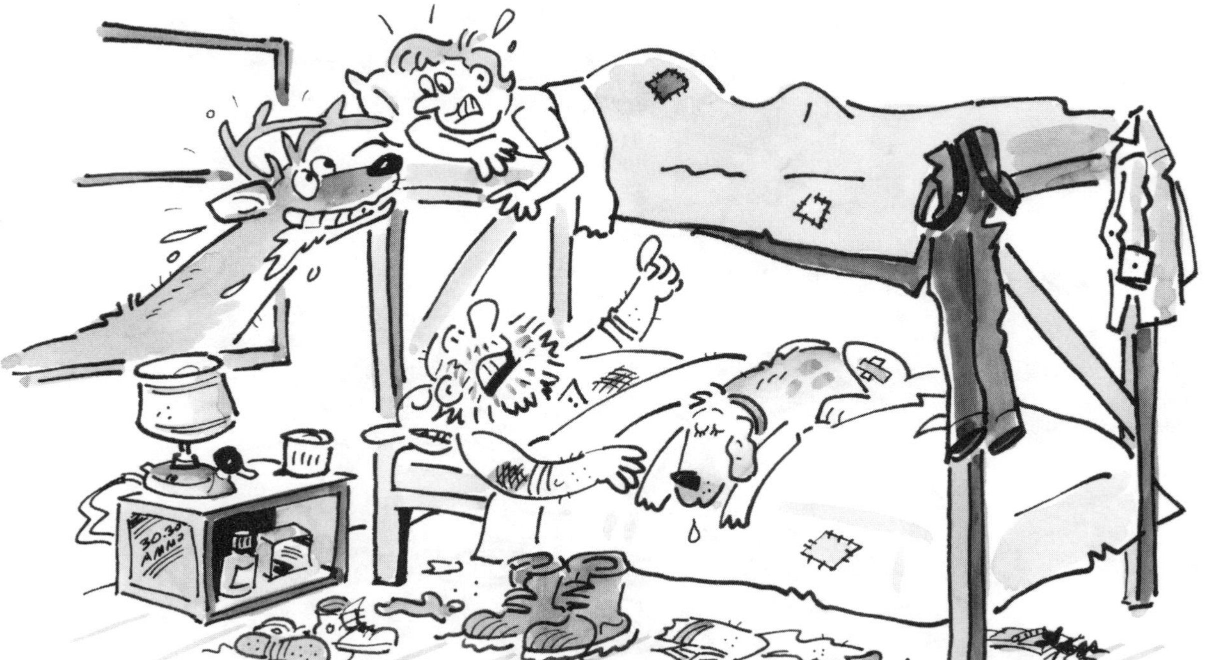
30-30 AMMO
COCHRAN!

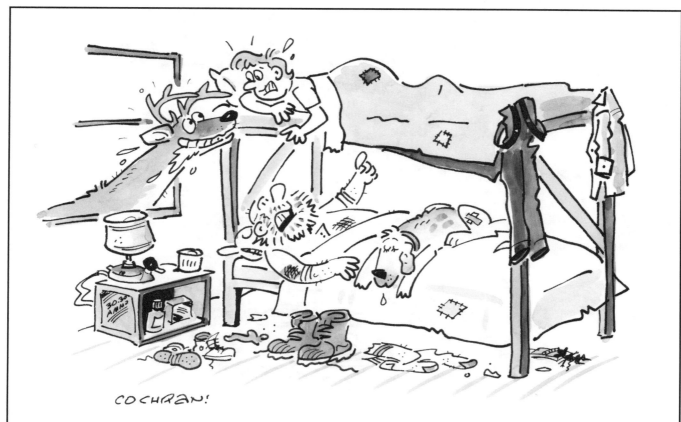

*"I told you to take off that shirt with the doe-in-heat stuff on it, kid!"*

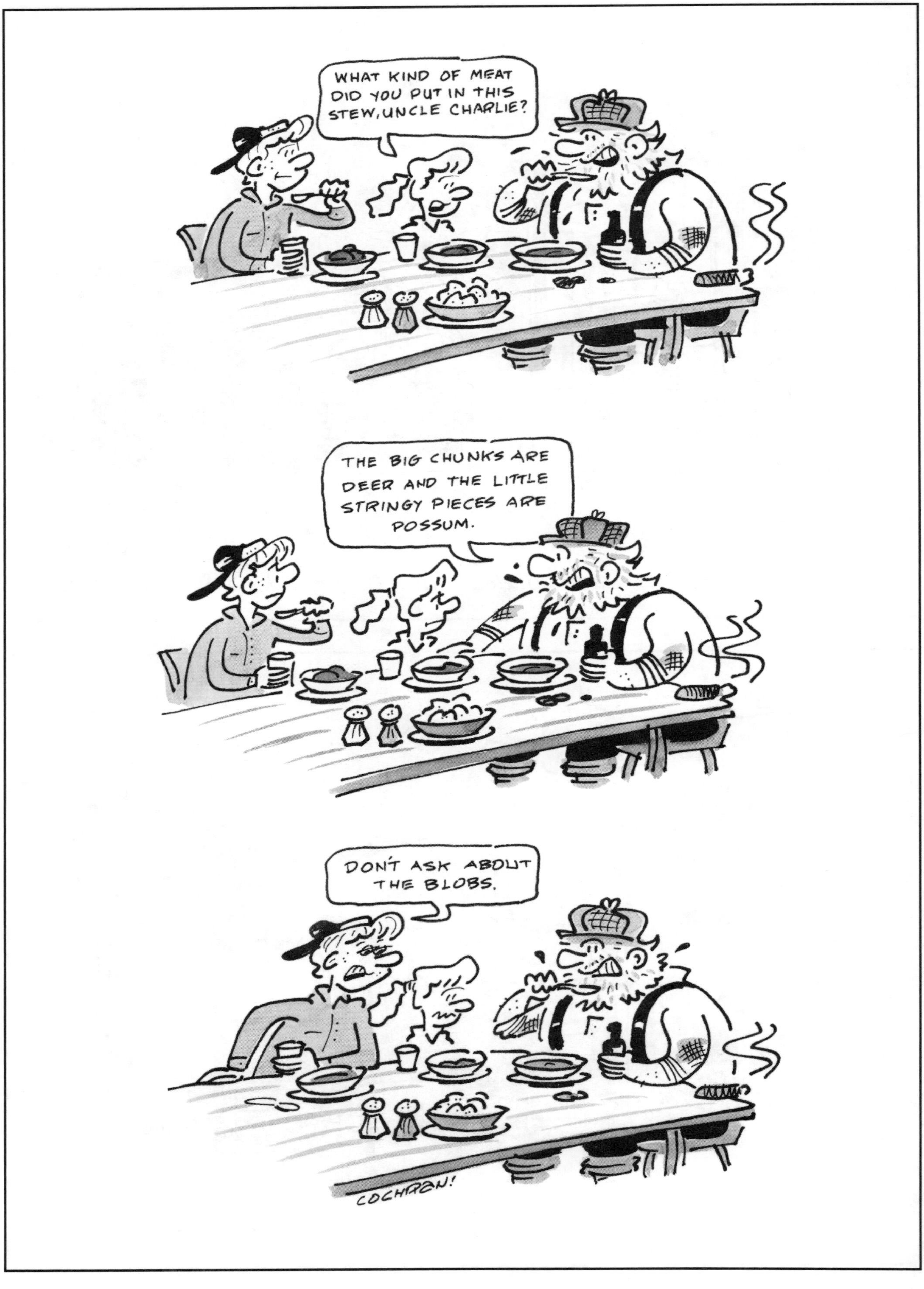
WHAT KIND OF MEAT DID YOU PUT IN THIS STEW, UNCLE CHARLIE?
THE BIG CHUNKS ARE DEER AND THE LITTLE STRINGY PIECES ARE POSSUM.
DON'T ASK ABOUT THE BLOBS.
COCHRAN!

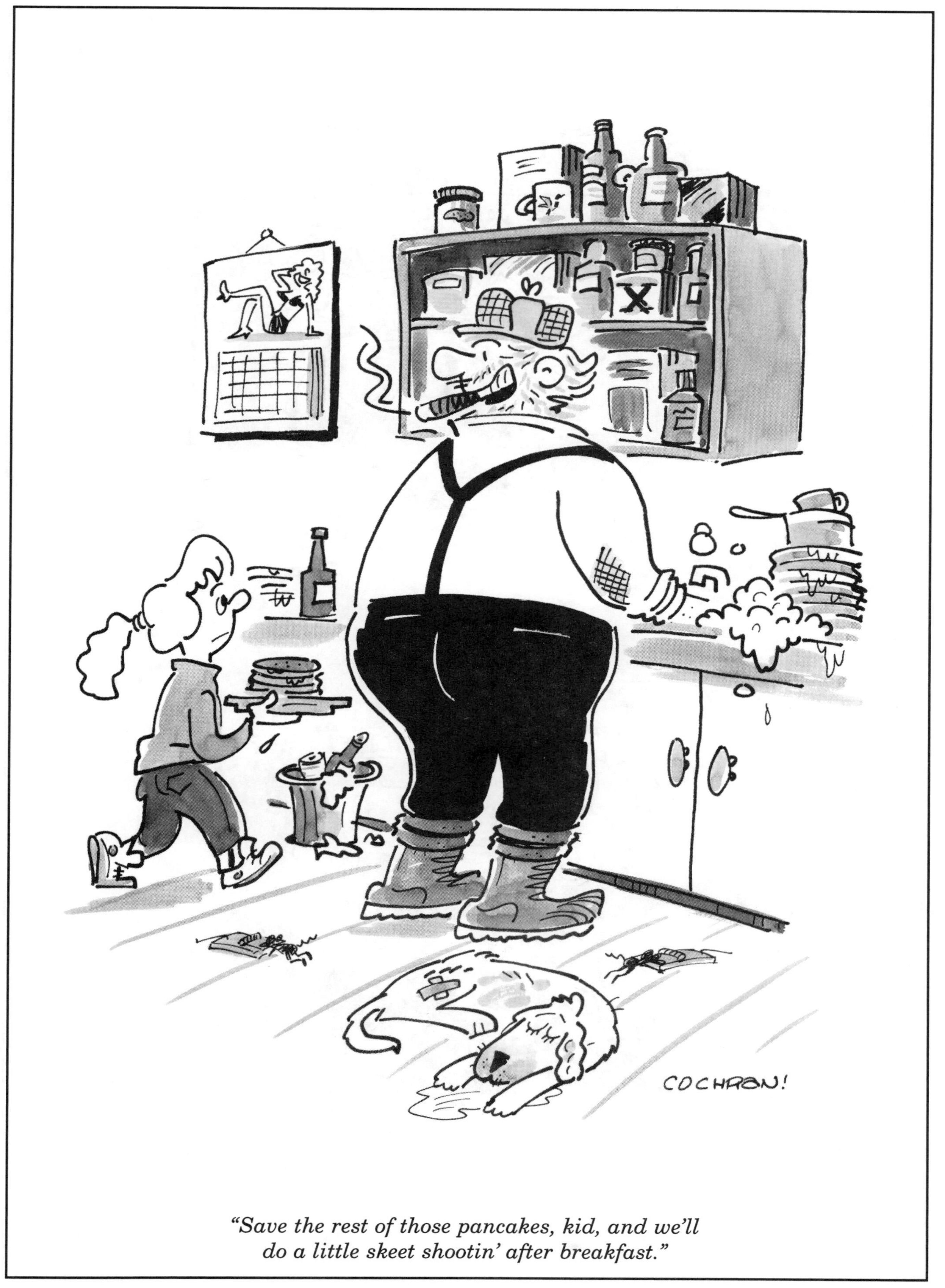
COCHRAN!

*"Save the rest of those pancakes, kid, and we'll do a little skeet shootin' after breakfast."*

YOU GUYS GO ON OUT AND HUNT. MY KNEES ARE BOTHERING ME TODAY.
IF THE LORD HAD JUST PUT GREASE NIPPLES IN THE DAMN THINGS THEY'D HAVE LASTED ME LONGER.
COCHRAN!

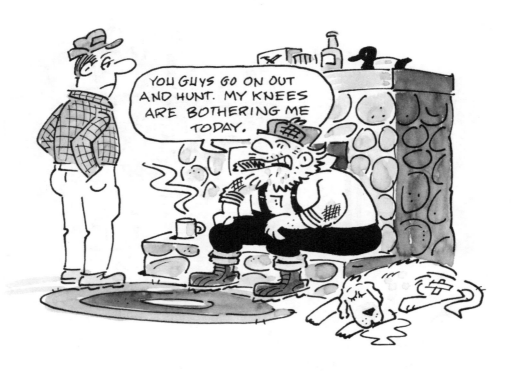

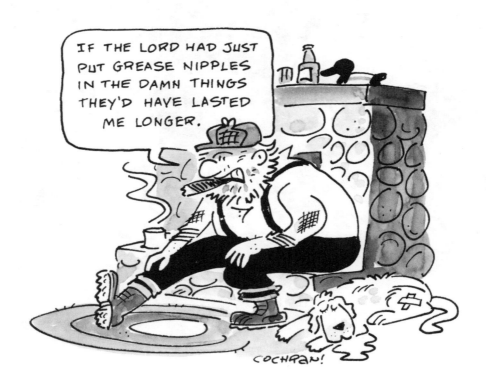

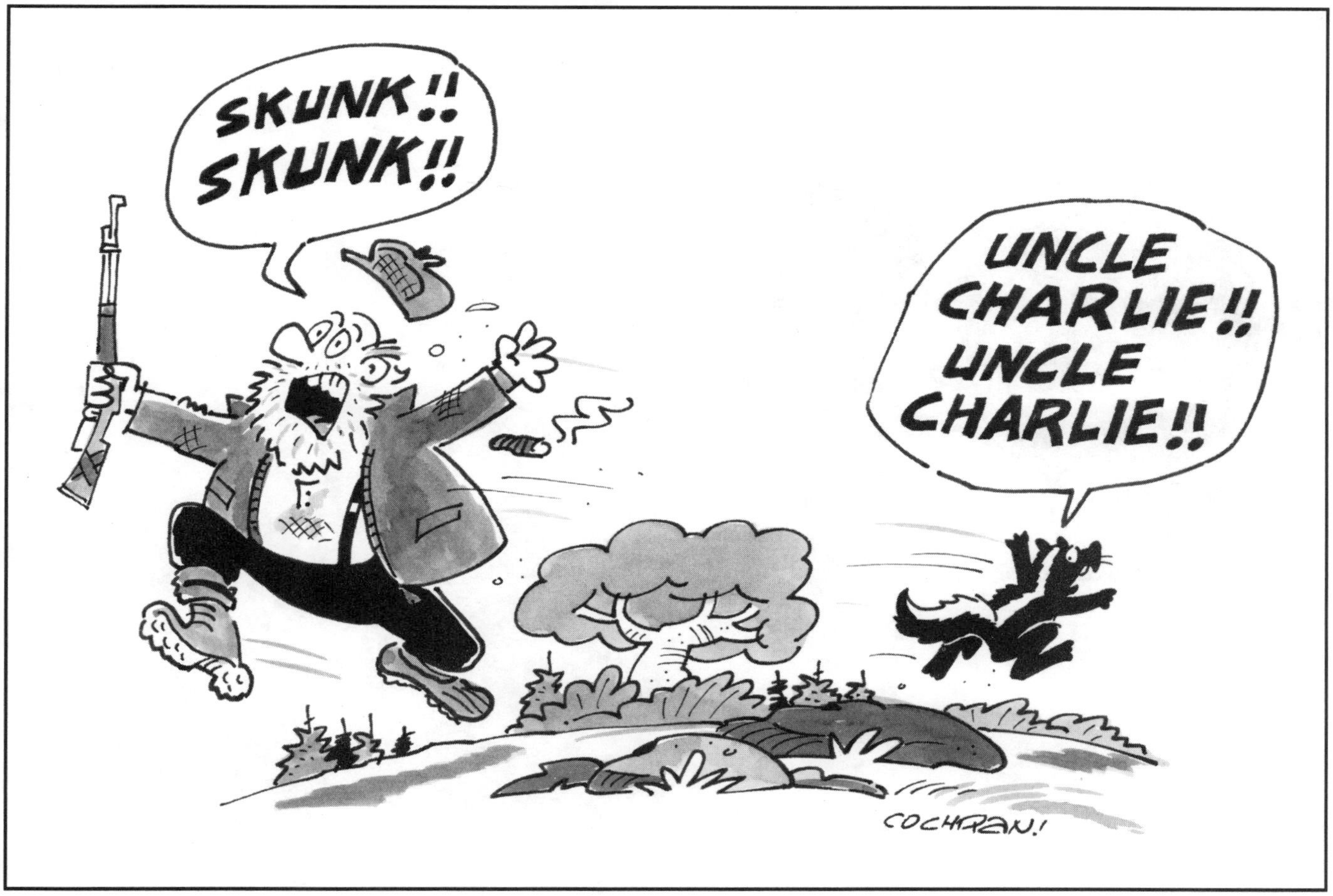
SKUNK!! SKUNK!!
UNCLE CHARLIE!! UNCLE CHARLIE!!
COCHRAN!

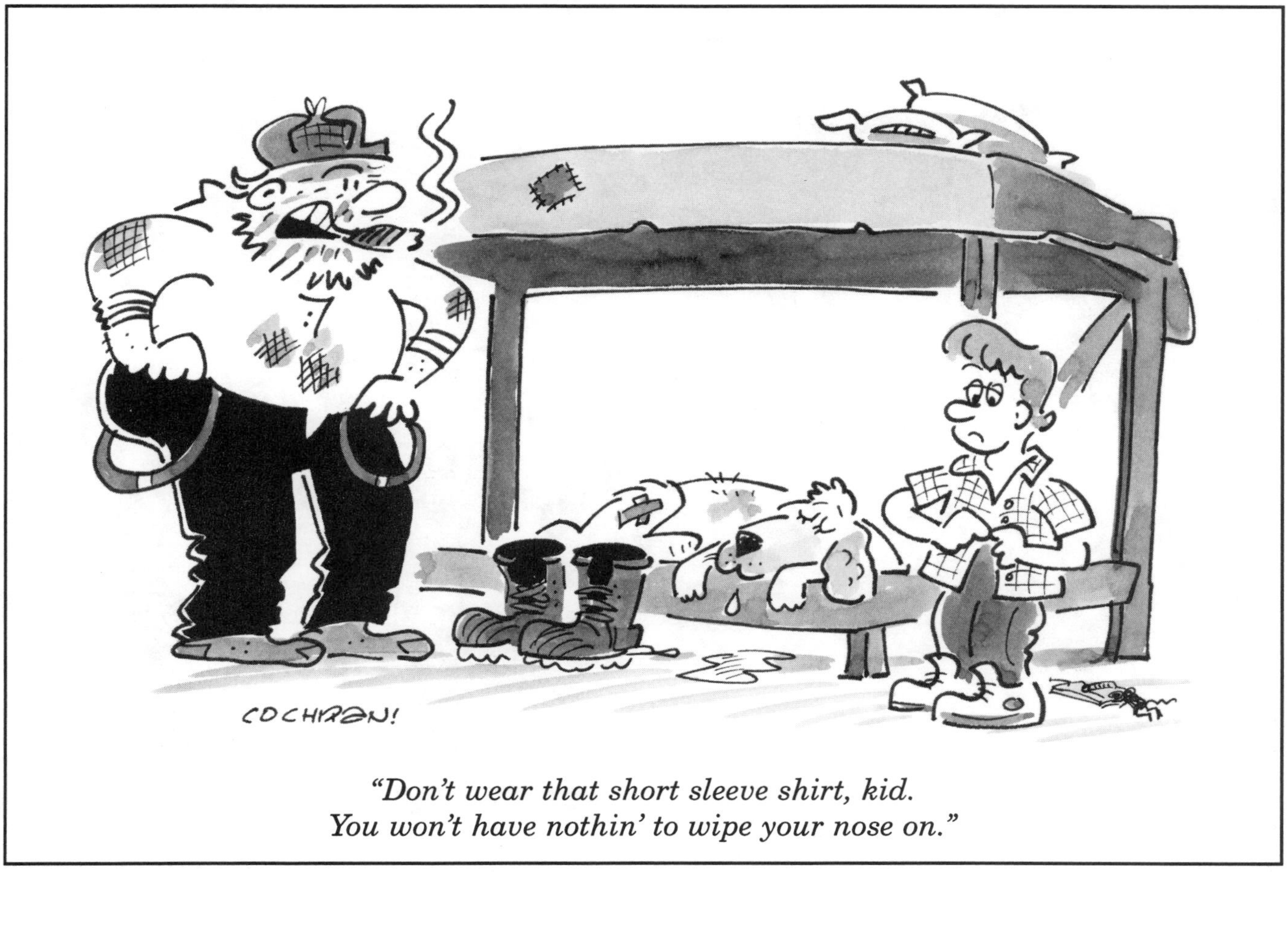
COCHRAN!

*"Don't wear that short sleeve shirt, kid.*
*You won't have nothin' to wipe your nose on."*

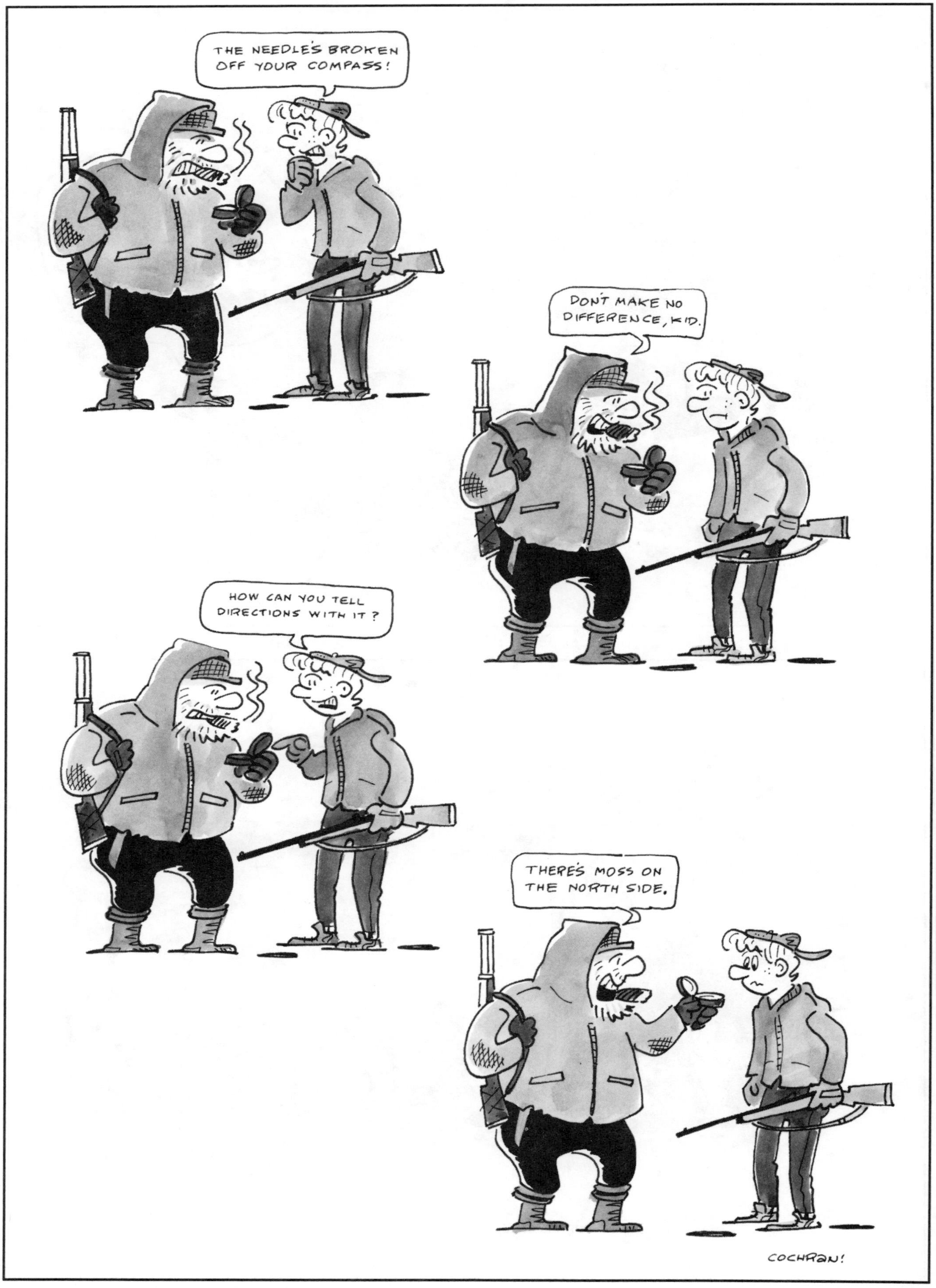
THE NEEDLE'S BROKEN OFF YOUR COMPASS!
DON'T MAKE NO DIFFERENCE, KID.
HOW CAN YOU TELL DIRECTIONS WITH IT?
THERE'S MOSS ON THE NORTH SIDE.
COCHRAN!

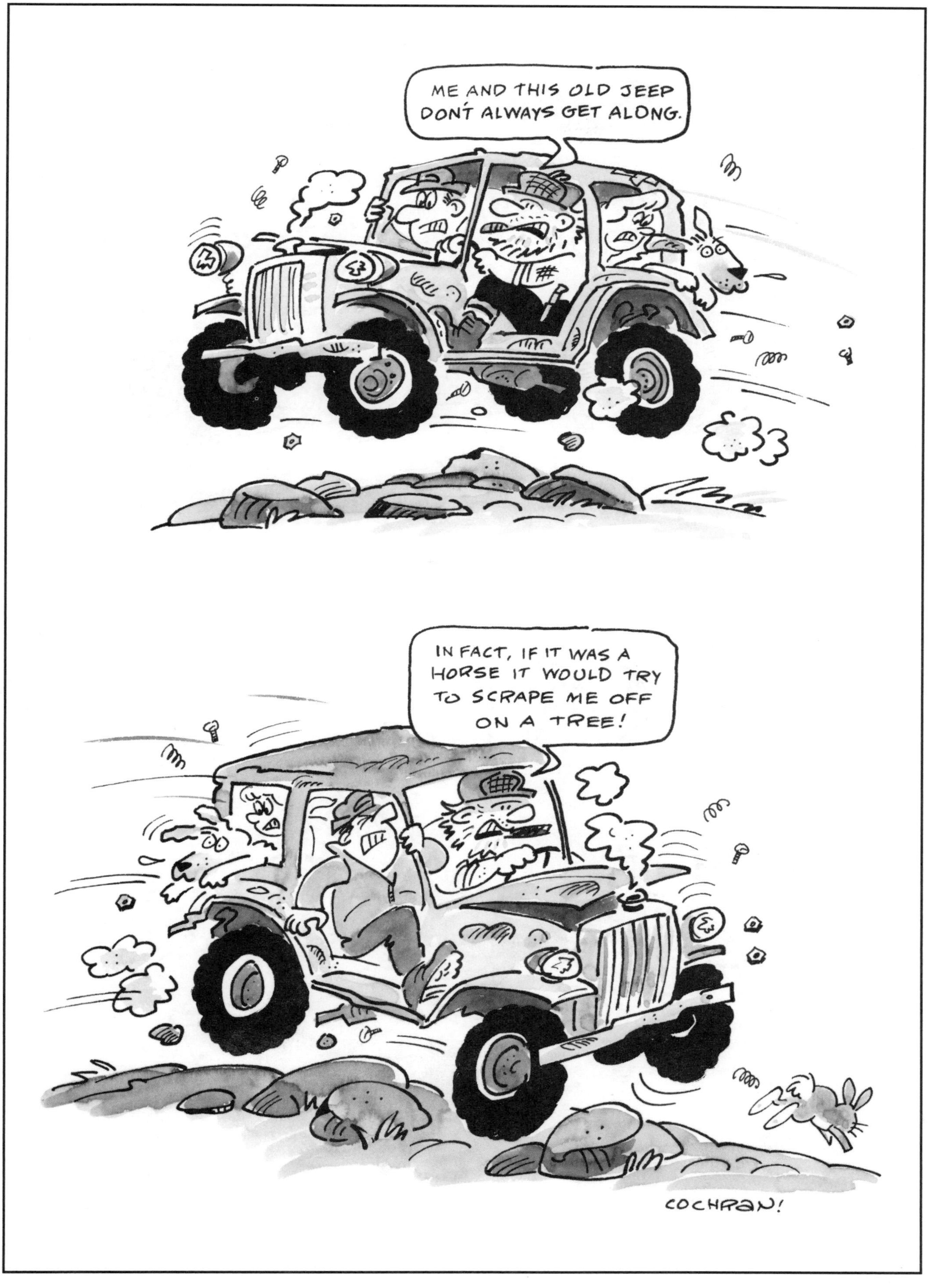

ME AND THIS OLD JEEP DON'T ALWAYS GET ALONG.
IN FACT, IF IT WAS A HORSE IT WOULD TRY TO SCRAPE ME OFF ON A TREE!
COCHRAN!

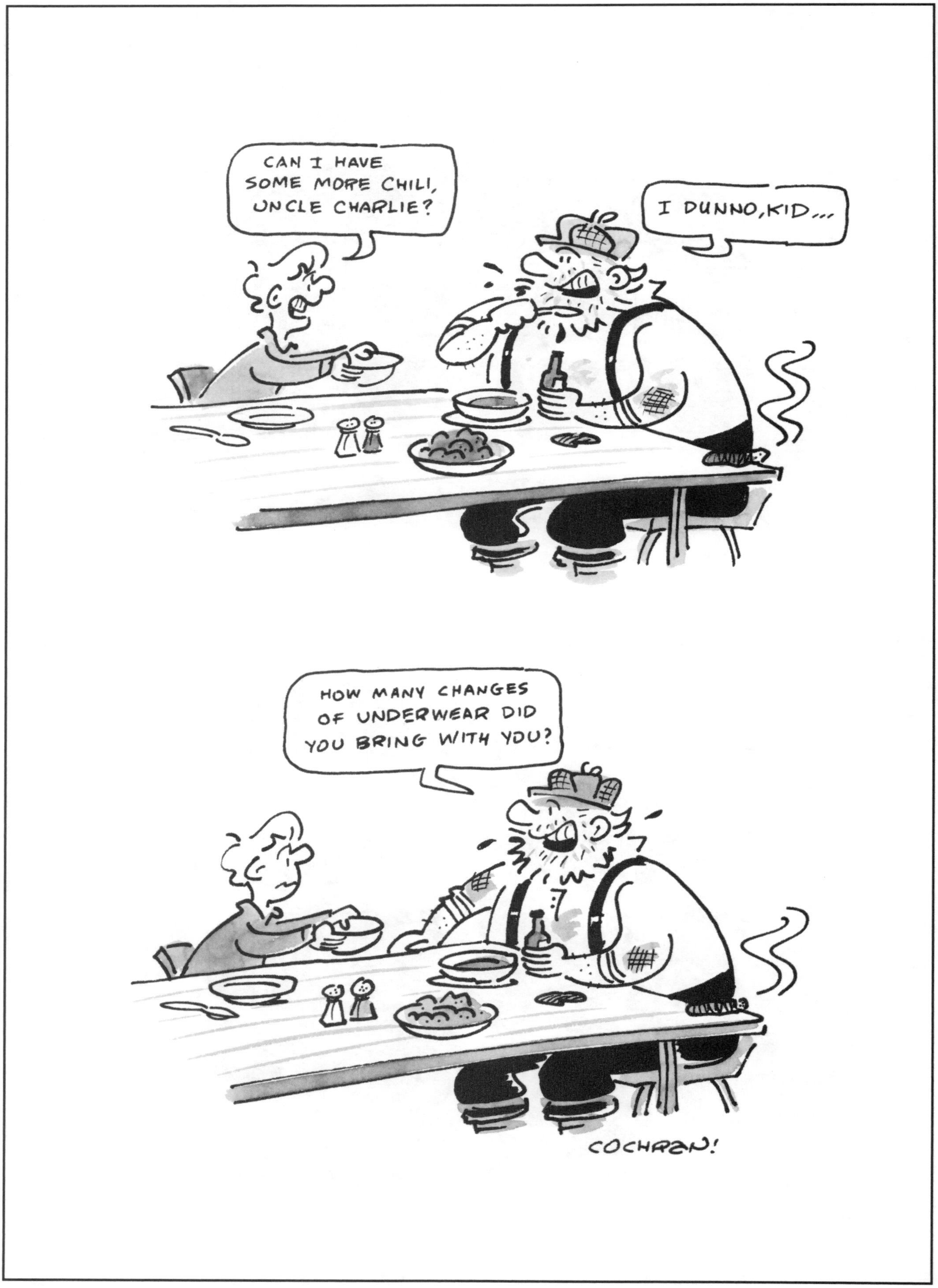
CAN I HAVE SOME MORE CHILI, UNCLE CHARLIE?
I DUNNO, KID...
HOW MANY CHANGES OF UNDERWEAR DID YOU BRING WITH YOU?
COCHRAN!

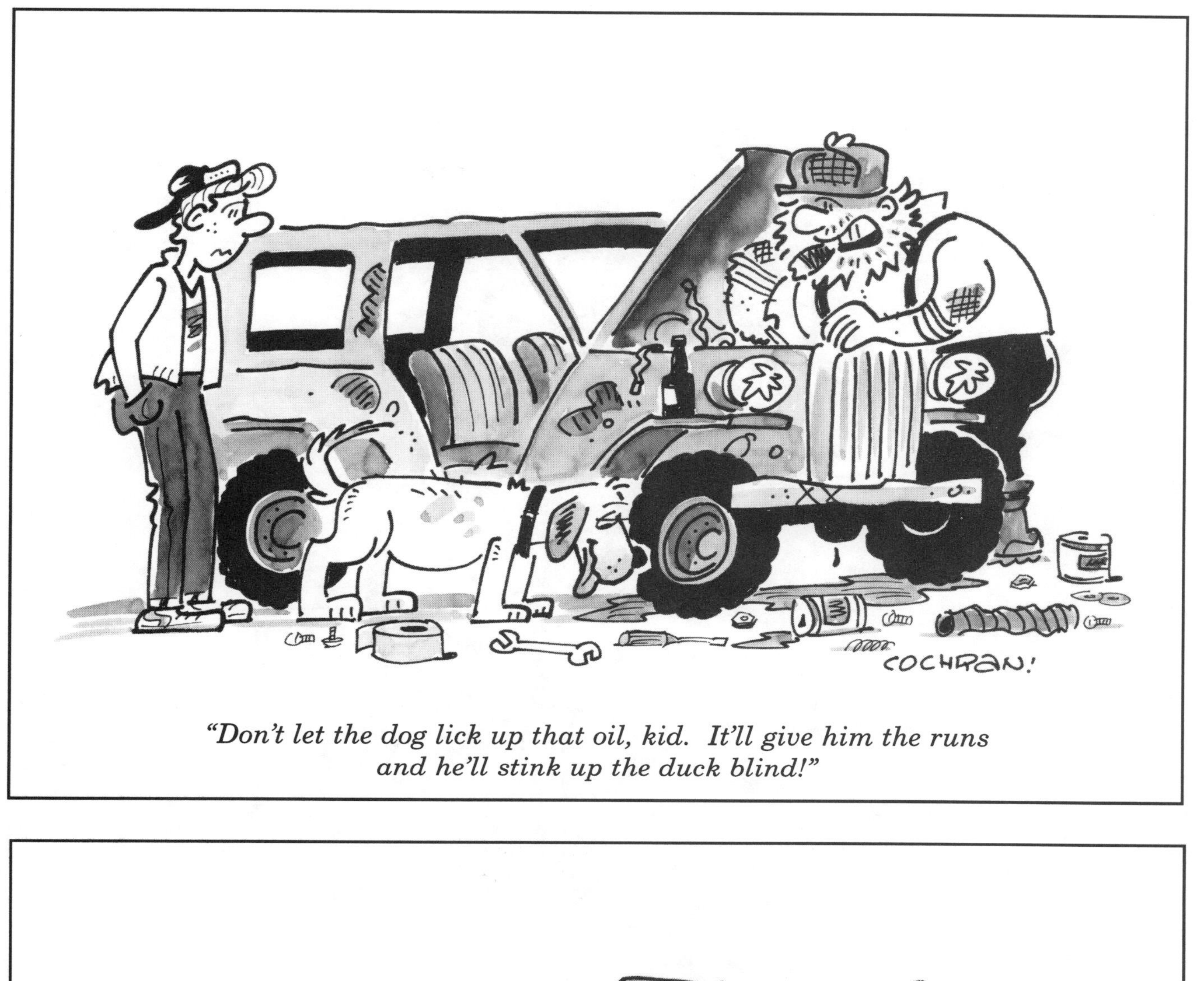
COCHRAN!

*"Don't let the dog lick up that oil, kid. It'll give him the runs and he'll stink up the duck blind!"*

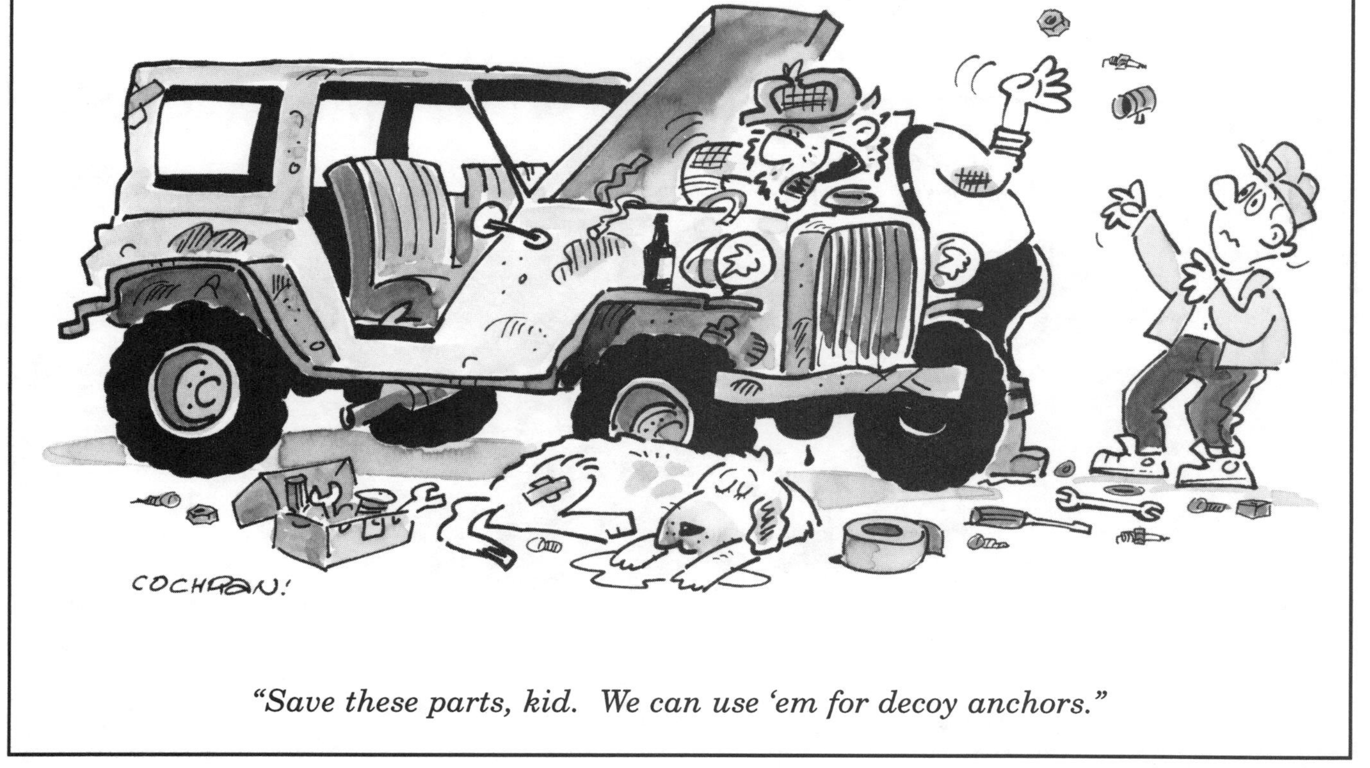
COCHRAN!

*"Save these parts, kid. We can use 'em for decoy anchors."*

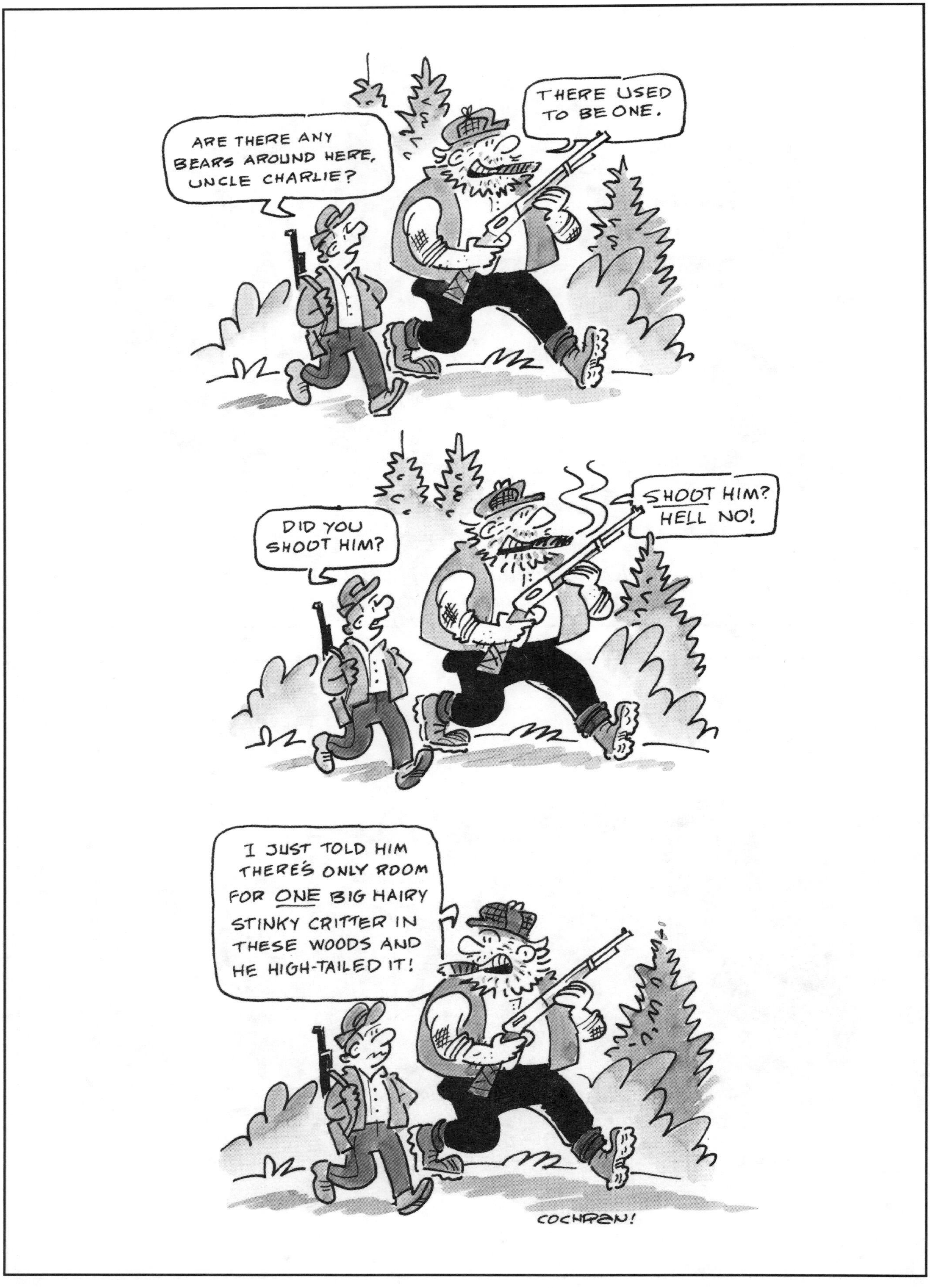
ARE THERE ANY BEARS AROUND HERE, UNCLE CHARLIE?
THERE USED TO BE ONE.
DID YOU SHOOT HIM?
SHOOT HIM? HELL NO!
I JUST TOLD HIM THERE'S ONLY ROOM FOR ONE BIG HAIRY STINKY CRITTER IN THESE WOODS AND HE HIGH-TAILED IT!
COCHRAN!

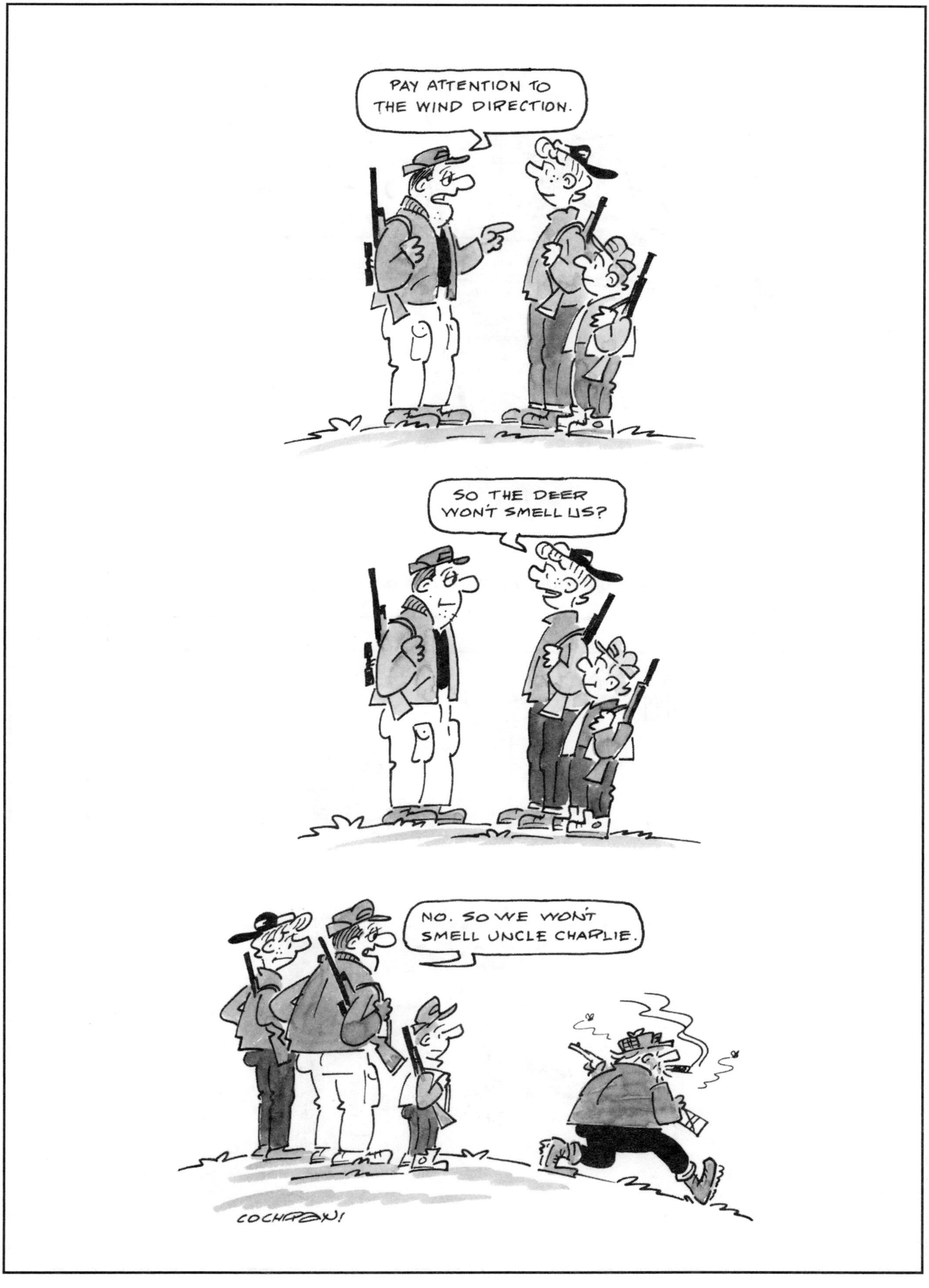
PAY ATTENTION TO THE WIND DIRECTION.
SO THE DEER WON'T SMELL US?
NO. SO WE WON'T SMELL UNCLE CHARLIE.
COCHRAN!

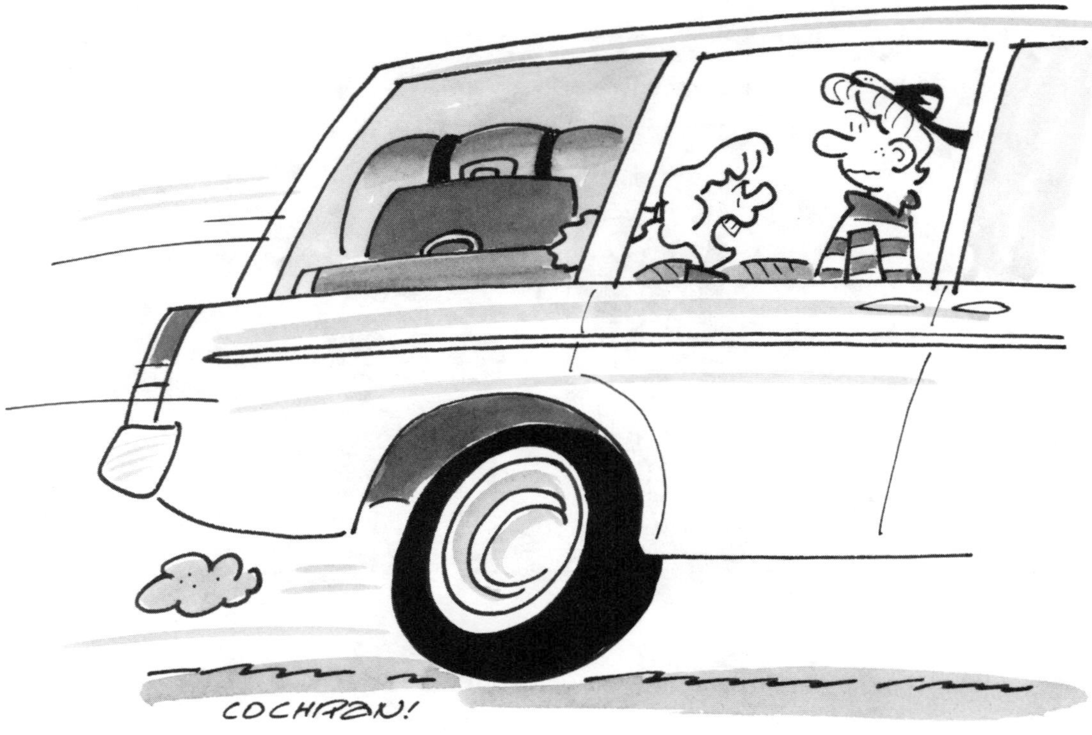
COCHRAN!

*"I can hardly wait to show mom how to cook a fish with a cigarette lighter."*

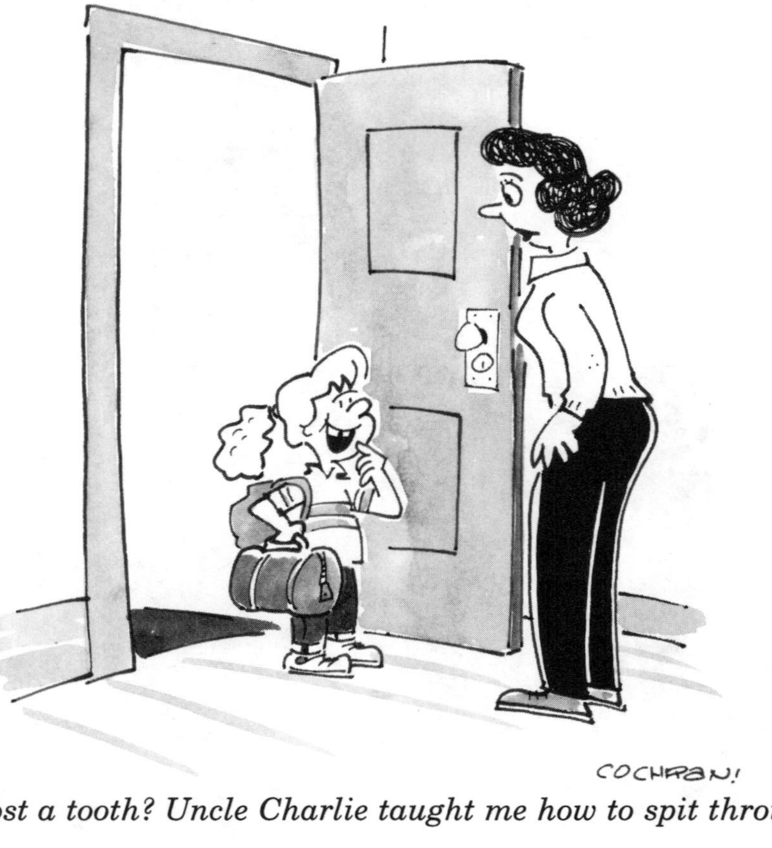
COCHRAN!

*"See where I lost a tooth? Uncle Charlie taught me how to spit through the hole!"*